CEREMONIES OF BRAVERY

CEREMONIES

OF

BRAVERY

OSCAR WILDE, CARLOS BLACKER, AND THE DREYFUS AFFAIR

J. ROBERT MAGUIRE

OXFORD
UNIVERSITY PRESS

OXFORD
UNIVERSITY PRESS

Great Clarendon Street, Oxford, OX2 6DP,
United Kingdom

Oxford University Press is a department of the University of Oxford.
It furthers the University's objective of excellence in research, scholarship,
and education by publishing worldwide. Oxford is a registered trade mark of
Oxford University Press in the UK and in certain other countries

© J. Robert Maguire 2013

The moral rights of the author have been asserted

First Edition published in 2013

Impression: 1

British Library Cataloguing in Publication Data
Data available

Library of Congress Cataloging in Publication Data
Data available

ISBN 978-0-19-966082-7

Printed in Great Britain by
Clays Ltd, St Ives plc

Contents

List of Plates

the fourth such being when Panizzardi confided
'the whole & entire truth' to him. BP.

26. Chez Mère Adèle, Montmartre, 1911/2: Maurice Gilbert,
    standing, with his wife Mary Beatrice seated on his left,
    and Rowland Strong, seated with his back to the camera
    next to his dog (Snatcher?), in the kind of convivial
    milieu frequented by Strong. BP.

27. Oscar Wilde at the Vatican, Rome, April 1900.
    The photograph by Robbie Ross, two years after
    Wilde's estrangement from Carlos Blacker, was given to
    Blacker by Ross, who remained a loyal friend to both. BP.

28. Drawing by the Spanish artist Ricardo Opisso of Oscar
    Wilde, Yvette Guilbert, and Toulouse-Lautrec at the Moulin
    de la Galette, Montmartre, 1898. Musée Tavet-Delacour,
    Pontoise. La Photographie Giraudon.

29. Oscar Wilde on his deathbed, with 'a few flowers placed
    there by myself [Robbie Ross] and an anonymous friend
    [Carlos Blacker] who had brought some on behalf
    of the children'. Photograph by Maurice Gilbert, 'taken
    by flashlight with a borrowed camera & inferior plate all
    obtained with great difficulty under trying circumstances',
    according to Ross. BP.

30. Empty envelope inscribed in Carlos Blacker's hand,
    among his papers at the time of his death in 1928. He had
    almost died of Spanish Flu in January 1920 while in
    Florence. The envelope may once have contained
    Wilde's last letter to him, in June 1898, which, in Blacker's
    words, 'put an end to our friendship forever'. Believing
    himself to be dying, Blacker may have been prompted to
    destroy the letter on the date inscribed. The envelope
    cannot be related to any of Wilde's surviving letters
    to Blacker. BP.

31. 'Photograph of W. R. Paton, my dear friend . . .
    announcing his death on the 21st April 1921 at Samos,—of
    pneumonia.' Note on back of photograph by
    Carlos Blacker. BP.

List of Abbreviations

Archives Nationales	National Archives, Paris
BN, NAF	Bibliothèque Nationale, Nouvelle Acquisition Française, Paris
Bosie	Lord Alfred Douglas
BP	Blacker Papers, Hand's Cove Library, Shoreham, Vermont
Carrie	Caroline Frost Blacker
CB	Carlos Blacker
CB Diary	Carlos Blacker Diary, Blacker Papers
CB Memo	Carlos Blacker, 'Private and Confidential' Memorandum on the Dreyfus Affair
Clark	The William Andrews Clark Memorial Library, University of California, Los Angeles
'De Profundis'	'De Profundis', in Merlin Holland and Rupert Hart-Davis (eds.), *The Complete Letters of Oscar Wilde* (London: Fourth Estate, 2000), pp. 683–780.
Holland	Holland Family Papers, Collection of Merlin Holland
King's College	The Papers of Oscar Browning, King's College Library, University of Cambridge
Letters	Merlin Holland and Rupert Hart-Davis (eds.), *The Complete Letters of Oscar Wilde* (London: Fourth Estate, 2000)
Linny	Henry Pelham Archibald Douglas Pelham-Clinton, 7th duke of Newcastle-under-Lyme
Nottingham	Manuscripts and Special Collections, Newcastle Collection, The University of Nottingham
OW	Oscar Wilde
PCOM	Prison Commission
Pip	Dr Carlos Paton Blacker
PMLA	Publications of the Modern Language Association of America
PRO	Public Record Office
Reading	Robert Harborough Sherard Collection, University of Reading

But man is a noble Animal, splendid in ashes, and pompous in the grave, solemnizing Nativities and Deaths with equal lustre, nor omitting Ceremonies of bravery, in the infamy of his nature.

Sir Thomas Browne, Hydriotaphia (1658)

Introduction

I

Shortly after his release from prison, Oscar Wilde in a nostalgic letter to Carlos Blacker ('My dear old Friend') paid rhapsodic tribute to what he refers to elsewhere as their 'ancient friendship':

> Often in prison I used to think of you: of your chivalry of nature, of your limitless generosity, of your quick intellectual sympathies, of your culture so receptive, so refined. What marvellous evenings, dear Carlos, we used to have! What brilliant dinners! What days of laughter and delight! To you, as to me, conversation—that τερπνὸν κακόν as Euripides calls it—that sweet sin of phrases—was always among the supreme aims of life, and we tired many a moon with talk, and drank many a sun to rest with wine and words. You were always the truest of friends and the most sympathetic of companions.[1]

The qualities so admired in Blacker were those that Wilde, surveying the wreckage of his life from his prison cell, had come to find so lamentably wanting in Lord Alfred Douglas, who, 'grasping often: at times not a little unscrupulous: ungracious always.... [lacked] simply the grace of sweet companionship, the charm of pleasant conversation, that τερπνὸν κακόν as the Greeks called it, and all those gentle humanities that make life lovely, and are an accompaniment to life as music might be, keeping things in tune and filling with melody the harsh or silent places'.[2] His 'unintellectual friendship' with 'Bosie' Douglas, in contrast to his friendship with Blacker, he viewed as 'intellectually degrading to me'.[3] Douglas, the target of this harsh indictment, retained only a dim memory of Blacker, absent abroad and a fading presence in Wilde's life by the time its focus shifted to Douglas. Many years later, in response to an enquiry about Blacker from A. J. A. Symons, who was writing a life of Wilde, Douglas could recall him only as a paragon cited by Wilde against whom to measure Douglas's shortcomings. 'I don't know anything about Carlos Blacker', Douglas wrote:

except that he was a great friend of Oscar's. I think they were at Magdalen together.... As a matter of fact I only met him once or twice about 35 or more years ago. He used to disapprove of me, according to Oscar's account, & Oscar used to quote him when he wanted to be disagreeable! 'Carlos Blacker says etcet.' To me he was always rather what Mrs. Harris was to Betsy Prig & I once said to Oscar 'I don't believe there's no sich [sic] person.' Subsequently I met him & found him quite amiable.[4]

The friendship between Blacker and Wilde had its beginnings at a period in Wilde's life that Max Beerbohm identified in his imagination with Wilde at his best ('Oscar was just in the mood I like him—very 1880', Beerbohm wrote on one occasion), and the friendship flourished through the 1880s.[5] Blacker's earliest surviving diary is for the year 1881, when he was twenty-two. Wilde's name first appears in an entry for 22 December of that year, which reads in its entirety: 'Oscar Wilde—.'[6] Max Beerbohm in his essay '1880', published in *The Yellow Book* in January 1895, eulogizes the watershed year that for many marked the end of the Victorian age and the dawn of a new era in the arts: 'The period of 1880 must have been delicious', he wrote of a time when he himself was eight years old.[7] This was the happiest time of Wilde's life in the opinion of his friend Vincent O'Sullivan.[8] Robert Sherard agreed: 'When I think over his life, I feel assured that the days when I first met him [in 1883] were the happiest days he lived.'[9]

Blacker was born in Peru where his English father had commercial interests and where, during his years of residence there, he married Blacker's Peruvian mother, Carmen Espantoso, in 1857. Among those who knew him, there is ample testimony to Blacker's great charm and his notably kind and generous nature. A brilliant talker and a versatile linguist, he was drawn to the company of intellectuals who shared his interests in literature, social anthropology, and comparative religion. He had no regular occupation or profession and, in approved Victorian manner, sustained the life of a man of leisure on a parental allowance. For his friend Salomon Reinach, the distinguished French archaeologist and philologist, Blacker's death in 1928 marked 'the end of a chapter' in his own life that he recalled had begun at Oxford in

1886. Citing Blacker's 'kindness, his love of truth and other admirable gifts', Reinach added wistfully: 'If only he had been obliged to work for a living, he might have become a renowned writer in several languages.'[10] In accounting for the apparent anomaly of Blacker's close friendship with Anatole France, who 'was so exclusively French that one hardly expects to find a foreigner in his intimate circle', Loring Walton, in his study of the correspondence between the two, points out that both were 'highly intelligent and cultivated Europeans', that Blacker's viewpoint 'was that of an enlightened citizen of Europe', and that moreover he was 'an amazingly genial man, endowed with a rare capacity for making friends and keeping them'.[11] In a letter to Walton many years after his father's death, Blacker's son, Dr C. P. Blacker, wrote that, 'My father had a great capacity for veneration and [Anatole] France was one of the few people he venerated. Another was Salomon Reinach.'[12] Like her husband, Constance Wilde held Blacker in the highest esteem: she thought that he possessed 'perhaps the greatest distinction of manner of all whom she had ever met'.[13] To Wilde, the arbiter of taste and fashion, Blacker was 'the best dressed man in London', and he commemorated their friendship in his dedication to him of *The Happy Prince and Other Tales*, the publication of which in May 1888 to general critical acclaim marked Wilde's debut as an established author.[14] To an observer, a long-time friend of both, Blacker was clearly Wilde's 'best friend'.[15]

2

Among Blacker's surviving papers are his diaries covering the years 1881 to the first month of 1907, with a gap of ten years. The missing years—1885 through 1894—cover the period of his greatest intimacy with Wilde and also a time when some 'tempestuous affairs' of his own were 'a source of immense worry and bother' to him. If diaries once existed for the missing years, they may have been among the records destroyed when Blacker's wife Caroline ('Carrie'), who strongly disapproved of the worrisome episodes in her husband's past, 'most drastically pruned' his papers following his death in 1928.[16] Of the surviving diaries, those from mid-1896 through January 1907 are written in an early form of Pitman shorthand in which Blacker was self-taught, apparently for its inaccessibility to the untutored eye. He records being 'reproached' by Carrie 'for writing this diary in short-hand because she was afraid that I never would write it out in long-hand'.[17] The shorthand diaries remained unread until 1989, when two dedicated experts in the Shorthand Analysis Department at Pitman's Central College in London, Olga Atkinson and Pamela Dunmore, undertook the formidable job of transcription, a challenging task that occupied them for seven years.

The intimate daily record provides a remarkable self-portrait of Blacker. Like Wilde, he had two sons, Pip and Robin, to whom he was a doting and loving father, as suggested by the following random diary entries made during the first six months of 1898, when Pip was two and Robin not yet one: 'Played with children after tea in drawing room making them dance'; 'I then had a tea party of milk and honey. Afterwards danced with Pip'; 'I took Pip, Robin on my knee together for the first time. Pip looked such a big boy. He took Robin's hand. I told him that he must always be nice, good to his little brother'; 'Pip knew names of different songs when I sang them showing that he has an ear for music'; 'Today Pip first showed indications of knowing how to rhyme'; 'Taught Pip March of Faust and Wedding March of Lohengrin while he was with us at tea'; 'Taught Pip Spanish song and dance'; 'I taught Pip two arias of the Valkyrie'; 'Pip learned Adeste Fidelis in my bedroom'; 'Pip learned Lohengrin March'; 'Taught Pip Commedia of Dante'; 'Taught Pip Plato'; 'Taught Pip Euripides'; 'Pip did tricks of singing repetition I had taught him'; 'Taught Pip *medio de fonte* of Lucretius'; 'Pip learned Aristotle today in my bathroom . . . Pip learned who was Queen of England'; '[Pip] learned name of President of French Republic Félix Faure'; 'Pip learned names of Evangelists'; 'Pip learned Virgil'; 'Pip learned Homer'; 'I taught Pip Epictetus'; 'Saw Pip climb into his bed with great courage and daring'; '[Pip] tested me about [quotation in Greek] saying it was by Epictetus'; 'Pip first learned to say Mr. Gladstone on the day he [Gladstone] died'; 'Made musical box play for children in nursery. Pip recognized Lohengrin'; 'Pip said, repeating after me, "to be or not to be, that is the question."'

Looking back on his early childhood towards the end of his life, Pip (Dr C. P. Blacker) recorded an indelible memory of his father:

My father had a quiet voice and very gentle manners. He could attune himself to children of different ages and knew exactly how to talk to them. He dealt with our questions about the Ten Commandments by telling Robin and me that these Commandments were directed to different people. Some were specially meant for children and others were more for grown-ups, but that in due course we would understand them all, and profit by them. In the meantime we could take it that all ten could be summed up in one comprehensive Commandment, which, if acted on by everyone, would make the world a much better place than it was. What, we asked expectantly, was this Commandment? My father hesitated a few seconds before answering. He then spoke the following two words: 'Be kind,' he said. After all these years I clearly remember the moment when he pronounced these words. It was a cold evening and we were standing near the seat at the top of the Schlossberg [in Freiburg]. My father was smiling with pleasure over what he was saying, and I saw his face in profile. His dark moustache was touched white with frost. He was wearing gloves and a cap. Robin and I wore mittens and woolen head coverings. 'Be kind to one another, especially to children younger than yourselves,' he said, and as he spoke, my father looked to us to be the kindest, wisest and best of men. Something of this well-remembered visual impression remained with me throughout the ensuing war.[18]

Pip's long-cherished image of his father is confirmed in its essence by Salomon Reinach, who counted Blacker's kindness foremost among his 'admirable gifts'. Alfred Douglas, after producing four contradictory books on his tortured relationship with Wilde, came in time to hold a similar view of Wilde, citing his kindness as pre-eminent among his many remarkable qualities. 'He was the kindest chap', he recalled in a moment of thoughtful retrospection, 'the kindest chap'.[19]

Sorting through 'old papers' before his death, Pip came upon a collection of letters that he found himself unable to destroy. 'In looking over old papers', he wrote in a note he deposited with the letters:

came to this box containing letters written by my mother to my father when they were engaged. When my father died at Dinard in 1928 my mother incinerated much correspondence. But when she came to this collection of letters, she was so moved by the rereading that she could not bring herself to destroy them. Nor can I do so today, though I am nearly ten years older than was my father when he died, and some 15 years older than was my mother when she left us. God bless them both![20]

The almost daily letters cover the period from the final months of 1893 through January 1895, for which diaries are missing, when the newly engaged couple experienced frequent lengthy separations, pending settlement of Blacker's 'tempestuous affairs'. In a letter to her future

husband dated '1 A.M., 1 January 1895', Carrie looked back on the
heartache the past year had brought them:

> The year that is gone was ill omened from the beginning of it to the end;
> when I saw it first come in my heart was like lead within me, and now that it is
> past it is hard to say which is sadder, it's coming or it's going. If you remember,
> Carlos, it was not till after the beginning of 94 that anything really painful and
> heart breaking came to disturb our love, & since then nothing, no nothing, has
> gone well with us.[21]

Blacker's principal tormentor in his troubles was his erstwhile intimate
friend Henry Pelham-Clinton, the youthful duke of Newcastle. In
1890, Blacker embarked on a speculative venture in America in which
he suffered a ruinous financial loss, the source of his 'tempestuous
affairs'. The duke, a modest investor in the venture at the urging of
Blacker, his 'most excellent of pals', was unwittingly caught up in the
subsequent collapse at great unexpected cost to himself when the
enterprise failed. In righteous anger, he freely voiced his suspicion of
the irregular means that had been employed to involve him in the
debacle. As rumors of the ugly charges were whispered about London,
posing a serious threat to Blacker's forthcoming marriage, he succumbed to a debilitating depression and, overwhelmed by his troubles,
chose to leave England and join his sister and her family on the
Continent. In helpless despair, he turned to Wilde, his self-described
'oldest and most faithful friend',[22] who readily agreed to act for him in
securing a retraction and apology from Newcastle—a welcome reassurance for Blacker's distraught fiancée. 'I feel happy for I know you
are in good hands with Mr. Wilde', she wrote with relief to her future
husband.[23] Although the 'signal services' on Blacker's behalf performed by Wilde up to the time of his arrest produced some initially
promising results—Newcastle denying at one point (but later recant-
ing) ever having made, or even thought of, the slanderous remarks he
was being pressed to retract—the aggrieved duke was not soon to be
appeased.

3

A month before Blacker and Wilde were reunited in Paris in March
1898, after not having seen one another since before Wilde's arrest

three years earlier, each, unknown to the other, had become entangled in the Dreyfus affair, then at its high-water mark. Their presence in the famous case, if not the precise nature of their involvement, can be traced in the labyrinthine court records where the name of 'un homme de lettres anglais, M. Carlos Blaker [*sic*]' is linked by witnesses with that of another 'homme de lettres anglais, M. Melmoth [i.e. Oscar Wilde], qui connaissait un M. Blaker [*sic*]'.[24] Other witnesses refer to Wilde by name. Although their presence in the case has thus been known from the outset, owing in part to the obscurity of the official record but more to the studied silence maintained by both about their involvement in the great drama, they have been all but ignored in the vast literature of the affair. In what is widely considered to be the definitive modern history of the case, Jean-Denis Bredin's justly acclaimed *L'Affaire* (1983), neither is mentioned. A further indication of the obscurity that has shrouded Blacker's role in the affair is evident in a more recent exhaustive study, *L'Affaire Dreyfus* (2006), a 750-page *Dictionnaire* under the direction of Michel Drouin. The cover blurb, after noting that everything was believed to be known about the Dreyfus affair, poses the rhetorical question: 'But who was Carlos Blacker?'[25] While the chance involvement of Wilde and Blacker was to affect the course of events in the affair, it was at the same time to lead to the tragic breakup of their 'ancient friendship'.

Blacker arrived in Paris from his sister's home in Freiburg on the opening day of the trial of Émile Zola for the publication on 13 January 1898 of *J'Accuse*, his sensational open letter to the president of France. Zola accused members of the General Staff and other high-ranking officers of the French army of complicity in the wrongful conviction in December 1894 of Captain Alfred Dreyfus, a Jewish officer found guilty by a court-martial of selling military secrets to the German attaché in Paris, Colonel Maximilian von Schwartzkoppen. While the innocent man was serving a life sentence on Devil's Island, Zola accused the conspirators of protecting the actual traitor, Commandant Ferdinand Walsin-Esterhazy. The extraordinary hidden role that Blacker came to play in the affair was the result of his intimate friendship with the Italian military attaché in Paris, Major Alessandro Panizzardi, an active partner in espionage with his German counterpart and ally in the Triple Alliance, Schwartzkoppen. At a time when, in Blacker's words, 'three beings alone knew the whole & entire truth, namely God and the two Military Attachés', he became the fourth such being when Panizzardi confided 'the whole & entire truth' to him.[26] The two men thereupon embarked on a plan aimed at establishing the innocence of Dreyfus and the guilt of Esterhazy through the publication of incriminating documents in Panizzardi's possession.

4

In 1954, Allan Wade, with the cooperation of Wilde's son Vyvyan Holland, began work on a proposed edition of Wilde's collected letters. In response to a request from Vyvyan Holland, whose *Son of Oscar Wilde* appeared the same year, for copies of Wilde's letters to Blacker, the latter's son Pip was prompted to read them for the first time, as he informed a friend:

Last week I was most unexpectedly rung up by Vyvyan Holland, Oscar Wilde's son. He says that he is writing some sort of biography of his father and he wanted to know if I had any letters. Carmen [Pip's daughter] had some years ago found a small collection of seventeen letters. I went through these yesterday for the first time in my life. . . . My mother most drastically pruned my father's papers when he died in 1928, keeping but a fraction.[27]

Although Blacker received 'many beautiful letters' from Wilde, as he informed Constance Wilde's brother following her death, none of the surviving letters predates Blacker's marriage in February 1895.[28] Presumably, all correspondence with Wilde from before that time—the period when 'for many years up to 1893', according to Blacker, he saw Wilde daily—was among the papers destroyed by Carrie following her husband's death.

After the sudden death of Wade in July 1955, Rupert Hart-Davis took over the editorship of the proposed publication. In his introduction to the initial edition published in 1962, Hart-Davis states that 'except for three unimportant omissions, made to avoid giving pain to descendants and clearly indicated, Wilde's letters are here printed exactly as he wrote them'.[29] In the context of a collection of letters marked over a lifetime by what Bernard Shaw described as the invulnerability of Wilde's 'gaiety of soul', the omissions strike a discordantly rancorous note. All three omissions, restored in the later 2000 edition of the letters, relate to Wilde's friendship with Blacker and their bitter falling out, an episode that has remained as obscure as the roles the two

played in the Dreyfus affair. When in July 1986 a collection of Blacker's papers, including the surviving letters from Wilde, was sold by
Sotheby's in London, the sale catalogue referred to 'the never-fully-
explained ending of [Blacker's] friendship with Wilde'.[30]

5

One calamitous result for Blacker of his part in the Dreyfus affair was to
become the object of savage attacks in the anti-Dreyfusard press in
which Newcastle's slanderous charges were for the first time made
public. Blacker became convinced that Wilde, who alone had detailed
knowledge of the quarrel and related events, had been the source of
the information. The anguish and humiliation Blacker suffered at the
reawakening of a long-dormant nightmare, in which he had been
driven to a near-fatal act of desperation, prompted a self-imposed
silence rigidly maintained to the time of his death regarding the critical
role he had played in the Dreyfus affair as well as his breakup with
Wilde.

   At the time of the wounding press attacks, Frederick C. Conybeare,
quondam Fellow of University College, Oxford, one of four co-
conspirators with Blacker in the secret plan to establish the innocence
of Dreyfus, offered consolation in a letter to Blacker's wife Carrie:

When I read of great crimes in the past or witness such infamies in the present
as the Dreyfus case, a feeling comes over me—instinctive & I know not
whence but I am sure from the depths of a being in me that goes far outside
me & ultimately controls things—a feeling I say that someday and somewhere
justice will be done & the truth known even among those who now violate
and mock at the one & the other. If a minority of brave people can be found in
France to go on pleading for the right, I do not despair even of its triumph in
France within five years. Whenever the triumph comes I know that Carlos'
name will transpire and be in the mouths of thousands of French people as that
of one who, though he was an Englishman and had not the same interest &
duty in the matter as a Frenchman has, yet did not pass by on the other side of
the road. It may be momentarily painful to indulge one's generous instincts,
but in the long run one does not repent of having done so. . . . Pray Carlos
never to see that man [Oscar Wilde] (if I may so call one lower than the
animals) again.[31]

For Blacker, the consequences of indulging his 'generous instincts' in the Dreyfus case proved to be more than 'momentarily painful', as predicted by Conybeare. The resulting breakup of his intimate friendship with Wilde, a friendship nourished over years by a rare compatibility of intellect and temperament, was devastating to both of them. How this came about in the year that passed between Wilde's unique, post-prison tribute to an idyllic friendship and Conybeare's description of him as 'one lower than the animals' for his apparent betrayal of that friendship is the subject of this book.

I

'The Greatest Friendship of My Life'

I

Towards the end of an unhappy life, Lord Alfred Douglas looked back with a pang of nostalgia over half a century to a golden day in 'the wonderful summer of 1887, the year of the Jubilee of Queen Victoria', when as a schoolboy at Winchester he won the steeplechase. The acclaim of his peers that day was as heady and unfamiliar an experience as the equally unforgettable approval of an admired but distant father, whose pride in the victory prompted him to send five pounds. 'That Summer Term at Winchester remains ever memorable to me', Douglas wrote; 'life was simply one long dream of joy and fun', and Winchester, 'what an earthly paradise it was . . . how I loved it and love it still!' 'Decidedly, 1887, or its everlasting reflection', he concluded, 'will be the star-year of my eternity.'[1]

Like Douglas, in forever holding dear his refuge early in life from an unhappy home, Henry Pelham Archibald Douglas Pelham-Clinton, seventh duke of Newcastle-under-Lyme, retained throughout his life a strong emotional attachment to his old school and a profound nostalgia as well for the Jubilee Year 1887 when he formed what he came to regard as the greatest friendship of his life—his friendship with Carlos Blacker. Like his grandfather, the fifth duke, he entered Eton as earl of Lincoln and the following year succeeded to the dukedom at fourteen on the death of his father. He had suffered serious head and leg injuries in his infancy when he was dropped by his nurse who reportedly was too frightened to tell anyone of the accident. Lacking timely medical attention, in the ensuing complications the duke's physical development was seriously impaired. Although his mental faculties were unaffected, he failed to achieve normal growth, his height being estimated, by 'the least generous guess', at four feet six inches, with his head disproportionately large for his body. Finding his 'useless foot' a particular handicap, his left leg was amputated at his own wish when fourteen and he was fitted with a prosthetic limb. 'I am thankful that I had my leg off', he wrote from Eton to his guardian Gladstone, 'for I am able to do a great deal I could not do before.'[2]

Capable of only limited activity, it seems remarkable that he should have preserved such fond memories of the rough and tumble of school life ('a boy who is not happy there [Eton] would probably mope in heaven').[3] His Eton obituary notes that 'the ill health which oppressed him through life cut him off from many activities. As a boy here he could play no games: a little riding was all that could be managed for him. Yet to Eton he looked back as a centre of happiness.'[4] Identified by name with Eton's premier academic award, the Newcastle Prize, he enjoyed from the start a high degree of recognition and was fortunate in coming under the influence of a singularly humane and sympathetic housemaster, Walter Durnford, later provost of King's College, Cambridge, who provided a haven of security after the miseries of an invalid childhood passed in a troubled family circle.

His father, the profligate sixth duke, known from his title—earl of Lincoln—as Linky ('very worthless, I fear', in the opinion of Queen Victoria), was in the Bankruptcy Court a few years after assuming the title and had at one time to leave the country when he was unable to pay racing debts amounting to a staggering £230,000. Against the forceful opposition of his own father, the fifth duke, Linky had married Henrietta Adela Hope, the illegitimate daughter of the millionaire Henry Thomas Hope, who agreed to pay his gambling debts, which Linky heedlessly continued to incur on a ruinous scale. A year after his death in a London hotel at the age of forty-five, his widow, the then dowager duchess Henrietta Adela, married Thomas Theobald Hohler. Linky's son and heir, the young earl of Lincoln, known to his intimates in turn as Linny, became the ward of Gladstone, the fifth duke's Eton contemporary and life-long friend.

As guardian, Gladstone did much to restore the heavily encumbered estate at Clumber, subscribing generously to help free it from a crushing burden of debt. Such was his devotion to his friend the fifth duke that when the latter's wife, then Lady Lincoln, the granddaughter of

William Beckford, eloped to the Continent in 1848 with Lord Horatio Walpole, Gladstone went in pursuit. In the sweltering heat of an Italian summer, he followed the trail of the absconding couple from Naples to Lake Como in the vain hope of persuading the runaway wife to return to her duty to her husband and five children. When he finally caught up with her, she was about to give birth to Walpole's child and declined to see him. A scandalous divorce followed.

Eton remained to the end the center of Linny's life and the focus of his activity, together with his involvement in the affairs of the Anglo-Catholic Church of All Saints, Margaret Street, London. He deplored innovation in either institution. At Eton for the Winchester match in 1907 (he could 'never be there without violent movements of the diaphragm'), his 'conservative soul was smitten with dismay by a change of custom':

Hitherto the boys have always attended this match properly dressed with tall hat, etc. This year most of them appeared in 'half-change,' i.e., a loose jacket with the trousers belonging to their black coats and a straw hat! It did not look well and all wanton interference with old customs grieves me sorely.[5]

He experienced similar 'movements of the diaphragm' during his periodic attacks of 'Roman fever'—his recurring wish, following the example of his mother, to join the Church of Rome. 'Personally I am more than ever convinced of the truth of Catholicism and I think you are too, "au fond"', he wrote to Blacker towards the end of his life.[6] 'Altogether the Churches here [Paris] are giving me what you call "movements of the diaphragm" and a spiritual thermometer might indicate a touch of Roman fever, (strictly "entre nous")....It is possible that circumstances might arise when the step would be obligatory for me! Then, unless prevented, I'd be received at the Madeleine as I have often told you.'[7]

A month after fourteen-year-old Linny succeeded to the title, Clumber, the Newcastle ducal seat at Worksop, was seriously damaged by fire, with extensive loss of art treasures that had been collected there over generations. Fifteen of the seventy paintings that were damaged or destroyed had only hours before the fire been returned from the Royal Academy. Although the house was restored with great magnificence, Linny found the scene of his wretched childhood gloomy and uncongenial and was not often there except out of a sense of obligation. 'I spend Easter in London then ten days at Clumber as a duty!' he

wrote to Blacker on one occasion; and on another: 'I can't hold out
Clumber as an inducement because no normal person could be well or
cheerful *there*.'[8] His preferred residence was Forest Farm, Windsor
Forest, within easy distance of his beloved Eton, but even there,
during holiday-time, he found that 'Forest Farm is too dull with
Eton empty.'[9] 'Leaving Eton always fills me with profoundest sorrow',
he wrote in middle age: 'it is the one spot in the world I really love. If
Queen Mary thought "Calais" would be found on her heart after
death, I am sure "Eton" will be discovered on mine, not written,
but most deeply engraved.'[10]

At his death, following a solemn requiem at All Saints, Margaret
Street, he was buried in the Eton Cemetery. As reported in the *Eton
Chronicle* of 7 June 1928, 'A few months before his death someone
asked him what place he loved best in the world and his answer was
"Eton." It was the care of the last year of his life to devise how his body
might rest at Eton, and it was his dying wish that the arms and motto of
Eton should be laid on his breast.'[11] Described at the time as 'a man of
deep piety, and a staunch supporter of the Anglo-Catholic school in
the Church', and as 'one of the most retiring peers in England', it was
noted that he 'was prevented by delicate health, due to a fall in infancy,
from taking more than a small part in public life'.[12] 'A man of much
kindliness and charm, and a good talker in congenial society', he
cherished the memories of the opening scenes of his friendship with
his 'dearest friend' Carlos Blacker in the Jubilee Year. He was fond of
recalling an unforgettably happy day the two had shared at Brighton
that made the year forever memorable for him.[13] 'You know that
I have always looked upon you as my greatest friend', he wrote to
Blacker in 1920, and he begged him three years later to 'let one of your
good resolutions be to visit Paris in the spring, so that I may rejoice my
eyes in the sight of my dearest friend!'[14] They died within weeks of
one another in 1928.

2

The duke inherited many of the characteristics of his grandfather,
'the excellent, conscientious, laborious, unbusiness-like man' who
was the friend of Gladstone and served as Secretary of State for War
during the Crimean conflict.[15] Following Linny's death in 1928, it

was generally acknowledged that 'the little duke', as he was known, had achieved the goal he had set for himself early in life, as he had described it to Gladstone when he was fourteen: 'I do earnestly hope to grow up a good man, and gain the affections of my people and friends.'[16] In contrast, Linny's younger brother by two years, Lord Francis Hope, who was to succeed him as eighth duke, pursued a course in life more reminiscent of the career of their dissolute father, the sixth duke.

Early in the Jubilee Year 1887, Lord Francis turned twenty-one and in compliance with the terms of his maternal grandmother's will added the name Hope to his patronymic, becoming by royal license Pelham-Clinton-Hope. He thereby secured a life interest in Castle Blaney, Ireland, and estates in Surrey, Gloucestershire, and Warwickshire, with an estimated annual income of £20,000. Along with the notable library and collection of Old Master paintings, antique sculpture, and vases that had been assembled by his Hope forebears in the great neo-classical country house at Deepdene, Surrey, came the fabled Hope diamond and with it a full measure of the bad luck traditionally associated with its ownership. One of Francis's first acts on coming into his inheritance was to borrow £54,000 against the value of his life interest in order to pay £43,007 in succession duty and to discharge debts in the amount of £10,000. He was thenceforth rarely to be free from the grasp of money-lenders and by the time he was twenty-eight he was declared bankrupt. After mortgaging his life interest to secure his discharge, he found it impossible to live on the £2,000 a year allowed him under an arrangement with his creditors. Following repeated applications to the Chancery Court, he was finally given leave in 1898 to sell eighty-three of the Dutch and Flemish paintings from the collection at Deepdene, including Vermeer's celebrated *Woman Drinking with a Gentleman*, which had been acquired in 1774 by his great-great-grandfather, John Hope, and is now in the Berlin-Dahlem Gemäldegalerie. The sale of the Hope diamond and twenty more paintings from Deepdene followed in 1910. The great and final sale of the remaining works of art at Deepdene came in 1917, when 30 tons of sculpture and vases, 9 tons of books, and a number of paintings were sold at Christie's. Deepdene became first a hotel, owned at one time by the notorious Maundy Gregory, and subsequently, until 1966, was used as British Railway offices. During the latter occupancy, the once great house was reduced, in the words of an architectural historian, 'to an uniquely detestable state, disgusting beyond all powers of description'.[17] On Linny's death in 1928, Francis succeeded to the dukedom and Francis's son, the future ninth duke, inherited the famous library at Clumber, containing 50,000 volumes. Before his own death in 1941, Francis, described as 'a lonely, unconventional man', witnessed the final liquidation of his extensive inheritance. Following the sale by his son of the celebrated library ('several Caxtons, a first folio of Shakespeare, a first edition of Dante . . . ') over a period of several months in 1937 and 1938, Clumber itself was demolished in the latter year and its remaining contents dispersed in a series of sales.[18]

Heirs to a troubled family history, Linny and Francis had little in common other than their devotion to Carlos Blacker. The qualities of charm and intellect that so endeared Blacker to Oscar Wilde endeared him as well to Linny and Francis, to whom the handsome and urbane Blacker must have seemed everything the brothers were not. It is an indication of Blacker's sympathetic nature as well as his versatility that he was able to enter wholeheartedly into the very different spheres in which the two brothers pursued their widely divergent interests: Eton and Anglo-Catholic church matters with sober, pious Linny, and the theatre and other worldly attractions with pleasure-loving, profligate Francis. Linny could write at length—confident of a reciprocal interest on Blacker's part—of the Unitarian opinions of Reverend Stopford Brooke, one-time chaplain to the queen, whose life of the Reverend Dr Robertson Linny had received from Blacker shortly before the latter's departure for America in 1890.[19] Linny found Robertson's life a sad one, separated as he had been 'from both High and Low Churchmen by his undoubted heterodoxy'. He was sure that Blacker would 'be glad to hear that every night after dinner, I read the "beloved [the duchess]" one of [Robertson's] sermons; we are going through the first volume'.[20] Two weeks later, he was able to report that he had 'finished Robertson's Life: what a sad existence, and what a brilliant creature. . . . We continue to read a sermon every night: this evening it was the beautiful one on the Roman.'[21]

During the same period, twenty-four-year-old Francis was writing to Blacker of more worldly matters: 'I am so sorry that you are having such a dull time of it in Alabama; it will, however, give you a rare appetite for the pleasures of London. . . . What junkets we will have when you return. I mean to enjoy myself thoroughly this summer, and

I think success will crown my efforts.'[22] A boon companion of the two, the actor and *bon vivant* Norman Forbes-Robertson, added his own note of commiseration and encouragement to Blacker:

You talk of not having seen any women at Alabama worth looking at. I don't think there are so very many in most of the large towns in America. I do think you will see some pretty ones in New Orleans. I had a little musical here last Wednesday which I wish you could have attended. Most of the people as they went away said they had never seen so many beautiful women gathered together. I need not tell you that many of them were married. I had a good many 'smart' people too. I asked the Newcastle's & Francis but they were not able to come.[23]

As confidant and counselor to Francis ('Lothario' to Blacker) in his many romantic entanglements, Blacker wrote with advice from America, to which Francis replied:

Just a line or two to thank you for your letter of March 29th and to say in answer to your advice 'be firm,' that I have been so & I think it is all over between us now.—I have not seen the girl 'who served as a derivative junket' since that eventful night, & I am not sure I would know her again, but I have got her address.—You will laugh I am sure, when I tell you that I am smitten again, but this time it means marriage if anything. . . . I shall be in town on the 10th when I hope we will be able to arrange for some rare junkets.[24]

3

Early in 1882, when Linny and Francis were still at Eton, Johnston Forbes-Robertson, older brother of Norman, painted Blacker's portrait. Not yet twenty-three, Blacker appears a sophisticated man of the world, an elegant figure with an aura of glamour and a slightly melancholy cast to his handsome features, suggestive of the depression to which he was prone. 'How I do hate this day', he wrote to Linny on his thirtieth birthday, 'for it is the anniversary of my wretched birth, but it has the advantage of making one doubly conscious of the advance towards the end.'[25] He was elected when twenty-three to membership of the Garrick, a club founded for the object of enabling actors and 'men of education and refinement to meet on equal terms . . . and [as] a rendezvous offered to literary men'. At his debut in this brilliant circle, he recorded handing the porter a lavish £1 tip. A few months later, he was elected at Hurlingham, and duly noted the payment of the £21 entrance fee.

His diary entries for the year reflect the pleasant round of a life of leisure, carefree except for regular losses at cards (écarté, poker, and baccarat) and when romantic attachments became unduly stressful: 'Called on Blanche for last time;...flowers for Daisy 7/6'; 'Very depressed'; 'Flowers for Daisy 1/-'; 'watched Daisy fruitlessly'. While evenings at theatres and music halls (the Gaiety, the Alhambra, the Empire, the Lyceum) are regularly recorded, as well as disbursements to Blanche and Daisy ('Gave Daisy to pay off debts £3/10/0'; 'Paid Mrs Moore [Blanche] £3'; 'Gave Daisy £2'; 'Gave Daisy 10/-'; 'Gave Daisy 13/-'; 'Gave Daisy £5'; 'Daisy tip £1/2'), there is little evidence of application to the intellectual pursuits that underlay the broad erudition for which he was later known—with the exception of a visit to the Elgin Marbles with his close friend W. R. Paton. The following year, he records a 'row with D[aisy]', and the next day: 'Disclosures with B[lanche] M[oore]. Dined with B[lanche] at Paton's. Met D[aisy] by chance in Piccadilly. Resolved to part with D[aisy].' His regularly recorded expenditures for cigarettes ('Every day cigarettes cost 2/-, or 8/-') are interspersed with resolutions to stop smoking ('Left off smoking for good!'; 'Gave my promise to Dr. Mark to give up smoking for 6 months from today s.h.m.G.'; 'Discontinued tobacco finally'; 'Smoked my last cigarette'). By the middle of the decade, his good resolutions had been expanded, with no greater success, to include abstinence from port, wine, and coffee.

As was the case with Oscar Wilde, the 1880s were a halcyon period for Blacker. He lived with his parents in their London home, at 12 Sussex Square, and maintained his bachelor life on an allowance from his father of £750 a year. In the early years of the decade, there are only occasional references in Blacker's diary to Oscar Wilde, one four days before Wilde's marriage: '[25 May 1884] Dined at Bristol with N.F.R. [Norman Forbes-Robertson] & Oscar Wilde'; '[21 July 1884] Dinner at Bristol with F.R. & Oscar Wilde...dinner at Bristol £4/13/0.' It was not until the second half of the decade that their friendship reached the state of intimacy later described by Blacker to Wilde's brother-in-law, Otho Holland, when 'for many years up to 1893' they saw one another daily. This was a period in Blacker's life, prior to his marriage, which belonged to a past of which his wife Carrie strongly disapproved and which Blacker himself eventually wished to put behind him and forget. Diaries for the period are missing. If they once existed, it seems likely, as has been suggested, that they were among the records destroyed by Carrie following her husband's death in 1928.

4

In February 1889, Linny, then twenty-four, and seventeen-year-old Kathleen Florence May Candy, the daughter of Major H. A. 'Sugar' Candy, 'that notable figure in Victorian clubland and social circles', were married in All Saints' Church, Margaret Street, London. The bride was described as 'tall, with a fair complexion, brown wavy hair and bright grey eyes, and as with all Irish girls, inclined to laughter'.[26] Among the wedding guests were Oscar and Constance Wilde, who presented the newly-weds with a 'Japanese box'—presumably a gold and black lacquer box, an example of the *japonaiserie* fashionable at the time. Wilde, however, soon came to be, and remained to the end, a sore subject with Linny. Robert Sherard attributes this, without further elaboration, to a quarrel between the two that he says occurred about the year 1890. The ill feeling on Linny's part followed the course of his falling-out with Blacker, in which Wilde took an active part resented by Linny, whose dislike was further intensified by the scandalous circumstances of Wilde's subsequent fall. Many years later when Sherard was seeking to refute a charge that Wilde had been a snob, suggested by Frank Harris in his biography—based on Wilde's having allegedly claimed on one occasion that he was to be a guest at Clumber—Sherard wrote to the duke and inquired whether he had ever entertained Wilde there. 'It is, unfortunately, true that Oscar Wilde was an occasional visitor to Clumber in the late '80s', the duke replied, a month before his death on 30 May 1928, 'but I should be much obliged if you would let the matter rest and take no notice of the statement.'[27]

The distaste was mutual. Sherard describes a supper at the Garrick Club at which the duke was present when a house-party at Clumber was mentioned. Sherard 'casually said to Oscar as we were going home that [he] wondered who was going to Clumber for this house-party. "Oh," [Wilde] said, "the Duke will take a table of precedence and draw a line across it pretty high up, and those above the line will be invited, but not those below."'[28] Clumber was almost certainly the unspecified ducal house of which Wilde retained the unpleasant memory attributed to him by Laurence Housman in a pastiche of Wilde's conversational style:

I remember once, on a Monday morning, missing an unreasonably early train, and having to return for four hours to the bosom of a ducal family, when its exhibition hours were over. It was a charnel house: the bones of its skeleton rattled: the ghosts gibbered and moaned. Time remained motionless. I was haunted. I could never go there again. I had seen what man is never meant to see—the sweeping up of the dust on which the footfall of departing pleasure has left its print. There for two days I had been creating my public: the two days given by God to the Jewish and Christian world for rest; and from that breaking of the Sabbath, creator and created were equally exhausted. The breath of life I had so laboriously breathed into their nostrils they were getting rid of again, returning to native clay.[29]

In 1889, work was completed on a project dear to Linny's heart, the building of a Gothic-style church at Clumber, St Mary the Virgin, where, as was noted at the time of his death, 'the ritual observed has always been what is called "advanced"'.[30] As described by the duchess, 'on entering, the effect is that of a genuine fourteenth century Chapel untouched by the devastating hand of the so-called Reformation'.[31] The church was designed by the firm of Bodley and Garner and built at a cost of £40,000. Final settlement of the architects' account was delayed when Linny disputed a charge of £400 for work which he claimed was unauthorized. 'If Bodley brings an action against me', he confided to Blacker, 'I shall get George Lewis to defend me.'[32] As negotiations proceeded, Linny made an offer to settle on the basis of payment of the entire amount owing, less the disputed £400. 'If this is not accepted', he informed Blacker, 'I suppose the matter will go to the Courts, and good old George will be called to the defence.'[33] Bodley capitulated, however, and there was no need of 'good old George' this time. 'Bodley has eaten humble pie', Linny reported in triumph, ' . . . and cannot be pitied.'[34]

George Lewis had a long-established reputation as the foremost lawyer of his day, numbering among his clients the Prince of Wales and many of the most prominent figures in the upper reaches of society, politics, and the theatre, for whom he was friend and confidant as well as lawyer. 'He knows all about us', observed Oscar Wilde, 'and he forgives us all.' Lewis proved to be less forgiving in Wilde's case than the latter supposed. While he may not have known all of

Wilde's secrets, there was little that Lewis did not know about high-profile personalities in London, and what he knew of Wilde's private life in the years preceding his fall served to weaken the bond of their once close friendship. Having benefited from Lewis's wise counsel for many years, Wilde would lament the loss of it in his prison cell: 'when I was deprived of his advice and help and regard, I was deprived of the one great safeguard of my life'.[35] Wilde's troubles had started with the provocative card ('Oscar Wilde posing Somdomite') left for him at the Albemarle Club by Lord Alfred Douglas's maniacal father the marquess of Queensberry. When Wilde found it there ten days later, 'bewildered, incapable of judgment' and goaded by Douglas, he was driven to take what he came to regret as the 'fatal and idiotic step of beginning an action at law', resulting in his own criminal prosecution and imprisonment.[36] 'If you had come to see me in the first place', Lewis told Wilde following the collapse of the suit against Queensberry and within hours of Wilde's arrest, 'I would have torn up Queensberry's card and thrown it on the fire and told you not to make a fool of yourself.'[37]

In September 1890, the Prince of Wales invited Lewis to join his party for the autumn race meeting at Doncaster in Yorkshire. The members of the party were to be the guests of Arthur Wilson, a wealthy shipping magnate, at his country house, Tranby Croft. Had Lewis been able to be present on the occasion, it seems more than likely that the prince would have sought and followed his clear-sighted counsel and one of the great scandals of the Victorian era—the notorious Tranby Croft Affair—may well have been averted. During two evenings' play at baccarat, in which the prince, using his own distinctly marked counters, acted as banker, Wilson's son became convinced that one of the guests was cheating. The guest was Sir William Gordon-Cumming, a wealthy and prominent figure in London society, lieutenant colonel in the Scots Guards with a distinguished military record, and a long-time member of the prince's intimate circle. Young Wilson was able to convince four others in the party of his suspicions and the matter was brought to the attention of the prince. Gordon-Cumming, despite his vehement protestations of innocence, was coerced, in the interest of avoiding a public scandal that threatened his own and his regiment's good name as well as that of the prince, into signing an undertaking never to play cards again as long as he lived. In return, the ten other men present, including the prince, promised to remain silent with respect to the terrible charge and added their signatures to the document. Gordon-Cumming, the prince's traveling companion on the journey to Tranby Croft, was further humiliated by being made to leave the house early the next morning.

Inevitably, with so many sharing the secret, it leaked out and several months later rumors of it began to circulate in London. Gordon-Cumming, who had never ceased to protest his innocence, saw that he had no alternative but to sue his five accusers for slander. The prince, who from the outset had shown no sympathy for his friend Gordon-Cumming and to whom the entire experience was 'like a hideous nightmare', arranged to have George Lewis represent all of the defendants. Sir Edward Clarke appeared for Gordon-Cumming, as he was to do for Oscar Wilde a few years later in similar circumstances. The facts of the case, and the absence of any clear motive on the part of wealthy Gordon-Cumming to risk honor and high position for a negligible sum, point to his innocence. Despite this, Lewis was able to secure a victory for the defendants that, although unpopular with the press and the public, was received with gratitude by the Prince of Wales. The following year, Lewis was given a knighthood and ten years later, at the coronation of Edward VII, he was made a baronet. Gordon-Cumming, on the other hand, was dismissed from his regiment, expelled from his clubs, and spent the remaining forty years of his life socially ostracized in retirement in Scotland. The lesson of the case and the fate of Gordon-Cumming were not lost on Linny, as he was to demonstrate two years later when he quarreled with Carlos Blacker.

2

'Sadness, Disappointment, Upset, & Weariness'

I

On coming into his princely inheritance in 1887, Lord Francis Hope embraced the opportunity to focus his full attention on 'the pleasures of London'.[1] He was soon joined by Blacker who left his parental home in Sussex Square and moved into rooms at 161a Piccadilly, designated his 'Albemarle Chambers', at the corner of Piccadilly and St James's Street. The building, demolished to make way for the Royal Insurance Building in 1907, was among vanished landmarks identified with the early years of his friendship with Blacker that Linny recalled with recurring nostalgia. 'In St James Street, too, much is being done', he wrote to Blacker toward the end of his life; 'the dirty little house where we had our jolly Xmas party in 1887 has gone'.[2] From his new address, Blacker in November 1888 sent a twenty-year-old American acquaintance, 'Miss Frost'—destined to be his future wife Carrie—a large paper copy of Wilde's *The Happy Prince*: 'I once heard you say that you liked the stories & so it affords me great pleasure to offer them to you in their best dress.'[3] Blacker's friendship with the author was flourishing at a time fondly recalled by Wilde years later ('What marvellous evenings, dear Carlos, we used to have! What brilliant dinners! What days of laughter and delight!')[4] In the intimacy of their daily association, not only was Wilde moved to dedicate his first popular published work to Blacker, he granted him as well an extraordinary authority over his future literary output, as Blacker reported to Linny:

Our friend Oscar was impenetrable yesterday to my attacks on what 'you wot of' & laughed it all away. It has now been however arranged that all his manuscripts are in future to be submitted to me for approval, & I shall make a wholesome slaughter of his humours & tempers, when the occasion deserves it. He had no excuses to offer & disarmed me by his extreme hilarity, saying he had foreseen & anticipated my strictures.[5]

For Blacker, added to the enchantment of carefree gaiety in the company of Wilde was his attachment to a woman identified only as Kate whom he treated 'as his wife, and had allowed her to be regarded as his wife by respectable women', according to Wilde, writing of a time when 'we had all stayed together, at the Hôtel d'Athenée, at the Hôtel de Normandie, at the Hôtel de deux Mondes, at many places together'.[6] The inadequacy of Blacker's paternal allowance to support 'la grande vie à Londres avec la belle Kate', as it was later referred to in a Paris newspaper, was a problem for which two American friends, the brothers Dillwyn and Alfred Parrish, appeared to offer a solution.[7] A corporate venture envisioned by the brothers for the purpose of developing land and mineral rights in the State of Alabama held promise for Blacker of an assured means of securing his financial position. 'We have been working out a scheme for developing Alabama', Blacker informed Linny, 'which I am in hope may yield grand results.'[8] Totally lacking in business experience, he became a promoter and director of the North Alabama Land Development Company and agreed to underwrite £7,000 of the company's debentures. Among the first with whom he sought to promote the enterprise was newly married Linny. Having only recently settled the disputed claim for payment of the costly new chapel at Clumber, Linny was shy of any further expenditure. The success of his conscientious efforts to clear the ducal estate at Clumber, home to some 250 workers and tenants, of the heavy burden of debt inherited from his spendthrift father had been owing to his own fixed habits of fiscal discipline and prudence acquired under the tutelage of his guardian Gladstone. He eventually agreed to a modest investment in the company but was grateful not to have to come up with immediate payment for it in full. 'By this post I am sending the hundred quid to your bankers', he informed Blacker; 'much thanks for your consideration, for in my present financial condition it would have ~~made~~ been severe to fork out £300'.[9] In response to Blacker's importuning, Linny turned to Thomas Hohler who, through his marriage to the dowager duchess, had become his stepfather and adviser. Hohler found it 'most difficult' to offer advice in the absence of more specific information about the project 'and above all the real honesty of the borrowers', adding parenthetically '(By the way, I remember warning you at Clumber against lending our friend more money & you took my advice)!!!' Dismissing letters furnished by Linny by way of background to the proposed investment as those of 'an idiot or a drunken man', Hohler concluded that, 'Of course if the Parents can offer you such security as will insure you repayment of *both* your liabilities—then I should advise your going on with further help; but I personally would do *nothing* before ascertaining from the *Parents*, in *their* *own* handwriting the proof certainty & security of this.'[10]

In February 1890, Blacker sailed for America with high hopes for the success of the Alabama venture. In response to an optimistic letter from him a month later about the company's prospects, Linny remained non-committal:

I am glad that things are doing so well with you and with the Company. . . . I am much impressed by what your last letter says concerning the future of 'Rivertown', and if it really lies in my power to do anything for its spiritual welfare be sure that I will do it. Of course, as you know, I am not altogether unhampered with claims at home; but if the embryo city puts oof into my pocket, I shall consider that the said prospective town has the first call upon me for that cash. . . . Your old friend forever Newcastle.

Linny sorely missed the companionship of Blacker and wished that he 'were back that we might have a good old yapp in 161a'.[11] As the months went by, the company failed to prosper. 'This is a most savage life', Blacker noted despondently to Linny from Alabama, '& if you add a temperature of 85 & countless malevolent insects you will guess that the financier's life is not a happy lot.'[12] Deeply discouraged and depressed, Blacker returned to England in June. 'I grieve to see how low your spirits are', Linny wrote on the eve of his return; 'Oh! If you were only back, any engagement but a royal one I will chuck to meet you at Liverpool. . . . Longing for your return.'[13] To Blacker's disappointment, however, Linny's heartfelt sympathy did not extend to his making any further financial commitment. 'The gloomy silence which you are maintaining', Blacker wrote a month following his return, 'causes me to imagine that you must be finding your time very much absorbed & engrossed, but this will be in a pleasant manner as opposed to the feverish flutter of the financier's lot.' Turning to a less problematic subject, he cited the appearance in the July number of *Lippincott's Monthly Magazine* of the 'Picture of Dorian Gray' and the challenge presented to his role as literary adviser to Wilde. 'You will be surprised to learn that O.W. is going to publish that damned story in a separate form in October, with additions but I fear no corrections. Have you ever known such abominable "Cussedness"'.[14] Two months later, continued silence on Linny's part in response to a direct appeal, convinced Blacker that no further financial help would be forthcoming:

I take it by your silence that you were unable to lend me the hand I asked you for. I trust my dear fellow that you have not thought me exacting or indelicate, for to you who have ever been the soul of kindness to me, such conduct on my part is indeed unmeant, for certainly I would have done anything rather than that you should think me capable 'd'abuser de vos bontés'.

However I will in future never disturb you in a similar fashion & will endeavour to appeal to the flinty sentiments of the trained financiers.[15]

The clouds continued to gather over Blacker's life as he spent the next two years in fruitless and dispiriting efforts to save the foundering Alabama enterprise. His own financial position grew steadily worse and was made more desperate by losses on the stock exchange amounting eventually to £2,000. In September 1892, faced with the imminent liquidation of the company and his obligation to take up his share of the now worthless debentures, he declared with resignation and despair that he was 'tired of the whole thing & to know the worst even would be a relief. . . . If it pleased God or the Devil or both to once again put me in a position to disregard everything connected with money worries, I shall enjoy that which I have never sufficiently appreciated before, PEACE with ecstatic enthusiasm.'[16] In order to meet his underwriting commitment and other obligations, he borrowed £10,000 from an insurance company, the loan secured by Lord Francis Hope, described in a later court proceeding ('The Affairs of Lord Francis Hope') as 'of 161a, Piccadilly, and Deep Dene, Dorking'.[17]

Under his worrisome burden of troubles, Blacker had in the meantime succumbed to a debilitating depression from which he sought relief in opium, the commonly prescribed antidote of the day for melancholy. With the brightness of his stimulating personality dimmed, he gradually withdrew from the ebullient company of Oscar Wilde, who, in contrast, was 'beaming with the inebriation of success, & is producing excellent plays with remarkable rapidity', as Blacker reported to his future wife Carrie.[18] In June 1892, however, Wilde suffered a serious reversal when the Lord Chamberlain banned the production of *Salomé*, which was to have featured Sarah Bernhardt in the principal role. In Bad Homburg for the cure and feeling unwell, he appealed to Blacker to join him. 'Oscar Wilde is in Homburg', Blacker informed Carrie, 'very miserable, because he sends me urgent appeals to join him there.—I fear our friend has tasted but a very little of what constitutes joy in the success of his play.'[19]

As the year 1892 came to a close, with 'American affairs' expected to end in a total loss, Blacker wrote that he had 'gloomy visions of the coming year, for though I am schooling myself to regard things with tolerable equanimity there are moments when regrets & apprehensions quite overcome my spirits'.[20] He had by then been almost totally eclipsed from Wilde's life by the fatally attractive Lord Alfred 'Bosie' Douglas, still an undergraduate at Oxford, who had accompanied Wilde to Homburg. Under daily pressure from his creditors, Blacker appealed to Wilde in desperation for prompt settlement of his interest in the latter's play, *Lady Windermere's Fan*, which had earned £7,000 for Wilde in its first year. 'My dear Oscar', Blacker wrote somewhat stiffly from 161a Piccadilly, 'I have waited quite long enough now, & I beg that you will do me the kindness to let me know in what manner, & when you intend settling my claim for the interest I had in your play. Pray let us arrange this quickly & amicably for the sake of old times.'[21] Responsive as he later proved to be to a more urgent appeal from Blacker 'for the sake of old times', Wilde, pressed by creditors himself, was in no position to honor a claim for immediate repayment. Two months later, however, when *Salomé* was published on 22 February 1893, he presented Blacker with one of fifty copies on hand-made paper, warmly inscribed: 'To Carlos Blacker from his affectionate friend, the author, in esteem and admiration'.[22]

When Blacker proved unable to repay his loan when it fell due in late 1893, the insurance company immediately looked to his trusted surety, on whom Blacker had totally depended to make good. In view of Francis's seemingly inexhaustible resources, his ability to fulfill his obligation as guarantor had been assumed without question at the time the loan was made. As a result of his reckless extravagance, however, a receiving order in bankruptcy had been entered against him in October 1893, to Blacker's horror, while Linny looked on

with mounting disapproval. A few months earlier, Francis had unsuccessfully sought relief in an application to the Chancery Court for an
order authorizing him as life tenant to sell the extensive Hope
collection of Dutch and Flemish paintings at Deepdene. Linny and
his three sisters opposed the application and the court, noting that it
was Francis's own extravagance that had made it impossible for him
to live at Deepdene, refused to sanction the sale. Francis's mother, the
dowager duchess, attributed responsibility for his 'unlucky speculations' to the influence of Blacker. 'This is not the case as you know',
Blacker assured Linny, 'so it does not wound me.' A second charge
by the dowager duchess, that Linny had been 'seen at the theatre in
improper society', was similarly refuted by Blacker ('you know well
enough', he reminded Linny, 'that the society was not such as ever to
hurt you, or cause you to deteriorate. Therefore this second point
also leaves me unhurt').[23] 'During the years 1890–1893', *The Times*
later reported, Francis 'borrowed sums of money amounting to
£78,000, from Mr. Valentine Smith [a money lender]. . . . The
£78,000 had been expended in personal living, in loans to friends,
in payment of sums which he had guaranteed, and in financing the
Lyric Theatre.'[24] As to the 'loans to friends':

it was said that in contracting liabilities to the extent of £45,000 on behalf of
other persons without receiving any consideration the debtor had been
generous. He (the Registrar) was sorry that the debtor had been 'let in,' but,
dealing with the matter as a question of bankruptcy, he did not think it was the
kind of generosity to which the Court could give much weight in arriving at a
decision upon the application for discharge.[25]

With both Blacker and Francis unable to meet their obligations on the
note, the lending institution called upon Linny as apparent co-surety
to make good on the loan, totaling with interest £10,733. The dreaded
sequence of events that followed was devastating to Blacker. 'I am so
sorry', he apologized with mournful resignation to Linny in a brief
uncharacteristic penciled note, without salutation and suggestively
written on black-bordered stationery, as the duke was about to leave
for the Chicago World's Columbian Exposition:

& I feel damnably depressed at your going. If you do <u>not</u> go send me a
telegram to Piccadilly. I detest separations they are like anticipations of
annihilation. Peace! C.B.

Be good enough to let me know what my liability to you is from this place. Do not fail to do this.[26]

Stunned and enraged at the unexpected development, and unmoved by Blacker's appeal for 'Peace', Linny freely voiced the fact that there had been a serious irregularity in obtaining his guarantee without his knowledge. After grudgingly paying off the loan and unwilling to be placated, he made peremptory demands on both Blacker and Francis for immediate repayment.

Linny's own well-ordered life had in the meantime been subject to continuing disruption by a complication that weighed heavily on his spirits, as Blacker informed Carrie: 'Newcastle though enjoying far better health than is his wont, is almost disturbed beyond sufferance by domestic incompatibility, & Clumber is to him a cave of horrors.'[27] The incompatibility of Linny and his seventeen-year-old bride 'Tatta' had been apparent from the start. A month after the marriage, Blacker had noted in response to a report from Linny: 'is it not wonderful that there is no unmixed joy in this world, since your lady is suffering from objective aggressions. . . . Remember me to your lady for the riddance of whose ills I will offer up a prayer.'[28] While the young duchess asserted firm control over management of the Clumber estate, Linny sought relief from domestic turmoil in extended travels in America and Europe as well as in excursions in a 'land yacht' called the *Bohemian*: a twenty-five-foot-long caravan drawn by two sturdy dray horses, built to his specifications to include a wine cellar hung between the axles and space for a piano.[29] Thus equipped, he pursued his favorite pastime—'prowling about the country in a caravan, photographing. . . . He will be away for seven weeks . . . & I fear his wife resents it', Blacker reported to Carrie.[30] Linny's adventures as 'a gentleman gypsy' in his caravan, followed—with the advent of the motor car—by his acquisition of 'a wide array of . . . pioneering motor vehicles', and other suggestive circumstances, caused the chronicler of the ducal estate to speculate: 'Could our diminutive nobleman have been the model for the famous "Mr Toad" [of Toad Hall]', star of Kenneth Grahame's *Wind in the Willows*.[31]

Towards the end of the year 1892, before being called upon as co-surety, Linny, in quest of a more complete escape from the marital scene, had attempted to 'lure' Blacker into accompanying him to the World's Columbian Exhibition in Chicago and then on to further travels.[32] Blacker had declined the invitation and in a letter to Carrie, without reference to Linny's unexpected obligation on the loan, attributed what followed to 'spite, since by refusing to consort with him for a travel of 18 months he realized that it was irksome to me, & he sought revenge'.[33] It was not the first time the physically handicapped and retiring 'little duke' had been provoked to anger by his perception that he was being used by the handsome, sophisticated man-about-town Blacker. 'S'death, engrave this on the tables of your memory', Blacker had urged in response to the charge on an earlier occasion, 'the severance of our amity shall permanently & endurably date from the occasion on which you next assert that I treat you as a convenience.—Perish the thought!'[34] In the latest instance, Linny, in unabated rage, declined to follow Blacker's injunction to 'perish the thought' and relentlessly pressed the two defaulters on the loan for payment.

When Francis failed to meet his obligation as surety, Linny obtained a receiving order against him in September 1893, precipitating his eventual bankruptcy. Francis's statement of affairs showed gross liabilities amounting to £657,942 against assets estimated at £174,148. The official receiver found that 'the debtor's failure would appear to be attributable to extravagance in living, combined with betting and gambling, and more directly to liabilities and losses incurred in connection with and on behalf of other persons and a theatrical speculation'.[35] As the result of a succession of appeals and postponements, Francis's public examination did not take place until 31 October 1895. In contrast to the anguish and dread with which both Blacker and Wilde faced their own appearances before the Bankruptcy Court the same year, twenty-nine-year-old Francis displayed remarkable insouciance:

The Official Receiver.—Can you give me any idea how much was used for your personal expenses, in satisfying guaranters, and in financing the theatre?

The debtor (smiling).—I have never made any calculation, but perhaps I have received personally about £100,000.[36]

As petitioning creditor, Linny opposed his brother's application for discharge, and the order was suspended until not less than 10 shillings in the pound had been paid to creditors.

Although Linny was later to initiate similar action against Blacker, forcing him as well into bankruptcy, his immediate revenge took a more desperate form. In addition to casting slanderous aspersions on the legitimacy of the surety arrangement, aspersions with potentially criminal implications, in an incident that appears to have taken place at the Garrick Club and recalled the terrible charge that had so effectively ruined Sir William Gordon-Cumming, he accused Blacker of cheating at cards.[37] Like Gordon-Cumming, Blacker felt he had no alternative but to sue his accuser for defamation. In view of the disastrous consequences for Gordon-Cumming as plaintiff in the earlier case, there was little ground for hope of a satisfactory outcome.

2

Faced with the duke's charges, Blacker left London in a state of despair with the intention of settling in Paris. 'The fortune I have experienced in London has been so outrageous that it has almost become grotesque', he wrote at the time. 'I too am resolved to live in Paris & I am looking out for a convenient resting place for my books.' He confessed to feeling 'as I feel about most things in life sadness, disappointment, upset, & weariness'.[38]

The bleak, unpromising future brightened somewhat a few months later while Blacker was at Aix-les-Bains with his mother. Here in July 1893 he ran into his old friend, 'Miss Frost', with whom he had carried on a desultory correspondence since their first meeting five years earlier when Carrie was living in Dorset with her older sister Jane, the wife of Sir Lewis Molesworth. Sir Lewis, a friend of Carrie's brother Graham at Stonyhurst College, had met his future wife Jane when she was fifteen and he twenty, a guest at the time at Hazelwood, the Frost country home in St Louis. As in her own case with Blacker, it was love at first sight, according to Carrie, and Sir Lewis and Jane were married the following year. Subsequently, when Blacker was about to depart for America in 1890, Sir Lewis, at Blacker's request, had obliged him with 'a letter for St. Louis', leading to a renewal of the friendship. This was followed two years later by a happy interlude in New York in April 1892 when Blacker and Francis passed some carefree days in the company of Carrie and her younger sister Lily. Following the departure of his 'dear new sisters' on that occasion, as Blacker informed 'My dear Miss Frost' a few days later, 'like Patroclus, the sun has not been shining upon me'.[39] The respite from his worries had been all too brief and his thoughts had immediately returned to his troubles: 'Now, in the deadness,—the sickness,—& the pain of life to me, I find myself cheered by the thought that perhaps by accident, one or two such mornings as that of the 20th April may still be in store for me.'[40] Nine years older than Carrie and in a committed relationship with *la belle Kate*, he remained unaware that Carrie was in love with him. On the eve of their parting, she had gone to New York's St Patrick's Cathedral 'to pray & ask God for comfort. I cried . . . on that 24 of April', she later confessed to Blacker, 'because I loved you & was nothing to you.'[41]

Their chance meeting at Aix-les-Bains a year later seemed providential. In the weeks that followed, Blacker came to recognize the true depth of his feeling for her. 'For five years your love has been near me', he confided at last, '& it has taken five years for me to recognize it.'[42] By the end of the year, they had become engaged. While Carrie was able to look back gratefully on 'the old year that has brought us together & given us so much happiness', she was at the same time troubled by Carlos's alarming preoccupation with worries he felt unable to share with her.[43] 'How I wish it were in my power to unburthen myself to you but this is *impossible*', he agonized.[44] Mystified, Carrie began to doubt 'whether we have been wise, you in shutting me out, and I in consenting to be shut out from your confidence in regard to all that is troubling you. It gives me a pang to have you speak of things that are worrying you the details of which "cannot and will not concern" me.'[45] Blacker in response was adamant in his insistence that his troubles belonged to a past which did not concern her; he wished their 'New Life' to be free of them and the torment of his past life to be forgotten:

Under no circumstances whatever would it be right, expedient, or in accordance with the fitness of things as they should be, that you should have any knowledge from me of the things which trouble me.—

These belong to my past, they are in no way connected with you. I alone am responsible for them, & though the goodness of your heart may impel you to desire to give me comfort & advice, this is not within your domain, & I desire that it may never be.—

The future as I ambition it must be free from any of the elements of what has occurred to me in the past. It is to be the New Life, & the past forgotten.[46]

High on the list of worrisome 'elements' in his troubled past was the liaison with his long-time mistress. Seeking to terminate the relationship, Blacker warned Carrie that she might receive a letter intended to prejudice her against him and thus separate them.[47] Carrie assured him that if she should receive any such letter, she would send it unread to him to dispose of as he should see fit, adding that he could let the person who proposed writing to her know how futile this was as any such letters would not be read.[48]

Unable to bring himself to confide in Carrie, Blacker turned for solace and counsel to his 'oldest and most faithful friend', Oscar Wilde. At the end of November 1893, leaving Carrie on the Riviera with the Molesworths, Blacker went to Paris where he met Wilde at the Hôtel des Deux-Mondes, the scene of happy times in the past, in somber contrast to the present state of both their lives. As Blacker immediately learned, Wilde was as distraught as he himself, near the breaking point from 'the terrible strain of [Douglas's] companionship'.[49] The relationship that had at first so charmed and beguiled Wilde had become a torment to him. Bosie's terrible temper, his petulant tantrums, his mindless extravagance (at Wilde's expense), his uncontrollable rages and penchant for creating scenes: all had combined to make the strain of his company unbearable, causing Wilde 'to fly abroad and leave a false address to try and escape from him'.[50] Wilde later recalled his troubled state of mind at the time:

I remember that afternoon, as I was in the railway-carriage whirling up to Paris, thinking what an impossible, terrible, utterly wrong state my life had got into, when I, a man of world-wide reputation, was actually forced to run away from England, in order to try and get rid of a friendship that was entirely destructive of everything fine in me either from the intellectual or ethical point of view.[51]

'I found Oscar very dashed in spirits', Carlos informed Carrie:

but poor fellow he seemed to find comfort at being able to pour out his soul to me. He has much to make him unhappy but his grand spirit of optimism will ultimately I am sure carry everything before it. I have only heard his story so far, mine to him is to follow by mutual agreement. We lunched at the Café de Paris, ... We talked incessantly until 3, though Oscar remarked that my attention seemed to be distracted.[52]

Carrie was relieved to know that Blacker was with Wilde, and she hoped that he would persuade Oscar to stay on in Paris as long as Blacker remained there so as not to leave him alone. She regretted, however, that Oscar had brought his own troubles to Blacker. 'I am sorry to hear that Oscar has fallen on evil times', she wrote:

I hoped he would be in good spirits and make you forget your troubles, instead of listening to his. I am afraid from your account of how you spent your first day in Paris, that you could have done nothing about your own affairs, & by reason of not having written your letters as you intended, your return to me will be delayed by at least a day. However, if you were able to be of any use to Oscar, and I am sure you were, you will not mind the time.[53]

The reunion as anticipated proved a tonic to both Blacker and Wilde. 'Oscar has been very sympathetic and kind as he always is', Carlos wrote. 'He came here on his own affairs as you rightly thought, but he has been most ready to identify himself with mine, & will I am sure do me real services. . . . I am trying to urge [him] to remain.'[54] Wilde, however, could manage only five days ('He cannot remain, else he would'), after which he left 'with his mind more at rest & after speaking words of great judgment'.[55] Carrie was anxious about Blacker's being alone in his fragile state. 'Will it be necessary for you to remain in Paris for long after Oscar goes', she inquired; 'if so darling try not to be much alone and take all the care you can of yourself—Remember you made me a faithful promise to do nothing to excess, and to be more dear to yourself because you are infinitely dear and precious to me.'[56] Following Wilde's departure, Blacker wrote that 'until yesterday I was with Oscar but now I have to find some friend to talk to'.[57] To his reassurance regarding a principal concern of her own, his use of opium in his despondent state, Carrie replied: 'How good of you dearest, not to have taken any opiates—but remember that rather than have you suffer too much I would rather have you take something, more especially as when this is over, I hope & believe you will never have the occasion for anything of the sort again, and then we will break all bad habits, the habit of being unhappy first of all.'[58]

In the course of their mutual commiseration, Wilde agreed on his return to England to act on Blacker's behalf in negotiations with Newcastle and his formidable solicitor, 'good old George' Lewis. The immediate result was gratifying to Blacker who was able to report to Carrie not long after that 'Oscar Wilde has been doing me signal services.'[59] While immersed in this role, Wilde was simultaneously engaged in completing the last three acts of his play *An Ideal Husband*, which he had begun writing at Goring the previous summer. 'I became engrossed in writing it', he later informed Charles Ricketts, 'and it contains a great deal of the real Oscar.'[60] The 'real Oscar' is recognizable in the play in the character of the philosopher-dandy Lord Goring, who chivalrously comes to the rescue of his friend Sir Robert Chiltern, whose reputation and marriage are imperiled by the threatened exposure of a youthful transgression. Facing the imminent ruin of his happily settled life, Chiltern feels unable in his distress to confide in his rigidly moralistic wife, certain that their marriage could not survive the tarnishing of the image she has of him as an ideal husband. Lord Goring's successful intervention with the mischief-making Mrs Cheveley, a figure from Chiltern's shadowed past—thus saving the day—mirrors Wilde's like role in his dealings with Blacker's former mistress to avert the ruin she posed for Blacker in circumstances similar to those confronting Sir Robert Chiltern.

3

Proceedings against the duke, which were to drag on for more than two years, got off to a slow start. 'As you are aware the Duke is at present absent abroad & will not return for some months', Sir George Lewis informed Blacker's solicitor, H. Weller Richards, on 13 January 1894. 'I would therefore suggest the matter should stand over until he is back when I have no doubt there will be no difficulty in satisfying you.'[61] Richards passed the information along to Wilde with a request for instructions:

I append copy of the reply to my letter to Sir George Lewis of the 12th inst. It would have been more satisfactory if Sir George Lewis had attempted some explanation, but still I think the letter goes as far as could be expected. Will you kindly let me know if so far as you are able to judge, it will be advisable to fall in with Sir George Lewis' suggestion? Personally I see no alternative unless the proceedings are carried on, a course which we are all anxious to avoid.[62]

With greater prudence than he was later to display in his own dealings with Queensberry, Wilde concurred in Lewis's suggestion that proceedings be deferred until the duke's return. Meanwhile, he continued to act with full authority in instructing Richards on Blacker's behalf. 'If you are in London on Monday & can spare a few minutes', Richards wrote on 16 February 1894, 'I should like to see you on Mr. Blacker's matters.'[63] In May, Richards wrote to inform Wilde, 'I have an appointment to see the Duke's Solicitors on Monday at 1:45 & shall be glad to see you. Can you call at any time after 2 on that day?'[64] Shortly thereafter, Wilde met personally with the duke, who could only have found Wilde's intervention in the delicate matter a considerable irritation. This was not only the likely root of the ill-feeling that developed between Newcastle and Wilde, noted by Robert Sherard, but it is likely as well that it served to put further distance between Wilde and his once close friend and adviser George Lewis.

Another deeply concerned long-time friend of both Blacker and Wilde, William Roger Paton, wrote to Wilde from Smyrna, offering his assessment and advice:

I heard from Carlos that you had interviewed Newcastle about this matter of Newcastle's vile treachery to a dear friend. I am exceedingly of opinion that Carlos should continue to prosecute, in view of the horror of the crime & also in view of the station of Newcastle. I hope you agree with me & will urge this course on Carlos, who has a little & for a time lost his natural energy. It makes me cry much when he writes to me & tells me he is tired, because this means so much when he says it to me.[65]

In a follow-up letter two weeks later, 'fortified expressly by another appeal to a sacred thing—our friendship for Carlos', Paton assured Wilde that, 'above all I feel a sense of personal friendship to yourself & I want to maintain it by occasional correspondence, as I set great value on it'.[66] The point at issue in Blacker's legal proceedings against Newcastle became blurred when Sir George Lewis assured Blacker's solicitor, with regard to the slanderous remarks the duke was alleged to have made, that 'the Duke had never said such things or even thought them'. In addition, there were 'Newcastle's repeated assurances to Paton, Oscar & others that he had never said them'.[67] The duke continued to play a frustrating cat-and-mouse game with Blacker, alternately denying and reaffirming his charges.

Blacker's depressed and troubled state remained a source of constant anxiety to Carrie whose sole comfort, separated as they were at the insistence of her family pending their marriage, was in the knowledge that the matters that so harassed and worried him were in the capable hands of his faithful friend Oscar Wilde. 'My hope and prayer is that this may find you in a happy mood', she wrote to Blacker, 'for I do fear and dread your dark moments, dear, both on your own account and because they seem to turn you away from me. . . . I feel happy for I know you are in good hands with Mr. Wilde but I do long for you with all my heart.'[68] Seeking medical advice, he was diagnosed as suffering from 'an acutely morbid condition of the nervous system', for which his doctor prescribed the use of opium, 'which he pronounced to be the only drug that could assuage the fits of paroxysms of rage followed by helpless melancholy' from which Blacker suffered.[69] Notwithstanding the doctor's prescription, in view of his promise to Carrie, Blacker declined to take 'one single grain of opium, nor do I intend to do so'. Instead, he read day and night: 'all Shakespeare, Dante, & as much of Macaulay & Darwin as I have by me.—Also Pater. Alas how Pater who loved life so well & did so much to make it beautiful for others!—His death was a dreadful selfish blow to me.— Alas! Alas!'[70]

Just as rumors in the Tranby Croft affair had dogged Gordon-Cumming, so reports of Newcastle's accusations eventually reached Carrie's relatives in England, causing Carrie and Blacker to postpone their wedding. 'We would have been married last spring', Blacker later wrote with some bitterness to Carrie:

had it not been for the *manner* in which William [Carrie's brother-in-law, William Vernon] interfered in my affairs.—When he justified his desire to go to London by using the words 'There are some very ugly reports going about in the family about you' I allowed my prudence to overcome my rage & indignation, at the cost of not being married & allowing matters to remain as they are.—I have suffered much dear, but with clenched teeth.[71]

Matters were brought to a head by Blacker's 'unfortunate mistress', who in desperation appealed to Wilde. 'She came down to Worthing to see me and to implore my help', he confided subsequently in a letter to his friend Robbie Ross. 'For Blacker's sake, and to prevent her going to his father at his place of business, to his mother at her own house, . . . I gave her £25 at Worthing & subsequently in London I gave her £18, . . . and prevented her from making any trouble with Blacker's family.' 'What I did', he explained, 'I did from kindness, to Blacker primarily, and in the second place to a woman I had known intimately.'[72] She, however, unwilling to go as quietly as conceived by Wilde, pleaded her case in a series of letters to Sir Lewis and Lady Molesworth, revealing her continuing association with Blacker. The threat of her contacting either his or Carrie's family directly had long haunted Blacker, who later confessed to 'reprehensible' weakness on his part in failing to terminate the liaison decisively. Given the kindness recalled by intimates as his defining quality, not surprisingly Blacker proved unable to follow his own advice to Francis Hope—'be firm'—in similar circumstances. While admitting to Carrie that he 'may have acted with weakness', he explained that 'it was because I feared I might otherwise have acted with cruelty'.[73] 'I have heard <u>nothing</u> of the nature you suppose', Carrie assured him, with a note of annoyance at confronting again an unwelcome concern supposedly long-since settled, adding that, 'I pray God that nothing will be said to me, or that I shall hear nothing on that subject. I will bear anything for you but that, which is dragging my love so low.'[74] Carrie's sister Jane, Lady Molesworth, informed Blacker that it was in his power to make Carrie happy 'if he had a mind to'. 'You put an adder to my heart', he replied, 'when you tell me she is ill & anxious & worrying.'[75] Learning of the long-feared contact between his mistress and the Molesworths, with whom he had until then enjoyed a cordial relationship, Blacker dashed off an angry letter to Sir Lewis that the latter found to be 'grossly insulting' and accordingly declined 'to have any communication with Mr Carlos Blacker for the future'.[76] 'I am crying so that I cannot see but I must try to write you everything', Carrie wrote to Blacker after being shown his letter:

> [Sir Lewis] was very miserable & told me he had passed a most unhappy day as he knew what suffering must come of it. After that . . . I cannot stay any longer with the Molesworths nor with any of my people over here and my own sense of dignity and right will not let me accept your offer . . . of going to your family. It would be ruin to both of us, to you and to me, and would go against every feeling that I have of pride and self respect. Perhaps you as a man dearest cannot enter with these feelings but I know your Mother will.[77]

In 'the worst trouble I have ever known', Carrie could not bear the thought of seeing Blacker immediately 'with all these clouds between us. They <u>must</u> be cleared away now and forever.'[78]

At the breaking point following this latest trouble, Blacker, in one of his darker moments while on a visit to his sister Dolores in Eastbourne, came near to ending it all. 'Had it not been for Dolores's kindness', he informed Carrie, 'something dreadful might have happened in view of the state of my nerves.'[79] In a year of 'pain and intolerable misery', Carrie found cause to be thankful for 'the one great fact that God has left you and spared you when he might have taken you on that dreadful ghastly night'.[80] While with his sister, as Blacker reported to Carrie, he received confirmation through Wilde of the implacable opposition of the Molesworths to their marriage:

I saw Oscar at Eastborne for a couple of hours yesterday and he is delighted at our plans as he is a very strong Carrieite as you know. I am happy to be able to tell you that he told me that Max Müller had told him that the Molesworths quite disapproved of your marrying me & that long ago they would have done *anything* to prevent it had they not seen how useless it was trying.[81]

Carrie's father, Confederate General Daniel Frost, had never entirely approved of the peripatetic way of life of Carrie and her sisters, 'wandering from pillar to post' in Europe. Informed of Carrie's engagement, but unaware as yet of the 'ugly reports' about Blacker, he urged Carrie to come back to the family country home, Hazlewood, in St Louis, to be married, given away by him, in the home in which she had been born and in which her mother had died and which she had not seen since her childhood.[82] Acquiescing in her father's plea, Carrie sailed for America in October, with Blacker to follow by the next available ship. On arrival in St Louis, Carrie was aghast to learn that her father had in the meantime been informed by the Molesworths of their strenuous objection to the marriage. Carrie's brother Graham was dispatched to New York with the family lawyer to intercept Blacker and give him an opportunity to respond to what was being said about him. The ocean voyage had been a nightmare for Blacker who, prior to his departure, had received a cable from Carrie's brother forewarning him of the ordeal that awaited him: 'You can come but be prepared to meet serious objections recently urged.'[83] Blacker had been apprehensive of the consequences of the Molesworths' intervention, fearing that Carrie's father might insist on his affairs being settled before the marriage could take place. 'It really would be <u>too</u> disastrous if I was to go to America & return unmarried', he wrote prophetically to Carrie shortly before she sailed. 'This would indeed be terrible, & though I do not for a moment anticipate that this could ever take place I do not for a moment doubt but that your dear sister will do her best to thwart us.'[84]

Blacker later recalled his reception in New York: 'On arrival I am met by two men who however charming were total strangers. For three days, I am submitted to a rigorous cross-examination on every possible subject & from every point of view.'[85] The 'charges' against him, as he reported to Carrie, were 'under three heads': his failure to press his suit for slander against the duke 'briskly' to a conclusion; his melancholy, 'with a tendency to suicidal mania', and his use of opium; and 'that other matter [his long-time liaison with his mistress]'. To the first charge, Blacker explained that his lack of animosity towards the duke and the disinclination of his family and some of his friends to his continuing the prosecution had inclined him to grow indifferent, but now he intended to carry the matter through to a conclusion. As for his use of opium, he stated that having promised Carrie to give it up he had with no difficulty freed himself from the habit and never intended to go back to it. He had been subject to melancholy all his life from earliest childhood and had 'repeatedly been assured that the only cure for this was marriage & great family interests', a prescription that did in fact ultimately prove effective for Blacker. Touching upon the third matter, the relationship with his former mistress, this was 'ended forever as God only knows it…absolutely banished from my mind & from my life'.[86] Following the interview, Carrie's father wrote to Blacker in New York:

I learn that you propose returning to England to prosecute your suit against the Duke of Newcastle to a conclusion. This being done with a result favorable to yourself would remove the insurmountable obstacle to any matrimonial connection with my family and I should no longer feel it to be my duty to actively oppose such a connection.[87]

The outcome, involving as it did his return to England unmarried, realized Blacker's worst fear. Indignant and especially resentful of the phrase, 'with a result favorable to yourself', he lingered in New York for a month in a state of helpless rage and deepening despair, exchanging passionate letters with Carrie in St Louis appealing to her fruitlessly to proceed with the marriage despite her father's objection and spare him the humiliating course insisted upon by her family. In the face of Carrie's reluctance to defy her father, finally, shattered and defeated, he left for England on the last day of November with a parting message for Carrie: 'ma vie sans toi est une angoisse'.[88]

3

'The Girl with the Foghorn Voice'

Francis had met with greater success in New York earlier in the year in his whirlwind courtship of an American music-hall actress, Mary Augusta Yohe, known as 'Madcap May' for her involvement in a number of highly publicized escapades. Following her stage debut at the age of ten, May had been a teenage chorus girl in a Pittsburgh burlesque show. At the age of eighteen, she was given the lead in a musical called *The Crystal Slipper*, which proved to be a great success. After several weeks, she eloped with the son of a wealthy Chicagoan but soon returned to the show when it turned out that he was already married. From then on, she enjoyed a considerable name in the theatre, her popularity sustained 'by her personal magnetism and by four remarkably rich low notes in her contralto voice which won her the appellation in London of "the girl with the foghorn voice"'.[1] A week after meeting Francis at a dinner party at Delmonico's in New York, she sailed for England, chaperoned by her mother, to star in the musical *Little Christopher Columbus*, in which her singing of 'Honey, Mah Honey' proved to be a show-stopper, winning her enthusiastic reviews from the London critics.

Shortly after May's arrival in England, Francis made a 'peculiar proposal' of a 'probation' marriage of five months, to which agreed, and the two set up housekeeping together. 'We were supremely happy', she recalled. 'I took a beautiful house a little way out from the city, and here Lord Francis came to be husband and suitor at the same time. My eighteenth birthday came along during the five month period.'[2] In Linny's horrified eyes, there could not possibly have been a less suitable prospect for marriage to the heir presumptive to the dukedom, and he was reported to have offered his brother $1,000,000 not to marry her.[3] Always short of money, it was never a compelling priority for Francis, and he and May were married in a quiet ceremony in Hampstead on 27 November 1894.

The marriage appears to have rekindled the duke's anger at Blacker whose influence over Francis in their intimate association he held accountable for the disaster. The charge was echoed four years later when Blacker came under attack in the anti-Dreyfusard press in Paris. A journalist writing for the *Libre Parole* posed the following question about him: 'Wasn't it he who abused his influence over a young lord, heir to one of the greatest names in the British nobility, to the point of having him marry an American singer of the most deplorable morals, both before and after marriage?'[4] While continuing to pursue Francis in Bankruptcy Court, Linny now petitioned for a receiving order against Blacker. The order was duly made a week after Francis's wedding, on 4 December, while Blacker was returning heartbroken from America, unsuspecting that yet another catastrophic blow awaited him. 'I learn that Newcastle has instituted proceedings to break me', he wrote to Carrie when news of it reached him. 'This must be sheer and wanton spite.'[5]

While Francis and May were 'supremely happy' in their 'probation' marriage, May grew restive in actual wedlock. She was reluctant to give up the theatre, 'the glamour of social prestige wore away' and she discovered in her husband 'certain shortcomings'—namely, a preoccupation with reading and hunting—that she felt caused him to neglect her. All would nonetheless have been well, she claimed, 'had it not been for the evil influence which threw Putnam Bradlee Strong across my path'.[6] Strong, the son of a former mayor of New York, was, in May's eyes, 'a fascinating man, with a suave gallantry which charmed women. I never have known a woman who, after being thrown in Captain Strong's company for a while, did not fall in love with him.'[7] No exception herself and powerless to resist Strong's fatal attraction, May eloped with him to Japan in 1901 as 'Mr & Mrs H. L. Hastings', 'taking with us eighteen trunks, five dogs and two servants'.[8] At the same time, Francis, heir to the legendary bad luck associated with the Hope diamond, had to have a foot amputated as the result of a hunting accident. In March 1902, he obtained a divorce from May on the ground of her 'misconduct' with Strong. The following month, he was back in the Bankruptcy Court, the largest claim being for $45,000 on a bill of exchange he had given to May when she was secretly preparing to elope.

Years later, during World War I, when May's wayward life had brought her to scrubbing floors as 'office janitress' on the night shift in a Seattle shipyard at $18 a week, 'quite often', she recalled:

I would hum while I worked, and sometimes, if the office were quiet I would sing snatches of my old songs—especially the one which helped me to become famous, 'Honey, Mah Honey.' Many times while I swung that mop I wondered what these men about me would say if they knew their janitress was May Yohe, who had been Lady Francis Hope, and whose throat, now covered with grime and perspiration had glistened white behind the great Hope Diamond and countless other gems men liked to hang upon it— the same May Yohe who might have become a duchess![9]

There is a poignant note of fantasy in her distant memory of her London triumph years before:

that opening night of 'Christopher Columbus,' with its song, 'Honey, Mah Honey,' at which pit and gallery joined the wildest demonstration ever given in a London theatre, when men threw pocketbooks and women their jewels at my feet and down from the gallery came that rare tribute, the shower of programs which is the final approval. May Yohe was the toast of London.[10]

May again made front-page news in 1924 when her third husband, Captain John A. Smuts, a cousin of the Boer leader Jan Christian Smuts, was found dangerously wounded by a bullet through his chest in the couple's 'cheap lodgings in the south end of Boston', leaving a note stating that he had shot himself 'because I was unkind to my wife, May Yohe, who has been the best in the world to me'.[11] Two weeks before, a roadside café and dance hall called the Blue Diamond Inn that the couple had opened in Marlowe, New Hampshire, had burned to the ground. May attributed her misfortunes to the 'curse' of the Hope diamond. When she died in 1938, her obituary noted that 'through a wide range of vicissitudes she maintained the engaging gaiety and unfailing cheerfulness which had made her a favorite with the theatregoers of the United States and Great Britain'.[12]

2

On his return from New York, Blacker joined his sister and her family in Freiburg. Here he received yet another blow when he learned that General Frost had written to his father in London 'a wounding letter', asking him to induce his son '<u>never</u>' to marry Carrie, urging 'among many other objections' Carlos's tendency to suicide and his 'shirking' of the action against Newcastle. The prospect of parting forever appeared more unthinkable to Carlos and Carrie as the drama of their situation unfolded. Family opposition served only to deepen their passionate need for one another. A flurry of letters from Carlos, full of misery and despair ('What misery all this is, Carrie dear. What hideous misery') was eventually followed by a letter from Carrie announcing her decision to go ahead with the marriage despite her father's objections and without waiting for resolution of the proceedings against Newcastle.[13] On 19 January 1895, accompanied by her former nurse ('dear old Murph, the best and most devoted friend of my life'), Carrie sailed from America on the *Umbria* for Liverpool where she was met by Blacker. About to embark on their 'New Life' together, he wished to dispel any possible lingering concern about his former mistress: 'One little care I must remove from your mind that it may never be referred to. The person who troubled us so much is married & provided for & can never trouble us again.'[14] Oscar Wilde claimed a share of the credit for the happy outcome ('she took my advice, and married a very rich young man').[15] Carlos and Carrie were married in London on 7 February in the presence of Blacker's family and immediately after the ceremony left for Paris. Their life together, so inauspiciously begun, was to prove a long and happy one during which they were never parted for a day, as Carrie noted following Carlos's death thirty-three years later.

Their long-deferred happiness, however, brought them only a brief respite from Blacker's troubles. The day after the wedding, his diary notes receipt of a '[8 February] worrying letter from Richards', and four days later he was adjudicated bankrupt in London. Summoned to England by Richards for a court appearance, the unwelcome prospect produced '[18 February] gloom at thought of return to London'. The following day, the eve of the scheduled court appearance, the couple

started from Paris: '[19 February] Comfortable journey, good cross-
ing—certain nervousness and worry... go to Sackville Hotel'.[16]

Meanwhile, with the opening five days before of his second phe-
nomenally successful play of the season, *The Importance of Being Earnest*,
Wilde had reached the zenith of his glory. He was then at the nearby
Avondale Hotel where Douglas had joined him the previous evening
on his return from Algeria. Before Wilde's own return from there to
London for rehearsals of his play two weeks earlier, the two had spent
several days in the company of André Gide, with whom Douglas had
stayed on at Biskra. Gide recalled later that shortly before Wilde
returned to London he had noted in his conversation 'a kind of
vague apprehension, a presentiment of some kind of tragic event
which he dreaded, but at the same time almost longed for'. '"I have
been as far as possible along my own road"', he quoted Wilde as
saying; '"I can't go any farther. *Something* must happen now."' According to Gide, he was sufficiently impressed by Wilde's 'actual
words' to have transcribed them at the time 'with absolute fidelity'.[17]
Alarmed by a recent attempt by Douglas's erratic father, the marquess
of Queensberry, to disrupt the opening performance of *The Importance
of Being Earnest* and uneasy about the ominous drift of events, Wilde
pleaded in vain with Douglas on the night of his return to inform his
older brother Percy of the true nature of their relationship. 'I implored
him to let us tell him (Percy) the truth', Wilde wrote to More Adey.
'He absolutely refused, and insisted on the comedy of his father's
delusions.'[18] Douglas's refusal was troubling, and Wilde was in an
unsettled state when the following day in response to Blacker's call
he came to the Sackville Hotel. In the magic presence of Wilde, the
'supreme consoler' in Douglas's considered view, Blacker's spirits
rallied: '[19 February] Dismal dinner—Oscar Wilde calls—endeavours
to dissipate general gloom—partial success.' 'One met him', Douglas
recalled years later, 'perhaps feeling gloomy and depressed as the result
of some trouble or setback, and in five minutes he had altered the
whole aspect of the situation and everything became couleur de
rose.'[19]

As Wilde pursued his fatal course, Blacker despondently awaited
his court appearance, noted by Carrie in her husband's diary: '[20
February] Sackville Hotel—nerves & worry—unfortunate postpone-
ment of examination—consequent depression partly due to effect of
London... general gloom'; '[21 February] Carlos, horribles in

court...Carlos *very bad*—temper & spirits'; '[22 February] Bad awaking—bad morning with "horribles"—bad luncheon.' Worse was to come when the date of his dreaded public examination in bankruptcy arrived on 6 March ('*Terrible*') and, worse yet, when 'the case stood over for further investigation'; '[7 March] Very much prostrated'; '[11 March] slightly bad temper... *Good resolution not to blaspheme or speak of death or use bad language.*' The ordeal finally came to an end on 14 March, and the harried couple sought needed diversion before leaving for Freiburg a few days later: '[15 March] *The Importance of Being Earnest*'; '[16 March] Avenue Theatre. May Yohe and Francis'. From Freiburg, Blacker, with a numbing sense of horror, followed the progress of Wilde's downfall in the press: '[5 April] Oscar Wilde's case first appears in papers'; '[6 April] Oscar's cross examination finished, very sad'; '[8 April] Oscar arrested! Friday last, dreadful, very upset... walked about, very low about Oscar'; '[9 April] Oscar at Bow Street, not allowed out on bail. Frightfully sad.'

3

Appalled by the catastrophe that had overtaken Wilde as the consequence of his ill-advised suit against Queensberry, Blacker, shortly after his return to Freiburg, may have received another sobering reminder of the perils involved in pursuing his action against Newcastle in the person of Sir William Gordon-Cumming, whose family name appears in Blacker's diary entries at this time.[20] By the latter part of May, with no stomach for pressing the action and wishing the matter over, he was ready to seek an 'arrangement' and wrote accordingly to his solicitor H. W. Richards. The latter offered little encouragement, noting that 'the subject bristled with difficulties'.[21] With Wilde under arrest and unavailable, Blacker enlisted the aid of another intermediary, Canon Michael Barry, the priest who had recently officiated at his marriage, who had the merit of being a friend of the duke's. On 28 May, Wilde having been sentenced three days before, Blacker noted in his diary: 'Went with Carrie to buy book & all papers to see account of Oscar's conviction. After lunch wrote to Richards enclosing letter for Canon Barry with suggestion of document for Newcastle to sign.' Father Barry was not optimistic and in August sent Blacker a letter from the uncompromising duke, firmly 'refusing to do more'.[22] Letters from Richards saying he was pushing for an early trial date and 'telling me to prepare for the action & asking me for letters from Newcastle & pass book'[23] were regularly followed by delays: '[10 November 1895] Letter from Richards about action saying it could not take place during next fortnight.' Adding to the strain and uncertainty was a letter from Blacker's mother, advising him to have the action against Newcastle put off until after Christmas 'in view of Carrie's condition'.[24] With a baby expected the following month, Blacker wished more than ever, on whatever terms might be obtained, to be free of the nagging worry of the suit which was receiving attention in the press. On 16 November 1895, he noted in his diary having read of the action in the *Galignani Messenger*. The English-language newspaper published in Paris reported: 'Duke as Defendant: Pending Cause Célèbre: The Duke of Newcastle is defendant in a slander action, brought by a person named Blacker, which will shortly come before the High Court. It is stated that it will be of considerable social interest.'[25] Amid the gloom, he was heartened to receive a welcome letter from Francis, offering his services in the affair.[26] Everything having to do with the suit depended on Francis, as Blacker had informed Carrie the year before by way of explanation of the slow pace of the proceedings: 'With regard to my "action" this now depends on whether Francis has time & inclination to attend to anything but his own affairs. If he has time a solution will be arrived at, & if he has no time then it necessarily falls to the ground through no fault of mine.'[27]

Blacker was relieved to be able to unburden himself freely to his old friend and confidant William Roger Paton, the inseparable companion of carefree bachelor days in London in the 1880s, when the latter arrived from Greece for a fortnight's visit in early November. The two passed the days in long walks about Paris or sitting in a café over a glass of absinthe in the easy freedom of their long intimacy. In Paton, Blacker was assured of a sympathetic listener and a trusted adviser, and their conversations, as recorded in Blacker's diary, reflect the latter's preoccupations at the time, mainly, the 'state of things with Newcastle' and 'Oscar' and 'Oscar & life'. On 14 November, the time came for the 'last absinthe with Paton at the Café de Terminus. . . . Paton sad at leaving tomorrow'; '[15 November] Paton left for Oxford at 10 via Dieppe. I did not accompany him as it saddens too much.'

When four weeks later, on 7 December, Carrie gave birth to a son, the couple named him Carlos Paton Blacker, known through life as Pip.[28]

In late November came further happy news from Francis, announcing that he too was going to be a father. The joyful prospect proved to be short-lived, however, when May suffered a miscarriage, as Francis informed Blacker when writing to congratulate him a few weeks later on the birth of Pip:

I cannot tell you how pleased I was to receive your letter this morning & I heartily congratulate you on the safe arrival of a son & heir.—You will be sorry to hear that remaining on the stage & the excitement of a new town every week, caused a little accident to occur.—It is a great pity because if her contract had expired three weeks before it did, everything would have been all right.—However I shall profit by the lesson it has taught me.—I saw Richards yesterday and I am glad that your case is healthy-looking, I fail to see how my brother can possibly be saved from a complete rout.—Of course my position will not be a nice one, but when one comes to think that, at the time I made my statement to Lumley [Newcastle's solicitor] I was in no way hostile to my brother, it rather alters & puts a better appearance on the fact of my giving evidence against him.—I told Richards that I was going to do my utmost to get him to apologize amply & publicly, in fact I am going to see my uncle at Windsor today to see if he cannot bring pressure to bear.—I hope you don't mind my taking this course, but I feel that I must make an effort to avoid the stirring up of dirty mud, which must take place if the case comes into Court.[29]

While the Newcastle affair remained Blacker's overriding concern, the fate of Oscar Wilde was never far from his thoughts, as indicated in his conversations with W. R. Paton. When the year ended with a visit from another old friend of Blacker's and Wilde's from the charmed period of the 1880s, the actor Norman Forbes-Robertson, the conversation inevitably turned to Oscar: '[28 December] Norman & I dined alone, talking about Oscar nearly the whole time.'

A more recent albeit no less devoted friend than Paton and Forbes-Robertson was the Italian military attaché in Paris, Major Alessandro Panizzardi, to whom Blacker had been introduced at a tennis party during the summer. A popular figure in diplomatic circles in Paris, Panizzardi responded at once to Blacker's talent for friendship and was soon making regular appearances at the Blackers' dinner table. By year's end, a congenial intimacy had developed: '[18 December] Panizzardi to dinner. . . . Talk till one with P about his amours';

'[22 December] Panizzardi called in morning to ask advice'; '[23 December] Panizzardi called to say he could not dine on Xmas day'; '[27 December] Panizzardi called & we talked till past 12.'

Panizzardi's amours, and particularly his relationship with his German counterpart, Colonel Maximilian von Schwartzkoppen, had for some time been a matter of interest to the French intelligence service, which had compiled extensive dossiers on both military attachés. Serving the interests of member nations of the Triple Alliance, the two freely exchanged intelligence and cooperated in espionage matters, at times employing the same agents. Neither was aware that a letter addressed to Schwartzkoppen by Panizzardi had been intercepted by the intelligence service and had been illegally employed, in altered form, the year before to secure the conviction of Captain Alfred Dreyfus, then serving a life sentence on Devil's Island.

4

The stressful year 1895 having ended on a happy note with the birth of Pip, Carrie and Carlos welcomed the start of the new year with 'a merry dinner', at which their guests were their now intimate friend Panizzardi, Norman Forbes-Robertson and his sister Daisy, and another couple. The following evening, Francis and May arrived in Paris for a ten-day stay at the Grand Hôtel du Louvre, en route to the Riviera. Blacker and Forbes-Robertson met them at the Gare du Nord and the next day the four lunched at the Maison Dorée, 'where we talked about Newcastle and his family in general'. Bankruptcy had little discernible effect on Francis's daily routine in Paris, as Blacker's diary shows. Blacker called each day and joined the couple for lunch—at Maison Dorée, Durand's or the Grand Café. Although Francis and May were apt to get a late start on the day ('Francis and May at 12 just risen, so returned in cab home'; 'Went out . . . at 11 & walked to the Hôtel du Louvre, sat with Francis until he was dressed & then went with them to Grand Café'), there seemed always to be time for Lewis the hatter and Dumarest the jeweler. May sent Carrie flowers but Carrie was 'depressed at my offering to ask May to lunch'. With the Newcastle matter uppermost on his mind, Blacker 'spoke with Francis & May about action & advisability of considering witnesses insufficient', after which, 'very nervous', he 'wrote to Richards about

abandoning case, Carrie also writing & I enclosing Francis's letter'. On
11 January, 'said good bye to Francis & May who left by 5:30 train for
the Riviera'. The following day, 'after lunch thought of resolutions to
avoid cigarettes before dinner after the 7th February [his and Carrie's
wedding anniversary] & wine before dinner as soon as Newcastle affair
is settled'.

The initial response from Blacker's solicitor H. W. Richards on 15
January was maddeningly disappointing: '[15 January 1896] Long letter
from Richards about course to be adopted with regard to that damned
action, showing as usual hesitancy and indecision. . . . I remained in
and wrote to Richards telling him that I wanted the case to be closed if
possible and for the only risk by my withdrawing to be that the verdict
and costs would go against me which I did not care about. . . . A long
series of dull days made me a little depressed today, as also the letter
from Richards which we thought was unsatisfactory.' Richards indicated in reply that 'he would act in accordance with what I had written
to him', and a few days later came the welcome news that the long,
hideous nightmare that had been the cause of so much heartache had
finally come to an end: 'Letter from Richards enclosing letter from
George Lewis settling up the slander matter, at which I was delighted,
this unhappy business having now lasted for nearly three years and
having been a source of immense worry and bother to me.' While
Blacker was greatly relieved, the terms on which the action had
been settled fell far short of what Carrie's father had set as a condition
of his consent to the marriage. Richards expressed a lingering regret
about the capitulation: '[29 January 1896] Letter from Richards saying
he thought the course we had taken with regard to Newcastle was the
best but regretting he had not been able to give him the dusting he
deserved.'

4

'He Has Been Mad the Last 3 Years'

I

At the time of Wilde's arrest, 'the emotion of the great crisis', as Douglas put it, 'fanned the waning fires of our devotion to each other'.[1] Forgotten was the regrettable experience of their recent stay at the Avondale Hotel following Douglas's return from Algeria. Wilde later claimed that he had been prevented from leaving for Paris and for what would have meant freedom, as he had then wished to do, because, owing to Douglas's extravagance, he had been unable to pay the hotel bill and the management refused to permit his luggage to be removed until the account was settled. Douglas had brought to the hotel a companion whose presence Wilde found compromising. When requested by Wilde to ask his companion to leave, Douglas had created a violent scene and left with his friend for another hotel—the bill for which Wilde subsequently had to pay—from where he bombarded Wilde with abusive letters. On returning to the Avondale Hotel on the day he found Queensberry's provocative card, Wilde found 'a no less loathsome' letter from Douglas.[2]

And yet when he was alone in Holloway Prison five weeks later, abandoned on all sides and confronting the full horror of his predicament, Wilde found his only comfort in the daily letters and visits he received from Douglas, who, with characteristically rash courage, relished the excitement of thus openly defying public opinion. The intensity of the rekindled infatuation is evident in the hysterical tone of the impassioned letters Wilde addressed to Douglas at the time.

On 24 April, as his world crumbled, Wilde's household possessions and personal effects were dispersed in a scandalously conducted sheriff's sale for the benefit of his creditors. At the insistence of his counsel, and at Wilde's own urging, Douglas reluctantly left the country before the commencement of the trial on 26 April. When the jury failed to agree, a new trial was ordered and took place a month later. 'O sweetest of all boys, most loved of all loves', Wilde wrote to Douglas in his last surviving letter to him before his conviction, written on the opening day of his co-defendant Alfred Taylor's trial on 20 May, 'my soul clings to your soul, my life is your life, and in all the worlds of pain and pleasure you are my ideal of admiration and joy'.[3] The next day, he heard the ominous verdict of guilty pronounced against Taylor, who had been tried together with Wilde in the first instance but whose case was heard separately in the second trial. Later in the afternoon, with his own case to be tried the following day, Wilde was approached at the Old Bailey by retired Police Inspector Frederick Kerley who handed him the marquess of Queensberry's formal demand for payment of £677.3.8, which had been awarded him for costs in Wilde's unsuccessful libel suit against him. Failure to pay within seven days would constitute a statutory 'act of bankruptcy'. For Queensberry, snaring Wilde in the net of the Bankruptcy Court, from which he was never to free himself, added savor to his triumph in securing the criminal conviction that was to follow the next day. Found guilty of acts of gross indecency, Wilde was sentenced on 25 May to two years with hard labor and was immediately imprisoned.

In Freiburg, meanwhile, Blacker in deepening distress continued to follow the catastrophe as it unfolded in the press from day to day, while Carrie, horrified by the glimpse the case provided of a dark and unimagined world, grew daily more unsympathetic towards Wilde and his scandalous plight. Strong-willed and firm in her support of Blacker's resolve in their 'New Life' together to reorder an existence that had come close to ending in tragedy only months before, she was insistent that he sever all connection with Wilde. The difference in sympathy and outlook inevitably resulted in strain: '[14 April] Regrettable incident after dinner with Carrie touching the Oscar scandal.' Despite the discord, Wilde's fate remained Blacker's daily preoccupation: '[28 April] Church. Afterwards to railway station to buy *New York Herald* to see about Oscar case'; '[29 April] Went to station to buy *New York Herald* to read about Oscar's case, evidence very untrustworthy.' Two days later, the couple left for Paris: '[2 May] Arrived Paris. Settled at Bedford Hotel . . . Jury disagree about verdict on Oscar'; '[8 May] Oscar liberated.' Relieved, Blacker immediately wished to send a message of sympathy and encouragement but was deterred: '[12 May] Letter to Oscar disapproved by Carrie. . . . Much repentance & resolutions for future.'

The outcome of the second trial of Alfred Taylor's case was disheartening: '[22 May] Went to station with Carrie before lunch to buy *Galignani* & *Daily Telegraph*. Taylor found guilty'; and then came the dreaded news: '[26 May] Oscar sentenced yesterday to 2 years with hard labour. Bought all papers. . . . Wrote to Mrs Wilde.' '[28 May] Went with Carrie to buy book & all papers to see account of Oscar's conviction.' While Carlos was shaken with grief at the outcome, Carrie was all the more strongly confirmed in her hostile attitude and Wilde's fate remained a source of disagreement between them: '[30 May] Resolution to discontinue talking about Oscar at dinner. Carrie tired & with heavy head all day.'

In France, as in England and elsewhere, practically all of Wilde's friends abruptly dropped him. A French journalist, Jules Huret, writing in *Le Figaro* on 13 April 1895, named the writers Jean Lorrain, Catulle Mendès, and Marcel Schwob as *familiers* of Wilde. All three took offense at what they viewed as an implied insult and demanded satisfaction; on 17 April Mendès met Huret in a duel and was slightly wounded. A notable exception was Henry Bauër, a friend of both Wilde and Blacker, who, a week after Wilde's conviction, published a leading article in *L'Echo de Paris* in defense of the condemned man. Blacker met with him two days after the appearance of the article and together they planned a further statement: '[5 June] Met Bauër . . . & went with him to his room where we had long conversation about Oscar'; '[6 June] After lunch wrote draft of apology of Oscar for Bauër.' The result of their collaboration, 'Oscar Wilde en prison', appeared in *L'Echo de Paris* over Bauër's name the following week. Meanwhile, Wilde's terrible fate remained ever present in Blacker's thoughts: '[7 June] Went out before lunch to buy *Galignani* alone, notice from Governor of Pentonville that Oscar was not ill.'

Immediately after sentence was pronounced on 25 May, a Saturday, Wilde was taken to Newgate Prison, where he was held over the weekend. On Monday he was transferred in a prison van to Pentonville Prison where on 2 July retired Police Inspector Kerley, armed with an order for a special visit, made a second appearance and served Wilde with a copy of Queensberry's petition for a receiving order in bankruptcy. Two days later, he was moved again, this time to Wandsworth Prison. Here on 29 July he was examined by one of the official receivers of the Bankruptcy Court, Alfred Henry Wildy, who had been appointed receiver of Wilde's estate. 'Step by step with the Bankruptcy Receiver', Wilde recalled, 'I had to go over every item of my life. It was horrible.'[4] The creditors held their first meeting on 26 August at which a Statement of Affairs was presented which disclosed a deficiency of £3,591.9.9. The five largest claims, in descending order, were £1,557.16.1, due the trustees of Constance Wilde's marriage settlement (i.e. Carlos Blacker and Arthur Clifton) for a £1,000 loan made to Wilde on his wedding day in 1884, plus unpaid interest at the rate of 5 percent; £677.3.8 due to Queensberry; £500 due to Constance Wilde's brother, Otho Holland Lloyd, for a loan made in 1885; £414.19.17 due to George Alexander, the actor-manager, for advances against unearned royalties; and £70.16.11 due the Savoy Hotel 'for board and residence 1893–March 1894'. The rest of the claims were for relatively small amounts. There were no assets, other than the copyrights on Wilde's dramatic and other literary works, which had only a possible future value, and his life interest in his wife's marriage settlement, which was contingent upon his surviving her.[5] No proposal being offered for payment of the creditors, a resolution was adopted that Wilde be adjudicated bankrupt and, on application of the official receiver, the adjudication was accordingly made by order of the Bankruptcy Court on 31 August. Wilde's public examination was set by the court for 24 September. In Paris, Blacker, who had been following the proceedings closely through the summer, undoubtedly was mindful of his own painful ordeal six months before when he noted in his diary: '[30 August] *Times* bringing news of Oscar's having been made a Bankrupt & to appear on September 24 in public.'

2

Under prison regulations, Wilde was entitled to send and receive a letter and have two visitors upon completion of three months of his sentence, and similarly thereafter at quarterly intervals. His first regular visitor, on 26 August, was Robert Sherard, who had been interceding on his behalf with Constance Wilde, seeking reconciliation between husband and wife. Wilde himself appealed directly to his wife in a letter that her normally unsentimental and business-like solicitor, who had been urging a divorce, described as 'one of the most touching and pathetic letters that had ever come under his eye'.[6] Constance Wilde, encouraged in her hope of reconciliation, wrote in reply to her husband that she was prepared to forgive him. Since he had used the one letter allowed him to write to his wife, Wilde was unable to write to Douglas for at least another three months, by which time a deepening resentment on Wilde's part had led to their total estrangement. 'It seems to me *quite inconceivable*', Douglas wrote in disbelief when he learned how Wilde had used his initial letter-writing privilege, 'that he should prefer to correspond with his "*family*" than with me without some very strong reason of which I know nothing.'[7] Concurrently with her letter, Constance Wilde applied for and was granted an order for a special visit to discuss the matter of the divorce with her husband. 'It was indeed awful, more so than I had any conception it could be', she wrote to Robert Sherard of her visit to Wandsworth Prison on 21 September. 'He has been mad the last 3 years and he says that if he saw [Douglas] he would kill him.'[8] Constance asked Sherard to meet with her following the visit, and he learned in the course of a long conversation that 'her heart was altogether with him still, and that once his punishment was over, he would find a home with her and his children'.[9]

Sherard, quixotic and enterprising, obtained an order for a special visit, which took place on 23 September, through the intercession with the Home Secretary of the Hon. William Lowther, a friend of Sherard's father, the Reverend Bennet Sherard Kennedy. In his letter to Lowther, Sherard signed his actual name R. S. Kennedy (Robert Sherard Kennedy), presumably to confirm his identity as the son of the Reverend Kennedy, underscoring the urgency of his request by stating that he was 'leaving for Madagascar in three weeks and [had] no expectation of returning to Christendom'. The grounds for the requested visit were his wish to discuss proposals for averting both the prisoner's bankruptcy and his impending divorce and his wish to see the prisoner before his departure from England.[10] During the course of the visit, Wilde was angered to learn from Sherard that Douglas proposed publishing an article about him in the *Mercure de France* in which he quoted from three of Wilde's most intimate letters to him, written while under the terrible strain of the trials ('letters that should have been to [Douglas] things sacred and secret beyond anything in the whole world!').[11] At Wilde's request, Sherard intervened to have the article withdrawn. Dismayed and hurt by Wilde's reaction and annoyed at Sherard's interference, Douglas defended his intended use of the compromising letters: 'I think the publication of these extracts would have given thousands of people an entirely new idea about the man in the case, and nobody who was not an insensate hog would have failed to have been touched by the beauty of them and the utter unselfishness and braveness of them.'[12]

Wilde's drastic change of heart towards Douglas, which was to find such bitter expression in 'De Profundis', was the result of four months of solitary brooding on the ruin of his life in a terrible isolation from which the sole distraction was his involvement in the further ignominy of his bankruptcy proceedings. For this final humiliation, he held Douglas and his family directly responsible. His action against Queensberry, at a time when he hadn't the means of paying his hotel bill, had been taken in reliance upon the promises of Douglas's older brother Percy to pay half the costs and of Douglas's mother to pay any amount required. When it became apparent to them that any funds advanced would go to the despised Queensberry for his costs, the family demurred and ultimately did nothing. 'Their idea that it would be a sort of "score" off their father not to pay him his paltry claim showed how utterly blind they were to my feelings', Wilde recalled with bitterness. 'With regard to the whole question, the Queensberry family must remember that through them I am in prison, through them a bankrupt.'[13]

The day following Sherard's special visit, Wilde was brought up to the Bankruptcy Court for his public examination in the custody of two warders. He had lost twenty-two pounds, his weight having dropped from 190 to 168 pounds.[14] Although he wore his own clothes, they no longer fit him and his hair was uncut. It was on this occasion, described in a memorable passage in 'De Profundis', that Robbie Ross, waiting 'in the long dreary corridor', gravely raised his hat to him 'as hand-cuffed and with bowed head' Wilde passed him by.[15] He 'dreaded the examination in bankruptcy', Ross reported, 'more than anything he had gone through.'[16]

3

Constance Wilde's astute family solicitor, Sidney Hargrove, had recognized in the sheriff's sale in April a harbinger of Wilde's inevitable bankruptcy. He immediately wrote to Blacker in Paris, as trustee of the marriage settlement, proposing a plan designed to secure what was left of the property for the couple's children, Cyril and Vyvyan. The settlement produced an annual income of about £800, payable to Constance Wilde during her lifetime and, at her death, to her husband for his life, in the event he survived her, with the remainder to go to their children. Hargrove advocated a divorce as a means of terminating the marriage settlement, thus extinguishing Wilde's interest and placing the fund beyond the reach of his creditors. Fearful of the impending bankruptcy and in anticipation of the divorce, Hargrove urged that the debentures that constituted the principal of the trust fund be transferred to Constance immediately. Blacker readily complied: '[29 June] Carrie packed Debentures for Hargrove', to whom they were promptly sent.

When Constance decided against a divorce, Hargrove devised an alternative plan that had the additional merit of averting the public examination and annulling the bankruptcy while at the same time protecting the children's interest. In mid-September, he presented the new proposal to Blacker, who again expressed his ready approval. Providing as it did for payment of the creditors in full, Hargrove's plan had every prospect of success. It was presented to the Bankruptcy Court on 24 September by Wilde's counsel, John Peter Grain, who had been Alfred Taylor's counsel in the criminal trials, and was favorably received. It was found unnecessary to produce Wilde in court and his public examination was adjourned to 12 November, in order to allow time for the proposal to be implemented.

Central to the plan, and the key to its success, was satisfaction of the claim of the trustees of the marriage settlement, the largest single creditor. Both Blacker and his co-trustee Arthur Clifton, as well as Constance Wilde, concurred in Hargrove's proposal that the trustees withdraw their claim for the amount of unpaid interest, £557.16.2, as this was payable to Constance as income beneficiary, and she had delivered a receipt for it to Hargrove on behalf of the trustees.

Under the plan, the trustees would withdraw their claim for the remaining balance of £1,000 in consideration of Wilde's surrendering his life interest in the marriage settlement for the nominal sum of £5 and a covenant to pay £1,000 on demand, payment to be secured by a charge on the whole of his existing dramatic and other literary rights. Withdrawal of the claim of the trustees would reduce the deficiency to £2,033.13.7, which Ross and his friend More Adey undertook to raise by subscription among Wilde's friends and sympathizers. Douglas, on learning of the plan in Capri, complained in advance that 'they are making a filthy mess of everything in England; if they can't raise £2000 among his friends to pay his bankruptcy his friends ought to be shot. My brother who hardly knows him offers £500: can't some one knock up £1500 more? I am trying to *blackmail* my people to do something towards releasing him.'[17] Within a month, Ross was able to report that, 'of the £2,000 required, £1,500 has already been collected from friends and several strangers who have generously contributed'.[18] The success of the plan, which promised such favorable results for Wilde, seemed assured.

While Grain was presenting the proposal to the court, Arthur Clifton, who had accompanied Ross to the session, was unexpectedly allowed an interview with Wilde in his capacity as co-trustee of the marriage settlement. It was a 'very hot day', as Blacker's diary records on 24 September and the days following, and Wilde was unwell; again, '[25 September] Very hot day. Letter from Hargrove saying proposal to pay creditors might be accepted by the Court'; '[26 September] Letter from Arthur Clifton with his views touching Oscar's affairs & saying he had seen him.... Very hot day.' In response to Clifton's letter, Blacker wrote asking for more details. 'There is not so very much to tell after all', Clifton replied:

I was very much shocked at Oscar's appearance though scarcely surprised. Fortunately he had his ordinary clothes on: his hair was rather long and he looked dreadfully thin. You can imagine how painful it was to meet him! & he was very much upset and cried a good deal: he seemed quite broken hearted and kept on describing his punishment as savage. Of course I talked as much as possible about the future, about the friendship of his friends, about his plays and everything I could think of to cheer him up. He was very eager for news and I told him as much as possible of what had happened lately and really I suppose I did most of the talking.

As to business matters, he did not express any very decided opinion but thought he ought to be left something out of the settlement if possible, and I told him what I thought would be a good plan—namely that he should retain about a third of his life interest: and I told him I w[oul]d do my best to see that that was arranged. As I told you Mrs Wilde, whom I saw immediately after, quite agreed so there ought to be little difficulty.

He has been reading 'Pater' & 'Newman' lately; one book a week. I do not know what work he does.

He was terribly despondent and said several times that he did not think he w[oul]d be able to last the punishment out.

I was very fortunate in being allowed to see him, as his Trustee about his bankruptcy. He was in the care of two warders who were in the room all the time but I was able to sit quite close to him and talk quietly: a very different arrangement to any visits allowed at the Prison. The Prison Commissioners refused my application to see him about six weeks ago & gave me leave to write to him: however they returned my letter at once as not being only about business.

I wish I could give you a better account of what he said but really the conversation was very desultory and he wanted news much more than he wanted to talk.

I need not say that his eyes are opened to the foolishness of his life—at least of the part dealt with at the trial. Personally I believe he has been the victim of his enormous curiosity as to all sides of life—and that his part has been enormously exaggerated so as to shield others. The trial was a mere travesty of justice. I am going to do my best to get the punishment reduced but I think it is no good doing much yet.

I am sure you will consider this letter as private. I do not want any account of my visit to filter into the press and so I have to use some caution.

I think his best chance is in silence as far as the press goes. If it is made a party question or a means of badgering the Government I am afraid little can be done.

I shall make an effort to see him again soon and will tell him of your letter. I am sure he will be pleased.[19]

Clifton was technically qualified as a solicitor but was not in active practice, his interests tending more towards poetry and art. He became an art dealer a few years later and founded the Carfax Gallery in London, in which he was eventually joined by his close friends Robbie Ross and More Adey. He was obviously not conversant with the niceties of the bankruptcy law and what he off-handedly told Wilde that he 'thought would be a good plan—namely that [Wilde] should retain about a third of his life interest'—not only constituted a funda-mental departure from Hargrove's carefully thought-out arrangement but was manifestly not allowable under the law. The ill-conceived idea, which apparently originated with Clifton in the impromptu manner suggested by his letter, was eventually, under the equally uncomprehending advocacy of More Adey, to poison relations between Oscar and Constance Wilde, with fatal results for the reconciliation both ardently desired.

Throughout Wilde's imprisonment, Clifton displayed a cautious diffidence in dealing with the Police Commissioners and a lack of enthusiasm for visiting the prisoner that was in sharp contrast to Sherard's bold, imaginative flair. He may, like Ross and Adey, have felt himself vulnerable to the law under which Wilde had been prosecuted and was accordingly concerned that no account of his visits to the prisoner 'filter into the press'. After his application for a visiting order 'as acting Trustee of Mr. & Mrs. Wilde's settlement' was denied, as he informed Blacker, followed by the return of his letter by order of the Prison Board, he was apparently unwilling to risk another such rebuff. Three weeks later, he declined an offer from More Adey to join him in a further attempt to see Wilde:

Many thanks for your very great kindness in offering to take me with you to see Oscar. I only doubt if permission c[oul]d be got just now. Sherard is going and Mrs. Wilde I hear is likely to go. W[oul]d it not be better to let it wait a bit? As to the divorce and bankruptcy, the fear of both is at an end and so neither could be given as an excuse and besides it might complicate the arrangements if they were.[20]

Following the bankruptcy hearing on 24 September, the state of Wilde's health deteriorated steadily until early in October he was admitted to the prison infirmary. Here, on 14 October, Sherard, with a characteristic display of the kind of reckless loyalty that prompted Wilde to describe him as 'that bravest and most chivalrous of all brilliant beings', paid him a third visit, again as R. S. Kennedy. This time, his visit had unexpected consequences. The attending warder reported to the governor of Wandsworth that the visitor's conversation had been of a subversive tendency in that the visitor had informed the prisoner that something might be done to call attention to his case by means of an agitation in the *Daily Chronicle*. The newspaper had already reported, on Sherard's authority following his earlier visit to Wandsworth on 23 September, that Wilde was poorly fed and was suffering greatly from want of nourishment.

Kennedy (Sherard) was found to have abused his visitor's privilege, and the governor recommended to the Prison Commissioners that Wilde be removed 'to a country Prison, where he would be less accessible to such influences'.[21] The Commissioners accordingly ordered that Wilde be removed to Reading Prison as soon as his Bankruptcy Court proceedings were concluded. The incident, with its unforeseen consequences for Wilde, may have been a source of embarrassment to Sherard, who omits any mention of it in his enumeration of his several prison visits. It was his final appearance as R. S. Kennedy. His next visit, actually his fourth although he refers to it as his third, was to Reading, a regular quarterly visit in the company of More Adey, on 30 November 1895.[22] In the meantime, Wilde was in Blacker's thoughts as, amid the dreary surroundings of the infirmary, the prisoner observed his forty-first birthday: '[16 October] Today is poor Oscar's birthday.'

Preoccupied by the unsettled state of his own affairs and in the face of Carrie's unyielding opposition to his having any further connection with Wilde, Blacker readily acquiesced in Clifton's assuming the role of 'acting Trustee' of the marriage settlement, representing both of them. In response to Clifton's report that Constance Wilde concurred in his misguided idea that Wilde should be allowed to retain a third of his life interest in the marriage settlement and that accordingly 'there ought to be little difficulty' about it, Blacker agreed. Notified of this by Clifton, Hargrove wrote to Blacker at length explaining:

we think that such a proposal would be fatal to the arrangement which of course has to be sanctioned by the Court & Mr. Humphreys, Mr. Wilde's Solicitor, agrees with us in this, as it is the duty of the Registrar to see that the whole of the Bankrupt's Estate is realised for the benefit of his creditors & therefore he would probably veto any arrangement under which a third interest was reserved for the bankrupt.

After reciting the terms of his proposal, 'which was fully reported to you at the time [and which] was made in order that the public examination might be avoided', Hargrove, with more than a trace of irritation, reminded Blacker that 'these terms were approved by you & Mr. Clifton & also by Mrs. Wilde'. In an attempt to accommodate the substance of Clifton's legally unacceptable proposal, Hargrove doggedly came up with yet a third alternative, under which Wilde would surrender two-thirds of his interest to the trustees and the official receiver would sell the remaining third to Mrs Wilde for £50, leaving the latter free to settle the one-third interest on her husband if she chose to do so. 'We heard that Mr. Wilde was very ill', Hargrove's letter continued:

& imagined that the public examination which was adjourned . . . would be further adjourned on that ground but Mr. Humphreys tells us that Mr. Wilde is very much better & as he has not been able to obtain sufficient money to pay the other creditors in full he will in order to secure a further adjournment have to make an affidavit setting out what has been done & the terms which have been agreed with yourself & Mr Clifton.[23]

As the day set for the public examination approached, Ross and Adey were still short of the amount needed to pay Wilde's creditors in full and annul his bankruptcy. 'At the last moment fresh claims were made', Ross reported, '& it was impossible to collect £400 or so in 5 days'.[24] Humphreys attempted to secure a further adjournment, but, as Hargrove informed Blacker:

Mr. Humphreys writes us this morning that his affidavit was not accepted & as he is not in a position to pay 20 shillings in the £ the public examination will take place tomorrow [12 November] at 11 o'clock & the arrangement with the Trustees is therefore at an end. We think this is to be regretted as now Mr. Wilde's life interest under his Settlement will have to be sold for the benefit of all the creditors. We hope however to arrange for its purchase for the benefit of the children.[25]

As on the earlier occasion at the Bankruptcy Court, Clifton as trustee was permitted an interview; and this time Ross was accorded the same privilege, to discuss matters related to the prisoner's bankruptcy. 'After the proceedings by special privilege his Trustee (Arthur Clifton) & myself were allowed to see him in a private room for half an hour each', Ross continued:

You may easily imagine how very painful this was for both of us. I have not seen him since the day he was arrested. As you know I was with him at the time. Mentally his condition is much better than I had dared to hope, though his mind is considerably impaired. Physically he was much worse than anyone had led me to believe. Indeed I really should not have known him at all. This I know is an ordinary figure of speech, but it exactly describes what I experienced. His clothes hang about him in loose folds & his hands are like those of a skeleton. The color of his face is completely changed, but this cannot be altogether ascribed to his slight beard. The latter only hides the appalling sunken cheeks. A friend who was in court would not believe it was Oscar when he first came in. I cannot understand how any humane nation, the English being Protestant of course are not Christian, can keep him in this condition. He is still in the infirmary but told me he wanted to leave as he hoped to die very soon. Indeed he only spoke calmly about death. Every other subject caused him to break down.[26]

'There appeared to be no assets whatever', Hargrove reported to Blacker:

except the dramatic & other literary rights which are fully charged & therefore probably nothing will be payable to you & Mr. Clifton in respect of the £1000 due to you. As Mr. Wilde is older than Mrs. Wilde there is practically no market value in his reversionary life interest in the Settlement funds but the Official Receiver will have to sell the interest for the benefit of all the creditors & it is therefore important that it should be bought by friends of the family in order that either the whole or ⅔rds may be secured for the children.[27]

The Bankruptcy Court directed that Wilde return on 19 November to read and sign the transcript of the shorthand notes of his examination. This being done, the court proceedings came to an end and, as previously ordered by the Prison Commissioners, with the concurrence of a team of medical specialists sent to examine and report on him, Wilde was transferred to Reading Prison the next day. Unlike his trips to the Bankruptcy Court, when he was allowed to wear his own clothes, the train journey from London to Reading was made in mandatory convict dress. This resulted in one of the most painful incidents of his entire prison experience, when he stood on the center platform at Clapham Junction 'in the grey November rain surrounded by a jeering mob', vividly described in one of the best known passages of 'De Profundis'.

5

'Letters from Two Idiots
to a Lunatic'

Following the failure of Hargrove's efforts to annul Wilde's bankruptcy, the official receiver proceeded to marshal whatever assets there
were, to be sold for the benefit of creditors. Among the few assets left
after the ruinous sheriff's sale the preceding April was Wilde's life
interest in Constance's marriage settlement. A purchaser of the interest
from the official receiver would not be entitled to receive any income
from it until after Constance's death, provided Wilde were then still
living, and only for a period that would end with his death. The fund
would then go to the couple's children. In view of the fact that Wilde
was more than three years older than his thirty-seven-year-old wife,
with a shorter life expectancy, the possibility of his surviving her was
actuarially remote and his interest in the settlement consequently had
'practically no market value', as Hargrove had informed Blacker.[1] It
seemed unlikely that the official receiver would find a buyer for it and
consequently there appeared to be no obstacle in the way of its
purchase at public sale by Constance herself, or by 'friends of the
family' acting on her behalf, the object being that on Constance's
death the fund would pass directly to the children. Under Hargrove's
plan, Constance would commit to provide separately in her will, as
she eventually did, for her husband to receive an amount equal to the
suggested one-third of his life interest in the fund (or more, if she
chose) if he survived her. Hargrove outlined his proposal in a letter to
Wilde's solicitor, C. O. Humphreys, and sent a copy to Arthur Clifton
as the 'acting Trustee' of the marriage settlement for his and Blacker's

concurrence. Since the plan provided for a means acceptable to the court of achieving the result originally proposed by Clifton himself, no opposition was anticipated from the trustees. Clifton, however, with his uncertain grasp of the legal technicalities involved, promptly dismissed the proposal as unacceptable. 'It did not convince me in the least', he reported to More Adey, setting the stage for the debacle that was to follow.[2]

The only other asset of the bankrupt estate, the literary and dramatic works, which had a potential value, were partially charged to secure the claim of George Alexander, the actor-manager, who had production rights to *Lady Windermere's Fan* and *The Importance of Being Earnest* and who had made advances to Wilde against unearned royalties. In Wilde's own appraisal of his works, he singled out these two plays and *Dorian Gray* as still having 'money-making chances' and he hoped the official receiver would let him know what terms were offered for them.[3] In the event, George Alexander purchased the copyrights to the two plays from the receiver and later generously bequeathed them to Wilde's heirs.

Under the arrangement for the production of *The Importance of Being Earnest*, Wilde was entitled to 10 percent of gross weekly receipts up to £1,000, and 15 percent of anything over that amount, payable weekly. His royalties for the week alone preceding his 'fatal and idiotic' action against Queensberry amounted to £245.[4] The extraordinary success of *The Importance of Being Earnest*, and of the concurrently running *An Ideal Husband*, had enabled him to extricate himself from the Avondale Hotel, but holding his creditors at bay in the face of his mindless extravagance had become an increasingly unmanageable problem. 'My hotel is loathsome to me. I want to leave it', he had written to Alexander, acknowledging receipt of £300 advanced against royalties and asking for 'the balance as soon as possible. . . . I am sorry my life is so marred and maimed by extravagance. But I cannot live otherwise.'[5] With an annual income in excess of £2,000, he had been financially insolvent for more than two years and by the end of February 1895 he had been served with writs amounting to over £400. On the brink of disaster, having obtained a warrant for Queensberry's arrest for criminal libel on 1 March, he raised £10.2.6 by pawning some jewelry on 12 March and the following day, heedless of impending danger, set off for Monte Carlo for a holiday with Douglas, prepared on his return 'to fight with panthers'.[6]

On the assurance of Douglas that legal expenses of the action would be paid by his older brother Percy and his mother, both of whom were temporarily out of London, Wilde met the immediate demands of his solicitor by borrowing £500 from Ernest Leverson, scarcely more than an acquaintance at the time although the latter's wife Ada was one of Wilde's closest woman friends. Any possibility of repaying the loan within the promised period of 'a week or ten days at most' vanished when the funds guaranteed by Douglas failed to materialize. The Leversons nonetheless stood by him loyally, sheltering him in their home when he was free on bail between the first and second criminal trials and all doors in London were closed to him. He had identified his enemy with contempt three years before in an interview with a French journalist, at the time of the banning of *Salomé* by the Lord Chamberlain: 'The typical Briton is Tartuffe.... There are numerous exceptions, but they only prove the rule.'[7] Following his arrest, with the despised Tartuffe turned suddenly savage, he was heartened to find, in addition to the Leversons, another, more unexpected, exception to the rule.

Minnie Adela Schuster, the daughter of a wealthy German banker, was unmarried and lived a retired life with her mother in a spacious villa in Wimbledon called Cannizaro, passing the winters in Torquay. In the latter place she frequented the Pre-Raphaelite circle of Lady Georgina Mount-Temple (Constance Wilde's beloved 'Mia Madre'), whose house, Babbacombe Cliff, Wilde leased from November 1892 to March 1893. During half the lease-term, Constance Wilde had been absent on the Continent with her aunt and consequently had not shared to the same degree as her husband in the flowering of the friendship with Adela Schuster. When husband and wife became estranged following Wilde's fall, Schuster observed that she and Constance Wilde had 'never been intimate'[8] and that Constance 'probably classes me amongst her husband's friends',[9] although Schuster thought that 'he would naturally not know me by my real Christian name, which he has never heard in his life—he has never heard me called—or seen any letter of mine signed—by any other name than my nickname—too ridiculous to mention'.[10] She was known to her intimates as 'Tiny' ('Miss Tiny' to Wilde). Frank Harris, an old friend, later inscribed a copy of his *Oscar Wilde*: 'To "Tiny" Schuster who holds a giants' place in the heart & esteem of all who know her & an unique place in the affection & admiration of the author.'[11] She was a well-read, highly intelligent woman of cultivated taste who was charmed and fascinated by Wilde's conversational powers. With the exception of her friendship with Harris, she did not move in Wilde's more familiar circles and, given the occasional nature of their friendship, he could scarcely have had reason to suspect the depth of her admiration and affection. 'Personally I have a real affection for O.', she wrote when Wilde was in prison:

besides my immense admiration for his genius, and I do and always shall feel honoured by any friendship he may show me.... Personally I have never known anything but good of O.... and for years have received unfailing kindness and courtesy from him—kindness because he knew how I loved to hear him talk, and whenever he came he poured out for me his lordly tales & brilliant paradoxes without stint and without reserve. He gave me of his best, intellectually, and that was a kindness so great in a man so immeasurably my superior that I shall always be grateful for it.[12]

Aware of Wilde's financial embarrassment and that the state of his mother's health was an added source of anxiety in his painful circumstances, she placed £1,000 at his disposal. 'Kindly say nothing about it to anyone', she begged Adey; 'he [Wilde] asked for no secrecy, but I thought he would be less loath to accept it if he knew it would not be talked about. I had heard that his mother was ill and in need, and I knew he was penniless. But because I promised O, I would still prefer that no one should know it.'[13] In a note to Wilde accompanying the funds, she wrote: 'I desire this money to be employed for your own personal use and that of your children as you may direct.'[14] According to Wilde, he received the money after he had been served with the bankruptcy notice by Queensberry on 21 May 1895, which accordingly put the funds within the long reach of the official receiver.[15] Wilde, however, was reluctant to see the unexpected gift swallowed by his creditors and arbitrarily chose to designate it a trust fund, 'a sum of money left for my disposal, not for the paying of my debts, but for my own help, and support, and the help of those I love like my mother'.[16] He handed the money over to Leverson, whom he appointed 'trustee',[17] to administer the fund in accordance with the terms of Adela Schuster's note, which he designated 'the title deed of the trust'.[18] The arrangement was clearly vulnerable to the claims of the official receiver and was to prove troublesome for Leverson, as he later informed Wilde: 'I think, dear Oscar, you will remember how when you handed me this money I begged you not to speak about it. Through your indiscretion in this respect (pardonable, I admit) I have been caused much extra trouble and annoyance.'[19] The idea that the 'deposit fund', as Wilde termed it, would be available on his release to enable him to support 'at least eighteen months of free life to collect myself' nourished a dream that sustained him in prison. The discovery, on the eve of coming out, that it was no more than a dream was to prove a calamitous blow.

Throughout Wilde's imprisonment, Adela Schuster was unwavering in her devotion, working tirelessly to find means of mitigating his suffering. Although he was never to see her again, she remained enshrined in his memory as he described her in 'De Profundis':

a woman, whose sympathy and noble kindness to me both before and since the tragedy of my imprisonment have been beyond power of description: one who has really assisted me, though she does not know it, to bear the burden of my troubles more than anyone else in the whole world has: and all through the mere fact of her existence: through her being what she is, partly an ideal and partly an influence, a suggestion of what one might become.[20]

In his instructions to Ross regarding the manuscript of 'De Profundis', Wilde directed that two typewritten copies be made of specified pages, 'welded together with anything else you may extract that is good and nice in intention', and that one be sent to Adela Schuster and the other to Frances Forbes-Robertson. 'I know both these sweet women will be interested to know something of what is happening to my soul.'[21]

It was during Wilde's imprisonment that Robbie Ross discovered the vocation for which he is remembered as Wilde's incomparable friend: 'the Mirror of Perfect Friendship', as Wilde described him. There had been sufficient turbulence in Ross's own life as a homosexual to have caused his family at one time to send him into temporary exile from England. The shock waves of Wilde's fall prompted his family to press him once again to leave the country and he was in France with Douglas during the trials and the sentencing. On his return to England, he devoted himself to the effort to annul Wilde's bankruptcy, but when this failed, he went abroad again and rejoined Douglas in Italy in December and January. The always uncertain state of Ross's health led eventually to his undergoing major surgery for removal of a kidney in June 1896, requiring a lengthy hospital stay followed by a prolonged convalescence. This, together with the intermittent demands of his family, prevented him until the final months of Wilde's imprisonment from devoting himself with the same single-minded sense of purpose that he thenceforth displayed to the cause that was to remain the central concern of his life.

The management of Wilde's affairs meanwhile fell by default to Ross's partner William More Adey, a writer, editor, and art connoisseur ten years his senior, with whom Ross shared a home. Known to Wilde through Ross, Adey, from early in Wilde's imprisonment, in consultation with Ross and Arthur Clifton, handled Wilde's affairs with conscientious zeal and unflagging devotion. He was, unfortunately, as ill-equipped as Ross and Clifton, both temperamentally and by experience, for the demands of the responsibility. A grave and sober demeanor veiled an element of the irrational in him that at times skewed his judgment and betrayed him into incomprehensible acts of folly. Siegfried Sassoon, who came to know him years later, recalled that he 'sometimes suspected [Adey] of being rather dotty'.[22] Adey was in fact insane and confined to an asylum at the time of his death in 1942. When, on the eve of Wilde's release from prison, Adey finally presented an account of his stewardship, Wilde was aghast to learn how disastrously his affairs had been mismanaged, most regrettably with consequences fatal to the hope that he and his estranged wife Constance had cherished for reconciliation and a shared future.

2

In early February 1896 Wilde's mother, to whom he was deeply devoted, died, 'broken-hearted because the son of whose genius and art she had been so proud, and whom she had regarded always as a worthy continuer of a distinguished name, had been condemned to the treadmill for two years'.[23] In Paris, Carlos Blacker noted her passing: '[6 February 1896] Read in paper of Oscar Wilde's mother being dead. Poor thing, it appears she never rose from her bed after the conviction of Oscar in the month of May.'

Constance Wilde was aware of the anguish the breaking of this cherished bond would cause her husband. Compassionate and kindly disposed since their reconciliation at Wandsworth Prison the previous September, she had continued to nurture the hope that their marriage might survive. Despite the deteriorating state of her health, the result of injuries sustained in a fall on the stairs of her home the previous year, she traveled from Italy to break the news to him herself. A special visit was allowed by the Prison Commissioners on 19 February, and, in view of the circumstances, was permitted to take place 'in a room other than the ordinary visiting room'.[24] As on the earlier occasion, she was moved by compassion and pity at the sight of 'poor Oscar', whom she found to be 'an absolute wreck compared with what he was'.[25] Hargrove had kept her fully informed of the opposition he had been encountering from her husband's advisers to his proposal for securing Wilde's life interest for the benefit of the children. It was a source of annoyance to Constance that the matter had remained so long unsettled. She informed her husband of the arrangement proposed on her behalf by Hargrove, namely, that he receive from her an allowance of £200 a year during her life and one-third of the life interest (which she would purchase from the official receiver) under her will if he survived her. Wilde readily agreed to the terms, as well as to the arrangements proposed for her assumption of the guardianship of the children. She expressed her desire to have nothing done in a public court but to have everything settled privately by agreement between them. He was comforted and deeply touched by the kindness and gentleness shown him by his wife, whose suffering and agony of mind he recognized as no less than his own. 'My soul and the soul of my wife met in the valley of the shadow of death', he wrote of the meeting to Ross: 'she kissed me: she comforted me: she behaved as no woman in history, except my own mother perhaps, could have behaved'.[26]

The meeting was a solace to both and held bright promise for the future. On leaving the prison, Constance informed the governor that she intended to apply for another visiting order on the next allowable occasion. In order to ensure that everything he had agreed with Constance be carried out, Wilde used his next letter-writing opportunity to communicate his wishes in unequivocal terms to Ross:

I want you to have a letter written at once to Mr Hargrove, the solicitor, stating that as my wife has promised to settle one third on me in the case of her predeceasing me I do not wish any opposition to be made to her purchasing my life-interest. I feel that I have brought such unhappiness on her and such ruin on my children that I have no right to go against her wishes in anything. She was gentle and good to me here, when she came to see me. I have full trust in her. Please have this done *at once*, and thank my friends for their kindness. I feel I am acting rightly in leaving this to my wife.[27]

Ross replied immediately to say that his wishes would be carried out. He duly wrote to Hargrove as requested and informed Adey and Clifton and Leverson of Wilde's instructions.

Leverson agreed with Adey and Clifton that there were compelling reasons for not feeling themselves bound by Wilde's explicit instructions. Apparently acting on his own, Leverson called on Constance before her departure from London and presented a counter-proposal regarding the life interest. He explained that in light of what he and his colleagues perceived to be the demonstrated hostility of Constance's advisers, Hargrove and Sir George Lewis, towards her husband, they thought it too great a risk to rely upon her mere promise, however sincerely made, of settling the one-third share on him under her will. They considered it essential that the promise be secured by a guarantee, to ensure against a possible change of heart that might result from Wilde's future conduct; otherwise, they were prepared to proceed, contrary to Wilde's clear instructions, to bid against her for the life interest. Leverson's argument confirmed for Constance what Hargrove had told her of the determined opposition he had met with in his efforts to provide for the welfare of her children. Tempers flared when Constance told Leverson of what she thought would be Hargrove's response in the event her offer were not accepted. Hargrove had suggested that acts of criminal behavior by Wilde for which he had not already been tried might be made the grounds for a divorce, thereby exposing Wilde to the possibility of further prosecution. While the suggestion angered Leverson, it horrified Adey. The threat, together with what Adey perceived to be the malevolence of Constance's advisers, strengthened him in his conviction that Hargrove's proposal was unacceptable. As for Wilde's explicit instructions to Ross to the contrary, Adey felt that Wilde's friends could not 'regard any messages from Mr. Wilde sent while unacquainted with the circumstances as binding to them to act upon'.[28]

Adey had been in communication with Adela Schuster since the previous November when he had approached her, as a friend of Wilde's, about a petition he was preparing to the Home Secretary for the prisoner's release. He found in her an eager and resourceful collaborator in a series of measures aimed at alleviating the prisoner's suffering, schemes ranging from ways to 'get at' the Home Secretary through influential intermediaries to a plan for bribing the doctor at Reading to certify to the dangerous state of Wilde's mental and physical health. In furtherance of the latter plan, Sherard, during a visit to Reading with Ross in May 1896, advised Wilde in French not to appear to be too well. He succeeded 'admirably—Oscar, I think, quite understanding', Ross reported to Adey.[29] This was in contrast to an earlier visit the previous November when Sherard, accompanied on that occasion by Adey, had been prevented from speaking French when he had attempted to inform Wilde confidentially that Constance had changed her name to Holland. He was 'brusquely interrupted by the warder with a "Stow that, now! No foreign tongues allowed here."'[30]

While Adela Schuster viewed the dubious plan of bribing the prison doctor with caution, she was prepared to support the attempt if all else failed. 'I cannot think that there should be any question of "buying" the doctor till we have tried all other means', she wrote to Adey, 'but—if money is necessary I will certainly try to subscribe.'[31] The idea did not shock her: 'I am not the least shocked at your suggestion that means shall be tried (the money) if others fail, and if it can be done discreetly.... Please burn this letter at once.'[32] She had earlier contributed generously to Wilde's bankruptcy fund, which had been returned to the several contributors when Hargrove's plan had fallen through. In response to a new appeal by Adey for a contribution to a fund for purchasing the life interest, she immediately recognized the potential injury this might cause Constance and was circumspect in her reply: 'I would not hesitate to promise any moderate sum if I could feel quite certain that I were doing no injustice to Mrs. Wilde. I will hear her side of the question (I can learn it from others) before deciding.'[33] Adey sent her the letter that Ross had received from Wilde containing the latter's instructions, which removed any doubt she may have had that her initial misgivings were well founded.

Two days later, within a few weeks of the death of Wilde's mother, Schuster's own mother died. In her sorrow, she 'felt more deeply than ever for poor O's suffering—more especially because of his mother's death'.[34] Although distraught and in mourning, she wrote to Adey at length from Torquay with characteristically humane and common-sense advice, begging him to heed Wilde's instructions and not oppose Constance: 'I hasten to return you O's letter at once & I need not tell you that it has interested me deeply, and I am most grateful to you for allowing me to read it.... But I fear I cannot agree with you with regard to the life interest: I cannot too strongly urge you to heed Mr. Wilde's request and to let Mrs. Wilde purchase the life interest without opposing or outbidding her.'[35] Undeterred by Adey's refusal to be swayed in his judgment, Schuster, acutely aware of the disaster in the making for both Constance and Oscar Wilde, continued to the final moment to plead with him to abandon his ill-conceived plan.

3

In the long drawn-out contest between Adey and Hargrove over the life interest, the fact that it had practically no value was never in dispute. 'Oscar's chance of succeeding to [the interest] is very slight', Adey acknowledged, 'and certainly not worth to anyone financially more than £5 or £10.' In seeking an explanation for the bitter contention that ensued over such a negligible sum, one need look no further than the contrast offered between, on the one hand, Hargrove's practical considerations on behalf of Constance and her children and, on the other, Adey's idiosyncratic reasoning on how best to serve Wilde's interest. 'In the first place', Adey explained in justifying his position to Adela Schuster, 'I extremely dislike representing the common sense view of any question rather than the wider and generous view.'[36]

The stubborn refusal of Wilde's representatives to accept an offer that met the terms of Clifton's initial proposal seemed to Hargrove mischievous and perverse. As foreseen by Adela Schuster, Constance attributed the refusal to her husband and viewed it as a betrayal of the assurances she had received from his own lips. Her annoyance was compounded by Adey's role. When she learned several months later from Wilde's sister-in-law that Adey had been to Reading, she wrote her husband what he described as 'a most violent letter, in which she said . . . "I hear with horror that Mr. More Adey has been to see you. Is this your promise to lead a new life? What am I to think of you if you still have intercourse with your old infamous companions? I require you to assure me that you will never see him again, or any people of that kind."'[37]

Identifying the trustees of the marriage settlement with Adey's intransigence, Hargrove in exasperation recommended that they resign in favor of more impartial fiduciaries. He wrote to Blacker informing him that Adrian Hope, a relative by marriage of Constance, was prepared to take his place if he agreed. Blacker readily acquiesced, finding in the suggestion 'a source of intense relief'. Having abandoned his action against Newcastle a month before, his spirits responded to the prospect of freeing himself from this second worrisome involvement: '[23 March] After dinner told Carrie how fortunate & happy we were in everything.' The clouds were not long in returning, however, as Blacker from the experience of recent years had foreseen was bound to happen when things seemed to be going well. Shortly after dropping the action against Newcastle, his feeling of relief had been accompanied by a sense of foreboding: '[31 January] Today and yesterday I have been feeling particularly well and I do not know to what to attribute it. I hold it as certain, that in consequence of so feeling, I am sure to have something to trouble me very soon.' Two weeks after telling Carrie how fortunate and happy they were, the anticipated trouble arrived. Word came of the death in London of his father John Blacker, with whom he had not been reconciled since the onset of his troubles ('[6 April] Papa died. Regrets—remorse—'), and he and Carrie left immediately for England. While in London, he met with Hargrove and concluded arrangements for his and Clifton's resignations as trustees. On April 24, Adrian Hope and one Amy Wight were appointed successor trustees in their place.

When John Blacker's will was read following the funeral, Carlos learned that his share of the estate was the magnificent collection of Renaissance book bindings that had been his father's passion. The collection had been formed over a period of several years with the help of the well-known London dealer Bernard Quaritch and had an estimated value of £70,000. It now became Quaritch's unpleasant duty to inform Carlos that the bindings had proven actually to be the work of the highly skilled contemporary forger Louis Hagué, alias J. Caulin, and consequently were worth a mere fraction of what had originally been thought: '[13 April] Drove to Quaritch's . . . with whom I had the great & sad conversation anent the Caulin Hagué provenance.— Walked home dazed. Told Carrie. Remember no further details'; '[14 April] Waited in for Quaritch who came at 11:30 & he then before Carrie told us further particulars.' Quaritch's disheartening judgment was confirmed by experts at the British Museum: '[17 April] Carrie to British Museum & showed books to experts. Afterwards went to Quaritch's & told him result.' Quaritch eventually purchased the collection for £2,500. It was subsequently sold at auction in November the following year as 'A Remarkable Collection of Books in Magnificent Modern Bindings Formed by an Amateur (Recently Deceased)' and realized a mere £1,907.16.6.[38]

On his return to Paris, with 'things looking rather low', Blacker wrote to Quaritch, noting that 'for the sake of my poor father's memory . . . I am quite unable to shake off the thoughts of that terrible Caulin Hagué affair & it haunts me day & night'. Despite Quaritch's advice 'not to endeavour to pursue H.', who had reportedly died five years before, Blacker nevertheless 'went to call on Panizzardi in order to see whether he could not assist me in tracing H. but he had gone to Italy to his mother'.[39]

4

Adey remained unshakeable in his conviction that he was better able than Wilde to judge of the danger threatened by Constance's sinister advisers. In preparation for the bidding contest, he raised £170 by solicitation among his friends. 'These friends of mine have never been intimate with Oscar', he assured Adela Schuster, 'would be the last people to condone anything that he has done, and are fully sympathetic with what Mrs Wilde has suffered.'[40] He had been dissatisfied with the performance of Wilde's solicitor, C. O. Humphreys, and for the past six months had on his own been secretly consulting another solicitor, Martin Holman, 'a clever fellow and not decrepit like the old frog [Humphreys]'.[41] Ready on the advice of Holman to open negotiations with the official receiver, Adey was chagrined to find that Clifton had in the meantime grown weary of the struggle over 'the everlasting life interest'[42] and had changed his mind about the scheme he had authored, leaving Adey in the uncomfortable position of being the sole defender of the controversial proposal.

Although Adey claimed sole discretionary authority over the fund he had just raised ('I have received and paid into my bank the following sums to be used by me according to my discretion for the benefit of Mr Oscar Wilde'),[43] in countering Adela Schuster's impassioned pleas that he abandon his questionable course, he sought refuge in the notion that the ultimate decision was really not in his hands but rested with the anonymous body of 'friends and advisers,' the contributors to the purchase fund, at whose direction he claimed to be acting. As to who these advisers were, he explained further to Adela Schuster that 'the purchasers are not personal friends of Oscar's nor even acquaintances, but good kind people who have an admiration for his talents and a profound pity for his unhappy state'.[44]

The strain of his position was beginning to tell on Adey's health and on 21 May, with the matter unresolved, he left for a month's stay in France. Shortly after his departure, Wilde being again due a regular quarterly visit, Sherard and Ross went to Reading on a sweltering day for what Ross described as 'the worst interview I have had with Oscar, because Sherard was nearly breaking down all the time and shewed himself fearfully nervous. . . . I do not know why I am sure but he was much shocked by the change for the worse. . . . [Wilde] cried the whole time and when we asked *him* to talk more he said he had nothing to say and wanted to hear *us* talk.' When Ross brought up the subject of the life interest, 'he [Wilde] said he was not interested about the life interest. Asked if he had seen his wife lately? He said "No" but believed she was coming soon.'[45] The day following the unhappy visit, Wilde wrote to Ross explaining that 'I could not collect my thoughts yesterday, as I did not expect you till today. . . . Anything sudden upsets me.' He hungered for word of the familiar world from which he had been so totally cut off and asked for 'news of literature and the stage. . . . anything that will for an hour take my thoughts away from the one revolting subject of my imprisonment. . . . Has anything come of Carlos Blacker and Newcastle? The trial.'[46] He inquired of the affair in which he had once played a pivotal role, unaware that proceedings had been dropped and the matter settled four months before.

5

While More Adey and Adela Schuster remained adamant in their opposing views on the vexing question of the life interest, they were united in their concerted efforts to secure Wilde's early release on health grounds. They were joined in the attempt by Adela Schuster's friend Frank Harris. 'I *think* a very excellent person has been appointed to report on O's condition', she confided with high hopes to Adey: 'do not repeat this—Kindly *burn this letter*.'[47] After an hour-long interview with Wilde on 16 June, 'in the sight but not within hearing of an officer', Harris met with the governor and prison doctor at Reading, and subsequently reported his findings to the chairman of the Prison Commission.[48] Wilde followed with a formal petition to the Home Secretary in which he emphasized that 'forms of sexual madness ... [such as] the most horrible form of erotomania' from which he suffered were widely recognized on the Continent as 'diseases to be cured by a physician, rather than crimes to be punished by a judge'. He referred to the work of the German sociologist Max Nordau, who had used Wilde's case to illustrate 'the intimate connection between madness and the literary and artistic temperament'. Citing his 'fear of absolute and entire insanity', together with his failing eyesight and hearing, Wilde begged to be released: 'should his imprisonment be continued, blindness and deafness may in all human probability be added to the certainty of increasing insanity and the wreck of the reason'.[49]

On his return to England at the end of June, Adey applied to the Prison Commissioners for a special visiting order, supported by a petition from Wilde to the Home Secretary that Adey be allowed to see him on urgent matters connected with the guardianship of his children and his marriage settlement. In preparation for the visit, Adey set forth the matters he intended to discuss in a lengthy memorandum, written almost entirely in French, possibly in anticipation of adopting Sherard's strategy for communicating confidential information in the presence of the prison warders. He wished to warn Wilde of the evil intentions of his wife's advisers: 'they are all your avowed enemies, I mean her family, her solicitors and especially the big solicitor who you once thought was your friend [George Lewis]'. Even Sherard and Leverson were not to be trusted entirely in Adey's eyes, owing to their lack of discretion. With respect to the measures being taken to secure his early release, Adey's advice was to say nothing, 'especially [to] the excellent Robert and Ernest',[50] both of whom were strangers to the close brotherhood formed by Adey, Ross, and Clifton. Sherard had been unacquainted with any of the three before his arrival in London from Paris after Wilde's release on bail, when he first met Leverson as well.

'When you see Sherard', Adey reminded himself to caution Wilde, 'ask him not to provide the press with news of you.'[51] As one of Wilde's oldest and most loyal friends, Sherard was among the few people Wilde had expressed a wish to see when he regained his freedom.[52] Concerned about Adey's attitude towards him, Wilde pressed him about it. 'I hope you don't think I have any feeling against Sherard', Adey replied. 'I am on perfectly friendly terms with all your friends and get on particularly well with Sherard. I merely object to his frightful indiscretion which is a positive mania with him and, contrary to his affectionate intentions, does you harm.'[53] Although Wilde was relieved to learn this ('I am so glad you are friends with Robert Sherard: I have no doubt that he is very indiscreet, but he is very true'), Sherard was soon pained to find himself excluded from Wilde's confidence.[54] On his next and last visit to Reading, he later recalled:

[Wilde] asked me to absent myself for a few moments, whilst he talked to the gentleman [Adey] who had come with me. And in the grey gloom of the prison corridor where I waited till this conference, from which I was excluded, was over, it dawned upon me that my long friendship, fruitful as it had been in sorrow, might reserve for the future another sorrow, and the disappointment of a wasted effort.[55]

Deeply hurt, he did not come again.

On July 24, the official receiver notified Wilde's creditors of a meeting to be held 'to consider and deal with offers made to the Official Receiver and Trustee for the sale of the bankrupt's interest in his marriage settlement'.[56] Hargrove secured proxies from the new trustees of the marriage settlement as well as from the marquess of Queensberry, approving the sale of the life interest to Constance Wilde for the sum of £25. Adey had in the meantime appealed directly to Constance to write to the Home Secretary in support of Oscar's petition for release. She replied, agreeing to do what was asked, provided she was not opposed in her purchase of the life interest. Adey, ever mistrustful of her advisers and suspecting a possible ruse, was convinced that the letter had not actually been written by her. He sent it for examination to Adela Schuster, who assured him that she hadn't 'the faintest doubt'[57] that it had been written by Constance. She seized the opportunity to make yet another forceful plea for accommodation with Constance, setting forth in lengthy detail the disastrous results for both husband and wife that were bound to follow from the course he was pursuing, and from which she still hoped to dissuade him. 'I know that I am wearying you', she wrote in closing her long letter, 'most likely making myself ridiculous—but the matter seems to me important enough to make one quite frank, & so I dare to try and say exactly what I think.'[58] Fearing that her frankness in stating how ill-judged she viewed Adey's course to be might this time have gone beyond permitted bounds, her letter was followed immediately by a self-conscious apology: 'I believe I expressed myself much too strongly today at one moment about our mutual friend. I am afraid that what I said might have sounded contemptuous and might give you an entirely wrong impression. . . . It was merely the warmth of my defence of his wife that made me, for the moment, exaggerate the feeling that some other women—less gentle than she—might have for him.'[59]

Schuster's forceful appeal succeeded only in persuading Adey that the message he had received was indeed from Constance. With regard to the life interest, he remained adamant, prompting Schuster in frustration to take independent action. 'I think I ought to tell you that I have written to Mrs. Wilde', she informed him, 'though I don't wish to repeat to you exactly what I said to her. In fact this is meant to warn you that I am going over to the enemy in a very modified way, and, that *if* she replies to me, I may very possibly not tell you.'[60] Although their mutual regard for one another, firmly rooted as it was in their unquestioned devotion to Wilde, remained intact, their intense daily collaboration began from this point to slacken. At a meeting of the creditors on 27 August, the sale of the life interest to Constance for the generous sum of £25 was approved by a resolution adopted by creditors representing a majority of the indebtedness.[61] Adela Schuster made a last desperate appeal to Adey to step aside and allow the sale to Constance to go through: 'I hope most earnestly that even now you may be induced to throw up the tussle for the Life Interest and so induce Mrs. Wilde to write to the Home Secretary.'[62] Unmoved, Adey stubbornly entered the bidding, instructing Martin Holman, on behalf of 'O's friends', to increase the offer to £50 for half the life interest, with an option to purchase the remaining half, and, should the official receiver not agree to this, £75 for the entire interest—and finally, with total abandon, 'if absolutely necessary go up to £100 for the whole'.[63] Momentarily sobered by second thoughts about how far he had gone in this headlong commitment of Wilde's meager funds in the face of universal disapproval, he wrote to

Wilde: 'If you should hear of anything that I have done on your behalf without your knowledge of which you do not approve, I trust you will repudiate it in as strong terms as you please.'[64] After protracted negotiations, Adey ultimately succeeded in purchasing the life interest for the wildly exorbitant sum of £75, plus an additional £25 in related costs.

In order to discourage Hargrove from advancing the bidding, Adey instructed his solicitor Holman to inform him that a large sum of money had been collected on Wilde's behalf and was at Adey's disposal. The strategy backfired in producing the unintended effect of reassuring Constance, ever solicitous of her estranged husband's welfare, that he would not be in want of money on coming out of prison and that accordingly there was no need for her to consider reinstating the amount of allowance originally offered and agreed to by Wilde at the time of her visit to Reading the previous February. Since then, owing to Adey's perverse opposition, the amount originally offered had been reduced from £200 to £150 a year. Constance advised her husband to use the imaginary 'considerable fund' represented as being in Adey's hands for Wilde's benefit to purchase an annuity. As Adey persisted in his bid for the life interest, Hargrove, 'enraged at what seemed like double-dealing on [Wilde's] part', wrote the latter 'a violent and insulting letter',[65] informing him that unless the bid to purchase the life interest on his behalf were withdrawn, Constance's reduced offer of an allowance of £150 a year would be withdrawn altogether.[66] He indicated in addition that legal action was being taken to secure guardianship of the children. 'The tidings fell on me like a thunderbolt', Wilde wrote. 'I was aghast. I had been under the impression that my wife had bought the interest, or that at any rate everything had been arranged for her so doing, in the preceding March.'[67] It was the first intimation he had that his instructions to Ross seven months earlier had not been followed. 'What Hargrove's next move will be I do not know,' he wrote wearily to Adey, on whose judgment he continued to rely. 'If my wife leaves me absolutely without a penny I can only trust that for a year at any rate I will be looked after, and I may be able to write again.'[68]

6

On 27 February 1897, Wilde was by special permission allowed an hour-long visit in the solicitors' room with Adey, Leverson, and Ross, the latter now sufficiently recovered from his surgery after a long convalescence. Wilde was cheered by the prospect of the visit, as he wrote to Adey: 'We shall then surely be able to discuss all business matters. Business with you, seriousness with Ernest, nonsense with Robbie.' From Adela Schuster's 'deposit fund', thought still to be in the hands of Leverson, Wilde generously proposed that his 'debts of honour' be paid in installments, 'after I have seen that enough is forthcoming to give me at least eighteen months of free life to collect myself'.[69] While he was disappointed to learn that such preferential treatment of selected creditors would not be countenanced by the official receiver, he was consoled by what Adey had to tell him about his financial prospects following his release: 'I was touched and helped immeasurably by your telling me that some friends of mine have arranged that for eighteen months I am to have enough to live on: that gives me breathing space.'[70] The reassuring arrangement, so comforting to Wilde, was a figment of Adey's imagination, as he felt obliged to confess to Adela Schuster:

He seemed very anxious as to what he would have to live upon for the next year and a half, until he could again earn enough to keep himself. In order to relieve his mind I told him that I was sure that money would be forthcoming for him, so that he should not be in want during that time. I thought it better to say this, in order to save him present anxiety, even if he is disappointed when he comes out. As a matter of fact I know of no funds for this purpose at present.[71]

Having learned from Hargrove's 'violent and insulting letter' that his explicit instructions to Robbie Ross regarding his interest in the marriage settlement had not been followed, Wilde in a letter to Adey attributed to Ross 'the primary fault' for the disastrous consequences:

in not carrying out my own wishes and my wife's, conveyed to him in my letter of March 1896. . . . Everything has been wrong. So wrong indeed have things been that it looks to me as if Alfred Douglas had been directing the operations, desirous to 'score off' Mr. Hargrove, or my wife, or both. His sole idea seems to be to 'score off' people by sacrificing me. Please let me know am I right in discerning some of his sinister small nature in the whole transaction?[72]

Wilde was further angered by Leverson, who proposed to repay himself from the 'deposit fund' the £250 balance that remained outstanding on his loan. 'When he came here, he calmly told me that "money was tight in the City" and that he could not let me have the money that belonged to me! As if I cared whether money was tight in the City, or knew what it meant.'[73]

Like Adey, Wilde had become dissatisfied with his solicitor, C. O. Humphreys ('Nothing would induce me to see Humphreys. His advice would, I think, be worthless').[74] Another solicitor, Arthur D. Hansell, was engaged to act for him in negotiations with Hargrove to resolve the dispute with Constance over the marriage settlement and custody of the children. Agreement was reached in the final days of his imprisonment and on the eve of his release he signed a Deed of Separation under which he relinquished both the custody of his children and his life interest in the marriage settlement. In return, Constance agreed to pay him a yearly allowance of £150, contingent upon certain conditions aimed at ensuring that he live 'a respectable life and shall not annoy or molest the said Constance Mary Wilde . . . or be guilty of any moral misconduct or notoriously consort with evil or disreputable companions'.[75] Extraordinary authority was given his new solicitor, Arthur D. Hansell, to be the judge of any possible failure on his part in the future to abide by the terms of the agreement. Within six months, Wilde was to have reason to regret that Hansell was 'stupidly made arbitrator'.[76]

7

As the day of his release approached, Wilde reminded Adey that both he and Robbie had often assured him that sufficient funds were on hand to enable him to live 'for eighteen months or two years' following his imprisonment. He wished on the occasion of an up-coming visit by them to let him know 'clearly and definitely' what money there was. 'I have deferred asking the question till now. Now I must know.'[77] While awaiting the visit, Wilde wrote again to Adey with a detailed list of the articles of clothing and toiletry he would require, to be paid for out of a gift of £25 from an anonymous friend (Adela Schuster). As to the all-important question of where he would go to start life anew, he noted that 'Dieppe is relaxing, fashionable, and I am too well known there. I now see Havre is the best. There is a place close to Havre which is said to be *bracing*. I forget its name. Carlos Blacker used to be there a great deal.'[78]

On 11 May, the day arrived for Ross and Adey to present the account of their stewardship. As requested by Wilde, Adey had prepared and brought with him a written statement of Wilde's affairs, which he left in the care of the governor of Reading. When Wilde received it the following day, he read it 'with great pain, I need hardly say . . . of course I understand now why you did not allow me to read the paper of statement yesterday'.[79] In anticipation of the dreaded interview, Adey had prepared a memorandum headed 'Reason why I said enough for two years' in which he was hard put to fabricate a coherent explanation, citing a list of chimerical sources of funds: 'expectation of obtaining annuity; expectation of £500 from Douglas; assurance of Frank Harris; rumours of other moneys; promise of others, e.g. Gurney, Ricketts & McTaggart'. Under a separate heading, '£170 given to me by strangers to use entirely at my discretion', he listed the following purposes: '1st to stop bankruptcy; 2nd to buy life interest, as the only means of securing an annuity; 3rd for expences incidental to (1) and (2); 4th for other objects.' His accounting of disbursements from the fund showed: '£20 for legal expences to Humphreys connected with bankruptcy; £100 for life interest & part expences; £50 left for remainder of legal expences & other objects; £25 recently given by another person for pocket money exclusively.'[80]

Still in 'great pain' from Adey's memorandum, Wilde wrote to Ross two days later, referring to Adey in his letter as 'your friend', for whom he reserved his most withering judgment:

In point of fact, Robbie, you had better realise that of all the incompetent people on the face of God's earth in any matter requiring wisdom, common sense, straightforwardness, ordinary intelligence, More Adey is undoubtedly the chief. . . . In matters of business he is the most solemn donkey that ever stepped. He has neither memory, nor understanding, nor capacity to realise a situation, or appreciate a point. His gravity of manner makes his entire folly mask as wisdom. Every one is taken in. He is so serious in manner that one believes he can form an intellectual opinion. He can't. He is *extremely dense* in all matters requiring lucidity or imagination or instinct. In business matters he is *stupid*. The harm he has done me is irreparable, and he is as pleased as possible with himself. Now I have realised this, I feel it right, Robbie, that you should know it. If you have ever thought him sensible, give up the idea. He is incapable, as I have written to him, of managing the domestic affairs of a tom-tit in a hedge for a single afternoon. He is a *stupid man*, in practical concerns.[81]

In his exasperated letter to Adey ('My dear More'), Wilde advised him that 'the time is come when you should recognise one thing: that is that in all business matters even of the simplest kind your judgment is utterly incompetent, your opinion either foolish or perverted, and your capacity to understand the most ordinary circumstances of actual life absolutely *nil*'. Dumbfounded by the disastrous mishandling of his affairs, he concluded that, 'The entire correspondence of you and Robbie with me should be published. The best title would be *Letters from Two Idiots to a Lunatic*, I should fancy.'[82]

On 18 May, Wilde was moved from Reading to Pentonville Prison, from where he was released early the following morning. Owing to the distress Adey had caused him, he felt that he could not travel with him and he begged Reggie Turner to accompany him abroad. 'It is much better that More should not be with us', he wrote to Ross, 'as I know I could not restrain myself from discussing the terrible position in which I have been placed through his want of practical intelligence, and legal knowledge. . . . The result is quite awful.'[83] Turner, fearful that his allowance would be stopped should his role as traveling companion come to the notice of his family, felt obliged to decline; and in the end the hapless Adey, having faithfully attended to all arrangements, was there to meet him at Pentonville and accompanied him on the night boat from Newhaven to Dieppe. He brought with him a check from Leverson for £111.11.6, all that remained of Adela Schuster's 'deposit fund', and £80 in bank notes, representing a new loan from Leverson. Ross and Turner had gone on ahead to prepare for their arrival and were waiting at the landing stage to meet them at half past four on 'a magnificent spring morning. . . . There was the usual irritating delay', Ross recalled, 'and then Wilde with that odd elephantine gait which I have never seen in anyone else stalked off the boat.'[84]

6

'The Most Bitter Experience of a Bitter Life'

I

It was not in Wilde's nature to remain long under a cloud on his first day of freedom. He was instantly reconciled with Adey and wired to Ross from Newhaven not to mind 'the foolish unkind letters. More has been such a good friend to me and I am so grateful to you all I cannot find words to express my feelings.'[1] Any lingering rancor vanished in the glory of the magnificent spring day of his arrival in France. The Normandy countryside was resplendent viewed from the ramparts of Arques-la-Bataille where Wilde enjoyed 'the trees and the grass and country scents and sounds' in a way that Ross had never seen him do before.[2] After a week in Dieppe, where as he had foreseen he was soon recognized, he moved to the small village of Berneval, a few miles distant on the coast, where his incognito offered greater proof against discovery.

While the mismanagement of his affairs was quickly forgotten, the damage done to his relationship with his wife Constance was to prove irreparable and the source of lasting sorrow. She had left Reading prison following her emotional last meeting with her husband fifteen months before with renewed hope for a shared future. By the time of the signing of the Deed of Separation, however, her hopes had evaporated in anger and bewilderment at her betrayal over the marriage settlement. As the day of Wilde's release approached, she had written to her brother Otho: 'I have again had pressure put upon me to persuade me to go back to Oscar, but I am sure you will agree that it is impossible.'[3] Her susceptible heart softened once again, however,

when she received a long letter from Oscar, 'full of penitence'.
Blacker, to whom she showed it, found the letter 'very beautiful . . .
incomparably the finest piece of almost spiritual enthusiasm'.[4] Otho
Holland agreed, but 'thought its mood too overwrought and high
pitched to last'[5] and accordingly advised his sister to wait before taking
her husband back. She temporized, writing in reply to Wilde's peni-
tent letter that she would see him twice a year, with no mention
of permitting him to see his two boys, whose photographs she en-
closed: 'a terrible punishment', Wilde told Ross, 'and oh! how well
I deserve it'.[6]

Blacker had been out of touch with Constance since he had been
asked to resign as trustee of her marriage settlement the previous year.
He wrote to her shortly after Wilde's release, inquiring as to his
whereabouts. Constance was happy to hear from him and eager to
reassure Blacker that she did not associate him with her husband's
culpable advisers. It was illness alone 'and nothing else' that had
prevented her from writing to him earlier, she replied. 'Oscar's address
is SEBASTIAN MELMOTH, Hôtel de la Plage, Berneval-sur-mer, Dieppe,
and I hope you will write to him there. I am sure he will be pleased to
hear from you.' Ever at heart solicitous of her estranged husband's
welfare, she added in closing: 'I hope that you will write to Oscar as
soon as you can.'[7] On receipt of her letter, Blacker, amid the excitement of the birth of his second son Robin the previous day, wrote at
once from Freiburg: '[14 June 1897] Letter from Mrs. Oscar telling me
where she was. . . . Wrote to Mrs. Wilde. . . . Wrote to S. Melmoth.'

Wilde's instructions to Ross to make copies of certain pages of his
long prison letter 'De Profundis' for Adela Schuster and Frances
Forbes-Robertson were based on his assumption that 'both these
sweet women will be interested to know something of what is happening to my soul'.[8] Blacker he was sure would be interested as well.
'My dear old Friend', he wrote in reply to Blacker's letter, 'I need not
tell you with what feelings of affection and gratitude I read your letter.
You were always my staunch friend and stood by my side for many
years. . . . You will, I know, wish to hear about me, and what I am
doing and thinking.' As a record of a further stage in his soul's progress,
his letter—a lengthy, at times lyrical, description of his present state of
mind and body, in which, though his heart was broken, he often found
himself 'strangely happy'—echoes the self-examining theme of 'De
Profundis'. While he had learned many terrible things in prison, he

wrote, he had learned some good lessons as well that he had needed. Among others, he had learned gratitude for all the beautiful things that were left to him, first and foremost among which he counted 'loyal and loving friends'. Sympathy with suffering had taught him that 'the hard heart is the evil thing of life and of art'. He concluded with an earnest appeal to Blacker—one he was to repeat many times—to come and see him: 'I long to see you, dear friend. Could you come here with your wife? Or to Dieppe?... I must talk over my future, for I believe that God still holds a future for me, only I must be wise, and must see my way. Will you do this? It would help me very much to see you—more than I can say.'[9] They had not seen one another since before Wilde's imprisonment.

Blacker was deeply moved by Wilde's 'beautiful' letter and sent a copy of it to his friend and confidant W. R. Paton in Greece, who wrote in reply: 'As you know, the extent of my attachment to him far exceeds the bounds of our intimacy. Still I must write to him.' Some weeks before, Paton had found Wilde's eloquent letter to the editor of the *Daily Chronicle* about the terrible conditions of children in prison 'of the best augury' for Wilde's future ('I should not be surprised if some day or other he will be in Parliament') and he had been inspired on his own to launch a campaign for Wilde's 'social rehabilitation'.[10] Aware of Carrie's hostile attitude, he had appealed to her directly not to oppose her husband's support of the cause:

After writing my Sunday letter to Carlos, I had an Oscar Wilde soirée & wrote to Oxford, Cambridge & Berlin about his letter to the Daily Chronicle. What I feel so much is that Carlos & I are indebted to him for so much & that it is our duty to work for his rehabilitation. I am sure that you won't dissuade Carlos from giving his heart to this.... Please counsel him to give rein to his feelings about this matter, even if you have to fly in the face of the conviction of society.[11]

As a nucleus of activists for his campaign, Paton had turned to his friends F. C. Conybeare at Oxford and Oscar Browning, his former housemaster at Eton, now at Cambridge, both old acquaintances of Wilde's as well, and to Ulrich von Wilamowitz-Möllendorff, the distinguished German classical scholar in Berlin with whom Paton had had 'some interesting correspondence about Sappho & Oscar Wilde'[12] and who regarded Wilde's criminal conviction as barbaric. In his letter to Browning, Paton wrote:

You must tell me . . . exactly what you think about Oscar Wilde's letter to the Daily Chronicle which owing to floods I only saw yesterday. You don't, I think, know that his catastrophe was a personal catastrophe for myself, because it so happened that his best friend, his marriage trustee, was & is my best friend & I used whenever I went to London to have the inestimable privilege of hearing Oscar Wilde talk to us very intimately every day. Needless to say that although my friend & I were aware of his penchant for young men (notably Lord A. D.) & of his extreme imprudence in expressing his adoration we were ignorant of his excesses, which he unluckily concealed from us.

Now it seems to me that he has suffered for his sins (whatever they were) & that his letter is a fine expression of this. . . . I have written to my best friend (F. C. Conybeare) at the other shop in the same sense & partly in the same words. Try to propagate my sentiment in your I fear very hard ground.[13]

The response to his letters was not encouraging. 'I fear sympathy is too likely to stop at measures for his social rehabilitation', he reported to Blacker.[14] Disappointed at the failure of the campaign to gather momentum, he wrote to Wilde:

Carlos has just sent me a copy of a letter of yours, which it does me good to read. . . . I have always had the privilege of being very much attached to you (admiration apart—that is a smaller thing), & your catastrophe I felt as a cosmic blow in this little world of mine. For the future, if you feel yourself better than you were, you will have no difficulty in dismissing from your inmost heart the desire for social rehabilitation which I wish to God, all the same, were possible. My spirit is in loud revolt always against the barbarism which condemned & condemns you.[15]

While grateful for Paton's sympathy ('I have often heard from others of your sympathy and unabated friendship'), Wilde showed little patience with the idea of social rehabilitation: 'I don't dream of social rehabilitation', he informed Paton, 'nor do I want it, but I *do* want to do artistic work again, and I hope to do so.'[16] 'The Ballad of Reading Gaol', which was to be his final literary work, was then nearing completion.

2

Simultaneously with the receipt of Wilde's letter, Blacker received word from Constance that she was coming with her son Vyvyan to Freiburg where they were to be joined by her older boy Cyril, from his school at Neuenheim, towards the end of July.[17] 'I would willingly accept your kind invitation, & be your [guest] but I do not expect you would care for the 3 of us', she wrote. 'I should like to see something of Freiburg if you don't mind driving with me as I am unable to walk. I am coming on purpose to see you, so I hope I shall see you.'[18] A week later, to prepare him further for the deterioration in her physical state, the result of progressive spinal paralysis, she wrote to say that she was 'supposed to keep perfectly still so I am afraid you will find me utterly incapable of doing more than taking short drives'.[19] Blacker was shocked at her condition and reported it to Wilde, who 'had no idea it was so serious'. He proposed coming to see her. 'I really think it would be better for her to see me, and have it over. I would only stay a couple of days', he wrote. 'Just try and advise me. I am so glad she is with you and your charming, brilliant wife.'[20]

Blacker could only have been dumb-struck by the prospect of Wilde's coming to Freiburg, where his presence would be bound to attract unwelcome attention and involve impossible complications. His nerves easily jangled, Blacker was still haunted by dreams of his own troubled past ('[6 December 1896] Dreams, nightmare about being in Saint Louis'). It had been only two weeks since Wilde's letter imploring him to come to Berneval or Dieppe with his wife Carrie to see him and talk over his future. In Freiburg, there would surely be an opportunity for such a helpful talk with his 'dear old Friend'. If Carrie had been 'depressed' some months earlier by the mere thought of asking Lord Francis's wife May Yohe to lunch, it was not at all likely, in view of her far more entrenched hostility to Wilde, of which the latter was unaware, that she would be prepared to receive the outcast in her home. Wilde's first meeting with his invalid wife since their legal separation promised to be an emotionally stressful encounter, with unpredictable results. In addition, Wilde's children, puzzled about their father's whereabouts and what had happened to him, presented an equally serious problem. What would they make of his sudden reappearance in their lives and his abrupt disappearance 'a couple of days' later? Blacker, in his response to Wilde's proposal to come to Freiburg, concurred with Constance's brother Otho Holland that a meeting at this time would be premature and his advice was to wait and come to his wife at the end of the summer when the boys had gone back to school and she was settled at Nervi in Italy. 'Of course I think it would be much better for Constance to see me, but you think not', Wilde replied. 'Well, you are wiser.' He professed to be 'simply heart-broken' over his wife's alarming condition. 'When I think of poor Constance I simply want to kill myself', he added in a note of despair that is in marked contrast to the frolicking tone and lighthearted banter of his letters to other correspondents at the time. 'I wish I could see you', he appealed again to Blacker, who had informed him that he could not come to France before the end of September. 'Where I shall be in September I don't know', Wilde replied. 'I don't care. I fear we shall never see each other again.'[21]

For Constance, Carlos and Carrie Blacker ('the kindest people and the nicest that I know') were an unfailing source of comfort and support. After spending a week with them in Freiburg, she and the two boys spent the month of August at the Gasthof Höchenschwand in the nearby Black Forest, where they remained in regular communication with the Blackers. 'The boys seem very happy', Constance wrote '& Cyril told me last night that he hoped every day would seem as long as yesterday.'[22] At the beginning of September, she returned with the boys to Freiburg for three weeks to be nearer the Blackers in a neighboring pension, the two families dining together regularly. Blacker and Cyril spent strenuous days bicycling while Carrie and Constance devoted hours to their shared interest in photography. When the time came for Cyril to go back to school, Constance left with her younger son Vyvyan for Italy and Vyvyan's return to his school in Monaco, after which she expected to be joined by her husband. Added to her constant physical pain was her anxiety about the future, her mental anguish aggravated by continued uncertainty about Wilde and a deep sense of loneliness on leaving Cyril and the Blackers. '[17 September] I afterwards went to see Mrs. Holland who had not come to dinner. [She] was very depressed on account of Cyril's having gone.' It was 'pouring with rain' on her last two days in Freiburg, which could only have added to the gloom of parting. Blacker went in the rain to pick up 'several things' for her, including some 'awfully sweet' little boxes that she had ordered. 'If we ever meet again, I will shew them to you', she wrote to Cyril from Basle the following day, underscoring the word 'if' four times, as though with a premonition that she had not long to live. 'The Blackers are exceedingly fond of you & I hope you will remain good friends with them all your life', she continued in a vein of weary resignation:

The Rhine is so lovely here; it simply tears along with waves like the sea, only they go always in one direction. I should not mind living here if I might always watch that restless river; it is unsatisfied [with] restless longing & desires only after that long journey to slip into the breast of the sea.[23]

While Blacker's concern and affection for Constance were fully shared by his wife, his ardor in the role of principal adviser and comforter was not always viewed with equanimity by Carrie. '[22 September] Letter . . . from Mrs Holland saying we were to go to Basle. Carrie took offence at this. We had a little rub about it. . . . At dinner Carrie spoke much about Mrs Holland, scolded me generally.'

From Italy four days later, Constance wrote to Blacker of her safe arrival in Nervi, adding: 'Not a sign of Oscar or a word from him, but I have an idea that he will turn up some day without writing.'[24] Unknown to Constance, Oscar had in fact turned up earlier in the week in Genoa, a few miles away, where he had spent the day en route to Naples in the company of Douglas.

3

By the time of his release, Wilde's declared intention to Constance at the time of her visit to Wandsworth Prison to kill Douglas if he saw him had undergone considerable moderation, owing in some measure it seems to the cathartic effect of 'De Profundis'. While Adey and Ross had been immediately absolved for putting 'an adder into my heart and an asp under my tongue',[25] by their mishandling of his affairs, Wilde's feelings towards Douglas were more ambivalent. He had emerged from prison psychologically off balance, his nerves shattered, his emotional life in chaos, and in a constant state of anxiety about his precarious financial situation. In a prescient assessment of his uncertain future, Constance wrote a few weeks prior to his release that 'his fate is rather like Humpty Dumpty's, quite as tragic and quite as impossible to put right!'[26] This was an insight that Wilde himself gradually came to accept in the course of his first unhappy year of freedom. 'Something is killed in me', he eventually confided to Ross. 'I feel no desire to write. I am unconscious of power. Of course my first year in prison destroyed me body and soul.'[27]

After a sleepless night following receipt of a 'revolting' letter from Douglas shortly after his release, Wilde wrote to Ross: 'To be with him would be to return to the hell from which I do think I have been released. I hope never to see him again.' His first day alone following the departure of Ross—Adey and Turner having already gone—was 'a very unhappy one', he wrote to Ross. 'I begin to realise my terrible position of isolation, and I have been rebellious and bitter of heart all day.'[28] A few days later, however, he was able to report that he had begun work on 'The Ballad of Reading Gaol'. 'It is very good for me to be alone,' he confided to Ross. 'I am working.'[29] Being alone, however, had never been a prescription for happiness for Wilde. After two years of terrible isolation, he was for the rest of his life to find the solitude requisite for creative work unbearable ('the one thing I cannot stand'). When the price of doing what was good for him involved resisting temptation, he had invariably found the price too high. Now, alone and 'in danger of *ennui*, that enemy of modern life',[30] the prospect of what he viewed as a return to hell with Douglas offered a fascination and an excitement that proved to be irresistible. He was soon in daily correspondence with Douglas, whom he assured, a week after informing Ross that he hoped never to see him again: 'Don't think I don't love you. Of course I love you more than anyone else.'[31] Acquiescing in Douglas's entreaties to come to Berneval, Wilde invited him to join him there, cautioning, in the interest of secrecy, the use of an inconspicuous incognito—suggesting Jonquil du Vallon—and hoping that he would 'get quietly out of Paris'.[32]

Two days before the appointed rendezvous, Wilde was made alarmingly aware of the sword of Damocles that hung over him in the matter of the allowance he was entitled to receive from his wife by a letter from his solicitor Arthur Hansell, announcing his resignation. Acting on 'private information'—most likely supplied by Ross, alert to the danger a meeting with Douglas posed for Wilde—Hansell wrote as sole judge under the Deed of Separation, reminding Wilde of the consequences of any failure on his part to abide by the terms of the arrangement with his wife.[33] If, in Hansell's judgment, he were to be 'guilty of any moral misconduct or notoriously consort with evil or disreputable companions', he would forfeit the right to his allowance. The provision was specifically aimed at any resumption of the liaison with Douglas, as had been understood by the parties at the time of the signing. More Adey's solicitor Martin Holman had drawn his attention to an additional risk to Wilde of 'any further intercourse' with Douglas:

Lord Queensbury has made arrangements for being informed if his son joins Mr Wilde, and has expressed his intention of shooting one or both. A threat of this kind from most people could be more or less disregarded, but there is no doubt that Lord Queensbury, as he has shown before, will carry out any threat that he makes to the best of his ability.[34]

Wilde was 'so upset and distressed in nerve' by Hansell's letter that he called off the meeting with Douglas. 'A. D. is not here, nor is he to come', he assured Ross.[35] 'Later on', he wrote to Douglas, 'when the alarm in England is over, when secrecy is possible, and silence forms part of the world's attitude, we may meet, but at present you see it is impossible.'[36]

As summer wore on, the succession of visitors—and with it the revelry—slowed and the weather began to change. 'I am still here, though the wind blows terribly', Wilde wrote to Will Rothenstein in late August. 'I don't know where I shall go myself.'[37] In regular communication with Douglas, the two finally met briefly in Rouen towards the end of the month. 'I feel that my only hope of again doing beautiful work in art is being with you', Wilde wrote following their meeting. 'Everyone is furious with me for going back to you, but they don't understand us. I feel that it is only with you that I can do anything at all.'[38] The two made plans to go to Italy and live together as soon as Wilde could raise the money for the journey. Berneval, where three months earlier he was determined to make his home ('I adore this place'), had become hateful to him.[39] 'I simply cannot stand Berneval', he wrote to Ross from Dieppe. 'I nearly committed suicide there last Thursday—I was so bored.'[40] From Rouen in early September, he wrote to Blacker: 'The weather has been so dreadful at Berneval that I have come here, where the weather is much worse. . . . My last fortnight at Berneval has been black and dreadful, and quite suicidal. . . . I am greatly disappointed that Constance has not asked me to come and see the children. I don't suppose now I shall ever see them.'[41] Noting receipt of a 'letter from Oscar complaining of his wife', Blacker was skeptical and questioned Wilde's motives for going to Italy. Wilde replied on the eve of his departure: 'I cannot write here: the cold weather, the *ennui*, the dreary English, are all paralysing. . . . You are really wrong in your views on the question of my going.'[42] Blacker remained skeptical. '[16 September] I went to Mrs Holland to get her to write to him at once, tell him to join her at Nervi. I wrote to him also.' Constance, who was still in

Freiburg and shared Blacker's skepticism, was shattered by the news. '[16 September] Cyril to dinner alone…Mrs Holland came afterwards. Difficult, cried about her position in general, her affairs, about Cyril going into the navy.' Wilde had given Blacker his address in Paris where he counted on raising the money for continuing on to Italy. Douglas had apparently suggested his intimate friend Rowland Strong, a journalist, as a likely source of funds and Wilde attempted to make contact with him on his arrival in Paris. Unsuccessful in locating Strong, he obtained the travel money from Vincent O'Sullivan and left almost immediately to join Douglas at Aix-les-Bains from where the two continued on to Naples, arriving there on 20 September.

Constance wrote to the Paris address but in the following days heard nothing in reply—'not a sign of Oscar or a word from him', she informed Blacker ten days later.[43] The day after writing, she was stunned to receive a letter from Oscar from Naples, saying that hers had been forwarded to him from Paris. 'The whole thing seems to me to be rather hopeless', she wrote in despair to Blacker:

You say that I seem ballottée but so would you be if you were a woman & felt that you were being used as a cat's paw. However, Oscar says that he is coming to stay with me next month, & if he comes, he must come as my husband. The people who live here know my brother & know that I have no other. Besides, I hate telling lies more than this terrible thing called life makes necessary. I look forward to nothing. … Question. Has he seen that dreadful person at Capri? No-one goes to Naples at this time of the year. So I see no other reason for his going, & I am unhappy. Write to me & tell me what to do.[44]

Without waiting for Blacker's advice—which was to ask Oscar directly whether he had seen Douglas—Constance did exactly that, as she informed Blacker in a second letter the same day:

I have to-day written a note to Oscar saying that I required an answer to my question whether he had been to Capri or whether he had met anywhere that appalling individual. I also said that he evidently did not care much for his boys since he neither acknowledged their photos which I sent him nor the remembrances that they sent him. I hope it was not hard of me to write this, but it was quite necessary.[45]

As was the case with Constance, Blacker's letter to Wilde at his Paris address was forwarded to him in Naples. 'I know that all you have written to me about my coming here comes from the sympathy and loyalty of your great generous heart', Wilde wrote in reply, 'and

I am sorry that my being here gives you pain. . . . Had Constance allowed me to see my boys, my life would, I think, have been quite different. . . . I waited three months. At the expiration of that long, lonely time, I had to take my life into my own hands.'[46] Blacker sent Oscar's letter to Constance, who shared his exasperation at her husband's proffered reason for going to Italy: 'What is three months compared with all I have had to go through? But it grieves me to the heart that he should have behaved in this way. He is weak as water.' With Vyvyan back at school, she was alone ('excepting for a bad headache which keeps me company') and preparing to leave the hotel in Nervi where she had been staying to move to the nearby Villa Elvira, Bogliasco, which she had taken for the winter.[47] Here, still clinging to the hope that her husband would appear, despite the recent development, she made ready for his arrival.

There followed almost immediately a second letter from Oscar informing his wife of his intention to live in Naples with Douglas. 'Had I received this letter a year ago', she wrote, forwarding the letter to Blacker:

I should have minded, but now I look upon it as the letter of a madman who has not enough imagination to see how trifles affect children or unselfish enough to care for the welfare of his wife. It rouses all my bitterest feelings. . . . I think the letter had better remain unanswered and each of us make our own lives independently. I have latterly (God forgive me!) an absolute repulsion to him.

In closing, she added wistfully of her shattered dreams: 'I go on Monday to the Villa Elvira, where I have really hurried, thinking that perhaps Oscar was coming, borrowing linen from this Hotel, etc.'[48] Many years later, her son Vyvyan recalled his mother's 'joy when [Oscar] was supposed to be coming back, and I remember her misery when she found he had other claims upon his time'. She never saw him again.[49]

4

Among the 'good lessons' learned by Wilde from his prison experience, he had informed Blacker, were sympathy with suffering and the conviction that 'the hard heart is the evil thing of life and of art'.[50]

Despite the lesson learned, 'he really did not understand how cruel he was to his wife', Robbie Ross observed after Wilde's death, adding, 'but I never expect anyone to believe that'.[51] One who did not believe it was Blacker, who, while pained for Wilde's sake by his self-destructive course, was at the same time acutely aware of the suffering endured by Constance as the result of her husband's cruelty. 'Her memory I revere as a thing "enskied and sainted"', he wrote to her brother Otho after her death. 'Even to this day my wife and I are moved to tears when we speak of your poor sister, of her sweetness and kindness and above all of her generosity and wonderful sense of duty. She had a great and noble nature and she had grown to be a near and dear part of our own lives.'[52] Wilde begged 'dear Carlos' not to 'pass harsh judgments on me, whatever you may hear. . . . My friends in England are greatly distressed. Still, they are good friends to me: and will remain so, most of them at any rate. You must remain so too.'[53] Blacker, however, was convinced that in abandoning his wife and children for Douglas, Wilde proved himself to be utterly 'hopeless and beyond redemption' and in sympathy with Constance he resolved to sever all ties with him. He reported Wilde's distressing elopement to Naples and his own reaction to it to Paton, who claimed to have been 'physically & actually sick' on receipt of the news. 'It is very difficult for me to write about Oscar Wilde', Paton wrote in reply. 'As you know, I never really liked him & if I tried hard to persuade myself that he had a heart it was because you were fond of him. The thing is a somewhat shattering shock for us both, but from henceforth we abandon all relations with the man.'[54] On reflection, however, Paton had second thoughts about the finality of following Blacker's lead in their future attitude towards Wilde, as he expressed in a letter to Carrie a few days later:

I am not sure that I quite agree about the final abandonment of O.W. His fate has affected me much more than it should have done; for he was always very distant & always a little antipathetic to me. Still I feel an attachment & a debt to him, which will be permanent whatever his course of life be. Of course I think, as you do, that the course of action now imposed on us is to cut him.[55]

Blacker and Paton were not alone among Wilde's few remaining friends in condemning his conduct. In the face of universal disapproval, Wilde appealed for understanding: 'Stick up for us, Reggie, and be nice',[56] he begged Turner. 'Robbie has written me three unkind and detestable letters';[57] and 'people who have nothing to do with my life write long tedious letters to me informing me that I have wrecked my life for the second time'.[58] Robert Sherard was overheard in the Authors' Club in London expressing his disapproval. Reported to Wilde, the indiscretion earned Sherard a reprimand in terms reserved by Wilde to express his utmost contempt: he charged Sherard with playing Tartuffe. Their friendship, which had been strained by Sherard's exclusion from Wilde's inner circle of advisers at the time of Sherard's final visit to Reading Gaol, followed by a less than successful reunion in Berneval, never recovered its former intimacy. 'I have no inclination to propitiate Tartuffe, nor indeed is that monster ever to be propitiated', Wilde wrote to Vincent O'Sullivan in a note of thanks for rebuking Sherard at the time.[59] Within the year, Wilde was to apply the same contemptuous epithet to Blacker in the final scene of the breakup of their 'ancient friendship',[60] dismissing him with: 'So Tartuffe goes out of my life.'[61]

Well aware that in rejoining Douglas he risked forfeiting his allowance from Constance, Wilde reported shortly after his arrival in Naples that he was 'awaiting a thunderbolt' from her solicitor.[62] In the meantime, ever short of money he found 'the daily financial crisis . . . wearying'.[63] Under the strain, his letters to his publisher Leonard Smithers soliciting an advance on 'The Ballad of Reading Gaol' took on an uncharacteristically sharp edge for which he felt obliged to apologize and beg 'allowances for a man of wrecked nerves and life on the brink of many abysses'.[64] Finally, in mid-November, came the anticipated thunderbolt. Based on the letter he had written to his wife informing her of his intention henceforth to reside in Naples and 'keep house' with Lord Alfred Douglas, as her solicitor phrased it in his complaint, application was made to Arthur Hansell, as sole arbiter under the Deed of Separation, to declare that Constance was under no further obligation to pay the allowance. Wilde protested that at the time of signing he had never wanted to see Douglas again but since then circumstances had changed and accordingly he argued that the words of the agreement—so far as they referred to 'evil or disreputable companions', without specifically naming Douglas—should be construed narrowly. Not surprisingly, Hansell was unswayed by the argument and the allowance was promptly stopped. Added to the injury was the objectionable suggestion, which Wilde indignantly denied, that when he had informed his wife of his intention to live in

Naples he had used the expression 'keep house' with Douglas ('I thought "keep house" was only a servant-girl's expression').[65]

During the time together with Douglas, Wilde had managed to raise £120 for their joint support. With this gone and with Wilde's allowance stopped, the daily financial strain on their ménage in the Villa Giudice finally reached an unmanageable state. The £25 a month that Douglas received from his mother was insufficient for his own wants, as Wilde acknowledged, and consequently Douglas was unable to help him 'with either the smallest sum or the most meagre assistance'.[66] Under threat from his mother of stopping his own small allowance, Douglas, with Wilde's acquiescence, departed for Paris in early December. The affair that had been rekindled with such passion three months earlier in Rouen quietly succumbed in an atmosphere of fatigue, and a suggestion of boredom and relief, on both sides. Wilde saw no alternative but to stay on alone in Naples and try to settle down to literary work. Lady Queensberry agreed to pay him £200 towards the 'debt of honour' that Wilde felt he was owed by her family for legal expenses promised him at the time of his ill-advised suit against Douglas's father. As Wilde later reported to Ross, somewhat unfairly to Douglas—in a letter perhaps intended for Constance's eyes in an effort to persuade her to reinstate his allowance—when his money ran out and it came to Douglas's having to pay his share, 'he became terrible, unkind, mean, and penurious, except where his own pleasures were concerned, and when my allowance ceased, he left. . . . It is, of course, the most bitter experience of a bitter life. . . . I know it is better that I should never see him again. I don't want to. He fills me with horror.'[67]

Beyond putting some finishing touches to 'The Ballad of Reading Gaol' and preparing it for publication, Wilde never got round to the literary work he had proposed to undertake. A series of misfortunes befell him following Douglas's departure, as he reported to his publisher Leonard Smithers in early January: 'influenza, the robbery, during my absence in Sicily, of *all* my clothes etc. by a servant whom I left at the villa, ill-health, loneliness, and general *ennui* with a tragi-comedy of an existence, but I want to see my poem out before I take steps'.[68] He lingered on for another month in Naples until the publication date of the 'Ballad' approached, when he decided to return to Paris. 'My life has gone to great ruin here', he wrote to Smithers on the eve of his departure, 'and I have no brains now, or energy. I hope to make an effort in Paris.'[69]

1. Carlos Blacker, *c*.1882, 'the best dressed man in London', according to Oscar Wilde, while Constance Wilde thought that he possessed 'perhaps the greatest distinction of manner of all whom she had ever met'.

2. Oscar Wilde at the height of his success, 1892. Photograph presented to Carlos Blacker ('always the truest of friends and the most sympathetic of companions').

3. Carlos Blacker and Lord Francis Hope, aboard the *Majestic* in New York Harbor, 20 April 1892.

4. 'Linny', 7th duke of Newcastle, was twenty-four at the time of his marriage on 20 February 1889 to seventeen-year-old Kathleen Florence May Candy, daughter of Major H. A. 'Sugar' Candy.

5. Carlos and Carrie Blacker, Cabourg 1902.

6. Carlos Blacker (1859–1928), portrait by Johnston Forbes-Robertson c.1882.

7. Carlos Blacker and his two sons, 'Pip' (Carlos Paton Blacker), then seven, and Robin, five, Cabourg 1902. Both boys later served as officers in the Coldstream Guards in World War I.

8. Caroline ('Carrie') Frost, daughter of Confederate General Daniel Frost of St Louis, and Carlos Blacker were married in London on 7 February 1895. 'From this time to the end', Carrie wrote following Carlos's death thirty-three years later, 'we were never parted for a day.'

9. Princess Alice of Monaco and Vyvyan Holland, younger son of Oscar Wilde, in the uniform of the Collegio della Visitazione, Monaco, which he attended from January 1897 until the death of his mother in April 1898.

10. Cyril Holland, older son of Oscar Wilde, killed by a sniper at Neuve Chapelle when serving as a captain in the Royal Field Artillery, 9 May 1915.

11. Oscar Wilde at a time when, as Carlos Blacker informed his future wife Carrie, he was 'beaming with the inebriation of success, & … producing excellent plays with remarkable rapidity'. Photograph (London, 1892) presented to Blacker.

12. Oscar Wilde's play *An Ideal Husband* 'contains a great deal of the real Oscar', as he informed Charles Ricketts. Having become 'engrossed in writing it', while at the same time performing 'signal services' for Carlos Blacker in his troubles, 'the real Oscar' is recognizable in the play in the character and role of the philosopher–dandy Lord Goring.

SALOMÉ

To / Carlos Blacker

from his
affectionate
friend,

the author,

in esteem and
admiration

13. Oscar Wilde inscription in copy of *Salomé*, published 22 February 1893, presented to Carlos Blacker.

14. Mary Augusta Yohe, known on the London stage as 'the girl with the foghorn voice' and as 'Madcap May' for her involvement in a number of highly publicized escapades, married Lord Francis Hope in November 1894.

15. Lord Francis Hope divorced May Yohe in 1902 for her 'misconduct' in eloping to Japan with the son of a former mayor of New York. Described as 'a lonely unconventional man', he succeeded to the title of 8th duke of Newcastle on the death of his brother.

16. Robin Blacker, 2nd Lt, Coldstream Guards, younger son of Carlos
Blacker, killed shortly after his eighteenth birthday in the battle of Loos, 28
September 1915.

17. Carlos Blacker and Anatole France, Hotel Majestic, Avenue Kléber, Paris, December 1915–January 1916.

18. Anatole France: to his 'très cher Carlos Blacker' (24 April 1918).

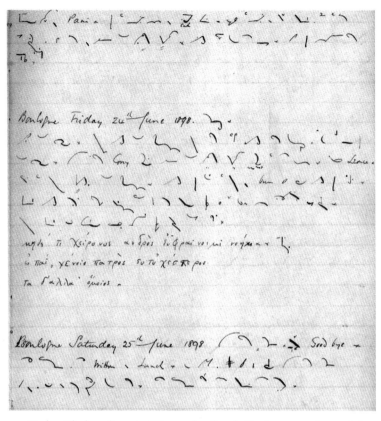

19. Carlos Blacker diary in Pitman shorthand: Boulogne 24 June 1898—
(including lines from the *Odyssey* and *Ajax*, written in Greek); 25 June
1898—Under the heading, 'Letter from Oscar saying Good bye', the entry
continues: 'After lunch just before dinner letter from Oscar which put an end
to our friendship forever.'

20. Ceremony of Degradation of Captain Dreyfus, Ecole Militaire, Paris, 5
January 1895. Adjutant Bouxin of the Garde Republicaine is seen tearing the
insignia of rank from Dreyfus's uniform, while the police van waits in the
background to take the condemned man to prison to await deportation to
Devil's Island for life.

21. Major Ferdinand Walsin-Esterhazy. The traitor was thought by his employer, the German military attaché, to be 'the most marvellous, audacious & wonderful canaille that it was possible to imagine, either in fiction or history, & capable of any & every villainy, including murder'.

Eug. Pirou   Paris. 23 Rue Royale

22. Salomon Reinach, in a secret report to the Chambre criminelle of his confidential talks with Carlos Blacker about the Dreyfus case ('he knows everything') wrote that 'Blacker confided in four persons: 1–Conybeare of Oxford; 2–Paton, an Oxford Hellenist resident on Samos; 3–myself; and 4–Oscar Wilde.'

Nos Contemporains

Paris (Le Prog.)

23. Joseph Reinach, sworn to secrecy by his brother Salomon as to the identity of Carlos Blacker, names him only once in his exhaustive seven-volume *History of the Dreyfus Affair* in a footnote unrelated to Blacker's plan.

24. Major Alessandro Panizzardi, Italian military attaché in Paris, standing, second from left, and Colonel Maximilian von Schwartzkoppen, German military ataché in Paris, standing, second from right.

25. Colonel Alessandro Panizzardi, Rome, 8 December 1899. At a time when 'three beings alone knew the whole & entire truth [about Dreyfus], namely God & the two Military Attachés', in the words of Carlos Blacker, he became the fourth such being when Panizzardi confided 'the whole & entire truth' to him.

26. Chez Mère Adèle, Montmartre, 1911/2: Maurice Gilbert, standing, with his wife Mary Beatrice seated on his left, and Rowland Strong, seated with his back to the camera next to his dog (Snatcher?), in the kind of convivial milieu frequented by Strong.

27. Oscar Wilde at the Vatican, Rome, April 1900. The photograph by Robbie Ross, two years after Wilde's estrangement from Carlos Blacker, was given to Blacker by Ross, who remained a loyal friend to both.

28. Drawing by the Spanish artist Ricardo Opisso of Oscar Wilde, Yvette
Guilbert, and Toulouse-Lautrec at the Moulin de la Galette, Montmartre,
1898.

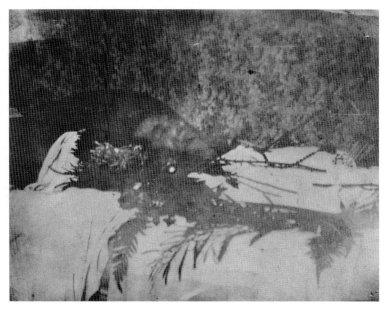

29. Oscar Wilde on his deathbed, with 'a few flowers placed there by myself [Robbie Ross] and an anonymous friend [Carlos Blacker] who had brought some on behalf of the children'. Photograph by Maurice Gilbert, 'taken by flashlight with a borrowed camera & inferior plate all obtained with great difficulty under trying circumstances', according to Ross.

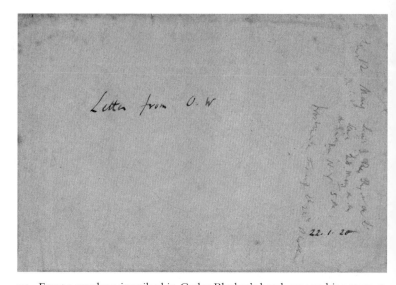

30. Empty envelope inscribed in Carlos Blacker's hand, among his papers at the time of his death in 1928. He had almost died of Spanish Flu in January 1920 while in Florence. The envelope may once have contained Wilde's last letter to him, in June 1898, which, in Blacker's words, 'put an end to our friendship forever'. Believing himself to be dying, Blacker may have been prompted to destroy the letter on the date inscribed. The envelope cannot be related to any of Wilde's surviving letters to Blacker.

31. 'Photograph of W. R. Paton, my dear friend … announcing his death on the 21st April 1921 at Samos,—of pneumonia.' Note on back of photograph by Carlos Blacker.

7

'The Dreyfus-case Paris Cannot Be Figured by the Paris of Today'

On the day Hansell's thunderbolt struck Wilde, a far more powerful one rocked Paris with the appearance of an open letter to the French Minister of War in which Commandant Marie Charles Ferdinand Walsin-Esterhazy was for the first time publicly named as the author of the document, the so-called *bordereau*, on the strength of which Captain Alfred Dreyfus had been falsely convicted as a traitor three years earlier for allegedly having sold military secrets to the German military attaché in Paris, Colonel Maximilian von Schwartzkoppen. The accusation of Esterhazy by the condemned man's brother Mathieu, signaled the beginning of the public phase of the complex Dreyfus affair, which rapidly split the nation along a deep ideological divide present in French society since the Revolution. Propelled by an incendiary and violently partisan press, events unfolded rapidly in Paris against a background of increasingly shrill daily polemics.

Following the public naming of Esterhazy, he was brought before a Court of Enquiry conducted by General Gabriel de Pellieux. In the course of the enquiry, Pellieux, on being privately shown a secret forged document, purportedly written by the Italian military attaché, Major Alessandro Panizzardi, to Schwartzkoppen and naming Dreyfus, became convinced of the latter's guilt and concluded that there was no proof against Esterhazy. Amid growing public interest and agitation in the press, Esterhazy demanded a court-martial which acquitted him on 11 January 1898. Two days later, the affair reached its frenzied fever-pitch with the publication of Emile Zola's inflammatory open letter to the president of the French Republic, *J'Accuse*, in which he accused members of the General Staff and other high-ranking officers of the French army of wrongful conduct in the trial and conviction of Dreyfus, then serving a life sentence on Devil's Island, and of protecting Esterhazy. Zola's stunning accusations immediately captured national attention, igniting through all levels of society from the capital to the provinces what Romain Rolland called a 'holy hysteria'. Zola was promptly prosecuted for criminal defamation on complaint of the Minister of War in a tumultuous trial that opened at the Palais de Justice on Monday, 7 February 1898. The same day, Blacker arrived in Paris with his family from his sister's home in Freiburg. Their arrival in 'very bad' weather was marred by an accident to two-year-old Pip: '[7 February] Poor little Pip at about 5:30, half an hour before we arrived in Paris, put both his little feet on the brass plate covering the boiling water to heat the carriage. He burned and blistered both his feet dreadfully and cried bitterly all the way driving to Mama's, 31 Avenue Kléber.... This was a most lamentable and pitiful affair, the first bad accident Pip has had.' It was an inauspicious beginning for the fateful months that were to follow.

When the case had been about to break with the public naming of Esterhazy, the German attaché, forewarned, had been instantly recalled to Berlin. In Freiburg, where Schwartzkoppen had spent the three years immediately preceding his posting to the German embassy in Paris in 1891, Blacker learned that shortly before his recall, Schwartzkoppen had stated in a letter to his former commanding general in Freiburg that Dreyfus was innocent. By the time of his arrival in Paris, Blacker had become deeply immersed in the case. He found the city on the opening day of Zola's trial 'in a ferment', and in the days following he read and talked of little else. Confined indoors with a bad cold for more than a week after his arrival, he wrote to his 'old & intimate friend Panizzardi, knowing that I would learn the whole truth from him'. Failing to receive an immediate reply, he noted in his diary that he was 'worried that Panizzardi did not answer my letter written on the 15th'. Since the recall of his ally and confidant Schwartzkoppen, Panizzardi had been left to face alone an increasingly hostile press and public, burdened with the terrible knowledge of Dreyfus's innocence. Deeply troubled over the direction of events, unable to sleep, his hair reportedly turned grey with anxiety, he had been 'meeting with scant courtesy from the Generals & officers he met'.[1]

As rumors of the existence of the forged document that had been privately shown to Pellieux—which came to be known after its creator, Lieutenant-Colonel Henry, as the *faux Henry*—and others connecting Panizzardi with Dreyfus, circulated, Panizzardi's position became increasingly untenable. Distraught, he wrote to Schwartzkoppen at the end of January to inform him of 'a whole lot of things you do not know yet... All this is horrible, but true.'[2] The Italian ambassador, Count Tornielli, 'could not let all this go on, since it affects me and not you.... So far, I have been the only one to suffer, for I am continually getting anonymous letters threatening me or telling me that everybody knows the part I played in this affair; I cannot sleep at nights now.'[3] Tornielli had informed the French Minister of Foreign Affairs that Panizzardi would be constrained to issue a statement to the effect that any communication purported to be written by him that referred to Dreyfus, either by name or by initial, was a forgery. He requested as well that Panizzardi be heard as a witness in a second Esterhazy enquiry conducted by Pellieux that had begun on 21 November 21 and lasted until 3 December. Reluctant to reopen the Dreyfus case and intent on preventing Panizzardi's appearance at all costs, General Le Mouton de Boisdeffre, Chief of the General Staff, in a note intended for the Council of Ministers marked 'secret,' stated among his reasons for insisting that the request be denied, that Panizzardi was a party with a direct interest in the matter and as such was necessarily suspect and that furthermore the General Staff had in its possession three compromising letters from Panizzardi to Schwartzkoppen—one of them being the *faux Henry*—referring to Dreyfus, which Boisdeffre, by implication, vouched for as authentic. In addition, Boisdeffre indicated, with telling effect, that the General Staff possessed letters 'of a very intimate nature' written by Panizzardi to Schwartzkoppen. In a correspondence remarkable for its ribaldry, the two military attachés are shown to have regularly mixed business with pleasure with a surprising absence of discretion, signing themselves to one another as 'Alexandrine' and 'Maximilienne'.[4]

Panizzardi had earlier written to Schwartzkoppen of his deep concern over the appearance in the newspapers of stories about the 'Schwartzkoppen–Panizzardi correspondence' that had been taken from the German attaché's flat:

They are confidential letters which you left in your clothes-pockets and which
have since had apocryphal matter forged and added to them. When Charles
went off in the morning to get the newspapers the porter's wife went upstairs,
ferreted in your pockets, and took possession of your letters. *I know that for
certain.* There is no need to return to this subject, but it is very regrettable to
think how falsified letters are being made use of to condemn an innocent man,
and all because these papers were not burnt.[5]

While it was widely rumored that certain letters had been altered to
confirm the guilt of Dreyfus, unsuspected by Panizzardi was the fact
that 'apocryphal matter' had been 'forged and added to' other letters to
nourish a 'Secret File' of correspondence between the two military
attachés revealing them to have had a homosexual relationship. The
potential scandal proved an effective deterrent to Panizzardi's being
allowed to testify.[6]

   Having had no direct dealings with either Esterhazy or Dreyfus,
Panizzardi was increasingly resentful of his isolated position and having
become the object of hostile attention in the press. His letters to
Schwartzkoppen, written under stress, produced a strain in their relations. 'You know well, that if anything upsets me I am very free in my
language', he wrote apologetically on 21 December, 'and you must
bear in mind that what I have told you and what is being said here
about me cannot be exactly pleasant for me.'[7] Nearing nervous collapse, at odds with Ambassador Tornielli for Panizzardi's having failed
to keep the ambassador fully informed in the past and under instructions from his government not to involve himself further in the affair,
he imprudently granted an interview to an Italian political columnist
named Henri Casella, unaware that the latter was acting in the interest
of Mathieu Dreyfus. Casella, informed that Panizzardi had in his
possession documents capable of establishing the innocence of Dreyfus
and the guilt of Esterhazy, had approached him with a view to getting
him to disclose the existence of this evidence. While denying that he
had any such documents, Panizzardi, in the reassuring presence of a
compatriot, declared his belief in the innocence of Dreyfus and spoke
unreservedly about the case. Armed with a letter of introduction from
Panizzardi to Schwartzkoppen, Casella left for Berlin on 22 December,
where the German attaché, relying on Panizzardi's assurance that
Casella was a personal friend and 'a thorough gentleman', met with
him and discussed the case with similar candor. When it was revealed a
short time later that Casella intended to publish the results of his

interviews with the two military attachés and that he offered to testify about them at Zola's trial, relations between Schwartzkoppen and Panizzardi were further strained. Nearing the end of his tether, Panizzardi was transfixed by the daily proceedings in the Zola trial, expecting at any moment that his name would be introduced by a witness. He could think of nothing else and Blacker's letter announcing his arrival in Paris remained unanswered.

When Blacker finally felt sufficiently well to leave the house, on 21 February, his first priority was 'to see if Panizzardi was in Paris; found that he was'. Finding the failure to receive a reply to his letter of the previous week inexplicable and worrying, he added, 'this depressed me'. Later that evening, however, 'after dinner while I was playing at bezique with Mama, Panizzardi appeared suddenly in the room, being the first time I had seen him since coming to Paris. He told us all about the Dreyfus affair and Esterhazy and remained until past 12.' Panizzardi was 'very excited & distressed. He seemed aged & worn, & he unbosomed himself to me without hesitation, seeming to find comfort in so doing.' The following day, Blacker 'woke at 7; could not go to sleep again thinking of what Panizzardi had told me last night. Got up, had my bath and went out to try to see [Salomon] Reinach but I was told that he was not in.' Disappointed at not finding his admired and trusted friend, the archaeologist and philologist Salomon Reinach, who like his brother Joseph was among Dreyfus's earliest and most active supporters, Blacker immediately turned to another close friend, the former Oxford don F. C. Conybeare, to whom he wrote the same day:

There is nothing (not even my own tempestuous affairs) that has ever excited me like this Zola affair. . . . Of course I could not rest until I had the truth in the matter & I have it & can prove it, & here is the outline.

Dreyfus did not write the bordereau.—It was written by Esterhazy who was in the pay of Germany & delivered over 200 secret documents to Schwartzkoppen of which about 30 are of the very first importance. . . . The point on which I wish to consult you is the following: I feel so strongly on this subject that I have offered to have some of the 200 documents I have mentioned reproduced in an English paper, if it will do any good & I come to you to ask you if you think it would do good & whether you would be willing to assist me in the matter.

Although I cannot ask you to keep what I have told you secret, I do ask you & charge you upon your honour not to mention my name to any one, as having given you this information, & as possessing the means to assist in redressing an infamous injustice.... I have been working at this for the last fortnight. Last night only I had the definite offer which I have mentioned, & if you agree I will go over to England & with you, do what you think best, with the documents which I would take over, in Esterhazy's handwriting & of the greatest importance.... This is only an outline, the particulars of the whole story are really almost incredible.[8]

The last straw for Panizzardi had been the testimony of General de Boisdeffre at the Zola trial on 18 February, in which the Chief of the General Staff had confirmed under oath the authenticity of the *faux Henry*. Frustrated and angry, Panizzardi had hit upon a plan to strike a retaliatory blow at Boisdeffre by demonstrating to the world that he was a liar. While Blacker, his more than enthusiastic co-conspirator in the high-risk plot, was writing to enlist the aid of Conybeare, Panizzardi wrote the same day to Schwartzkoppen informing him that in view of Boisdeffre's action he had come to the conclusion that 'something must be done', without disclosing exactly what he had in mind. Some indication of the effect his letter had on the German attaché is apparent in Schwartzkoppen's underlining of certain phrases, particularly the phrase 'something must be done', opposite which he added a question mark in the margin of Panizzardi's letter:

[Our] Governments, our Ambassadors, have given their word that Dreyfus has had nothing whatever to do with us; yet the Chief of Staff, Boisdeffre, has had the face in spite of everything to say to the court that they have received evidence of Dreyfus's guilt two years after his conviction, in a letter which has fallen into the General's hands.

He certainly had sufficient consideration not to mention our names and not to make any overt reference to us, but <u>everybody</u> [underlined by Panizzardi] knows that it is you and I who are concerned. If he had merely stated that this letter exists there would have been no harm done, for one can get any document one likes forged, but he gave his word and swore to the <u>authenticity</u> [underlined by Panizzardi] of this letter, as though he himself had confiscated it at your place or mine; in this way he not only disavowed our own and our Governments' statements but made us look like men without honour, indeed liars.

All this you will perhaps think of little importance! I regret to have to say that on this point I do not share your view, but feel absolutely <u>that something must be done</u> [underlined and queried (?) by Schwartzkoppen]. At the moment, however, it is no longer a question of saving a man and getting the real culprit convicted, but a question of <u>defending our honour</u> [underlined by Schwartzkoppen] and at the same time <u>giving this Mr. Boisdeffre a lesson</u> [underlined by Schwartzkoppen], putting him in his place and letting all the world and especially the French know how this man is lying, for on this point I no longer believe in his good faith. He knows <u>everything, everything</u> [underlined by Panizzardi] and speculating on our obligation of silence he is directing a strong attack against us, publicly saying that he is in possession of a document although he himself knows that it is a forgery.[9]

What made the task of establishing Dreyfus's innocence 'exceedingly difficult', Panizzardi informed Blacker, was the fact that 'the whole and the entire truth' had already been officially made known in confidential communications to 'the President [of France] & all the Ministers & most of the important political personages' by the German and Italian ambassadors under instructions from their respective governments—all to no avail. Official public declarations had similarly been disregarded. Zola's trial had demonstrated clearly that in the face of an impenetrable wall of resistance from the French government and the army General Staff, neither in the French press nor in the courts could the struggle for justice in the Dreyfus case be won. 'Panizzardi told me', Blacker wrote, 'that he had never himself had any relations with Esterhazy, but Schwartzkoppen, both as friend & member of the Triple Alliance, always communicated the important secrets he obtained from Esterhazy, without however mentioning "his man's" name.' Panizzardi offered to provide facsimiles of incriminating documents in Esterhazy's hand that he had received from Schwartzkoppen and Blacker undertook to arrange for their publication in the foreign press, together with details of the traitor's dealings with the German attaché, about which Panizzardi was well informed. Elated at the prospect the plan offered of establishing conclusively and irrefutably the innocence of Dreyfus and the guilt of Esterhazy, Blacker was impatient to confide the proposal to his revered friend Salomon Reinach. '[23 February] Went out in the morning to call on Reinach and had a long talk with him'; '[24 February] Read Zola verdict in paper. Also that Panizzardi was going to reveal the whole thing. . . . Panizzardi to dinner. Remained talking until 12:30. . . . Drank a little champagne with Panizzardi after dinner'; '[25 February] Went out to see Reinach but he was at the Louvre. . . . Went out after lunch to send telegram to Reinach telling him that I would go to him. . . . To Reinach's after dinner; remained there an hour.' Surprise being essential to the success of the plan, and for the personal safety of the conspirators, preparations were carried forward in the greatest secrecy.[10]

2

Unknown to Blacker, Wilde had arrived in Paris a week after his own arrival, on the eve of the second week of Zola's trial. As the compelling spectacle moved towards its dramatic climax, however, Wilde's attention was directed elsewhere. It was the publication day in London of 'The Ballad of Reading Gaol', the event with which he was now totally preoccupied, as he had informed Smithers.

Vincent O'Sullivan, Wilde's sympathetic friend and financial benefactor for the journey to Italy, had spent time with Wilde in Naples following Douglas's departure. He 'sometimes wondered', he wrote with hindsight long after, 'why [Wilde] did not stay in Italy, by what reasoning he persuaded himself to come back to Paris. Paris killed him. . . . In Italy he would have lived longer, and, I should think, happier. Paris, then, the Dreyfus-case Paris, cannot be figured by the Paris of today.'[11] Wilde had informed Smithers before leaving Naples that when his publisher came to Paris he could find him 'somewhere' in the Latin Quarter. On his arrival, he took a room in the shabby Hôtel de Nice in the rue des Beaux Arts, a quarter of the city familiar to him. Fifteen years earlier, when he had first met Robert Sherard, the appreciably more upscale Hôtel du Quai-Voltaire had been his home for several months, a short walk from the Hôtel de Nice but separated from it by an unbridgeable social and economic gulf. The contrast would have served as yet another reminder for Wilde on his promenades in the quarter of the irretrievable loss of the two things that, according to Robbie Ross, were 'absolutely necessary for him, contact with comely things . . . and social position'.[12] Although Sherard was then in Paris, Wilde, since the recent rift in their friendship, had no immediate desire to see him. 'His last years were supremely unhappy', Sherard wrote of the time. 'Towards me he became more and more distant. . . . In melancholy and solitary peregrinations on the boulevards, which fifteen years before we had trod so triumphantly, we sometimes passed each other in silence, with only a faint wave of the hand—like two wrecked ships that pass in the night.'[13]

In the days immediately following his arrival, Wilde's attention was devoted to making corrections for a second edition of the 'Ballad'. 'I see no one here', he reported to Robbie Ross, 'but a young Irishman called Healy, a poet.'[14] Chris Healy, a journalist and bohemian poet, was at the time acting as 'secretary' to Rowland Strong, Paris correspondent of the London newspapers *The Observer* and the *Morning Post* as well as the *New York Times*. Strong, who claimed descent from Chateaubriand, was described at the time of his mysterious death in Paris a quarter of a century later ('suspected foul play') as a member of 'a brilliant family'.[15] Both his older brothers, Thomas Banks Strong, bishop of Oxford, and Sandford Arthur Strong, librarian of the House of Lords and at Chatsworth, had distinguished careers. Grant Richards, the publisher, on his first visit to Paris six years before at the age of twenty recalled Strong, to whom he had a letter of introduction, as 'what the French call a type: he looked a Parisian; he had the fresh complexion of the Midi and the reddish beard of François I. . . . His interests did not seem to be either in literature or in painting, and his attitude was altogether one of cynicism and of being tired of what Paris in particular and the world in general could offer to a man of intellect.'[16] Despite his indifference to what life in the French capital had to offer, Strong subsequently produced a successful book on *Where and How to Dine in Paris*, published by Grant Richards in 1900.[17]

At the time of Wilde's arrival in Paris, Strong was totally caught up in the Dreyfus affair, regarding it as the world's most important news story. He recognized in Esterhazy the key to the mystery surrounding the case and was convinced that if he stuck to him closely enough and long enough he eventually would scoop the world press on the story. Wilde, who had tried unsuccessfully to get in touch with Strong when passing through Paris en route to Naples the previous September, apparently looked him up immediately on his return and thus met Healy.

The day following Wilde's arrival, Strong was introduced to Esterhazy at the offices of the leading anti-Semitic and anti-Dreyfusard newspaper the *Libre Parole* by Robert Sherard, who, according to Esterhazy, 'had demonstrated unquestionable proof of his loyalty and of his sympathy to my cause' by championing it some weeks earlier in a lengthy article in the *Saturday Review* in which Sherard had been sharply critical of the generally hostile attitude towards Esterhazy of his fellow English journalists. Sherard's spirited stance was sufficient to recommend him not only to Esterhazy but also to Esterhazy's closest ally among the representatives of the Paris press, François André du Quesnay de Boisandré, journalist with the *Libre Parole* and doctrinaire pamphleteer for the *Librairie Antisémite*. In the interest of improving Esterhazy's image in the English press, Sherard had offered to ask his friend and colleague Strong to interview Esterhazy sympathetically for one of the London newspapers Strong represented. Strong had already made an appeal for sympathy for Esterhazy in his account in the *New York Times* of the opening session of the Zola trial:

So much has been said about Major Esterhazy which is untrue that at least a truthful personal description of him might be of interest. He is neither tall, nor bent, nor gaunt, nor does he look the typical swashbuckler to which he has so often been compared. He is a little, old man, sad-faced and broken-down, badly dressed in thin, soiled clothes, with a wide waistcoat (when I saw him last) which was by no means fresh, and a battered silk hat, painfully over ironed.

'What has Zola got against me?' he asked pathetically. 'Why can't he leave a poor, broken-down man like me alone?'

Certainly if Esterhazy has sold secrets to foreign governments (a charge upon which he has been formally acquitted) there is nothing in his dress and appearance to suggest it.[18]

Esterhazy was then facing the unnerving prospect of appearing under subpoena as a witness in the Zola trial the following Friday, 18 February. Delighted to enlist the support of a second English journalist, he eagerly grasped the friendly hand extended to him by Strong. At the latter's suggestion, he and Sherard escorted Esterhazy to the Hôtel Continental to meet a compatriot of theirs, David Christie Murray, special correspondent for the *Daily News*, who Strong insisted was one of the most respected members of the English press and capable of influencing public opinion in England in favor of Esterhazy.[19]

Shortly before the opening of the Zola trial, the editor of the *Daily News*, E. T. Cook, had accepted the offer of David Christie Murray to go to Paris 'to see M. Zola and make such other investigations in the Dreyfus matter as may seem desirable'.[20] When Esterhazy consented to meet him, Murray later maintained, Esterhazy knew that he was to meet 'a man who was much prejudiced against him'. Undaunted and emboldened by the demonstrated support of Sherard and Strong, Esterhazy in the presence of Murray unhesitatingly launched into a heated diatribe, working himself into a paroxysm of rage with the prediction that 'the streets of Paris will be strewn with a hundred thousand bodies before the conclusion of this miserable affair', ending in a violent fit of coughing and spitting. 'I have only one lung', he explained to his astonished listeners when he recovered himself; 'I'm dying.' At Murray's suggestion, the group repaired to a nearby bar in the rue Saint-Honoré (undoubtedly Campbell's Bar, the preferred watering place of English journalists), where Murray, ceremoniously breaking some eggs into a glass 'with the air of an old provincial actor', concocted for Esterhazy a warm drink which he declared to be an infallible remedy. Esterhazy was further warmed by the 'ardent sympathy' manifested towards him by Murray and the party grew merry, for which Esterhazy was all the more outraged when Murray's interview appeared in the *Daily News* three days later, on the eve of his appearance at the Zola trial. 'He pulverized me', Esterhazy complained of the report, in which Murray quoted at length some of the more extravagant imagery from Esterhazy's tirade ('They want to kill me. Mark my words: it is I who will kill them; I will kill them like rabbits, but without a trace of anger; I would like to have a hundred of them locked in a room, with a stick in my hand: I would beat them to death'; 'I live now only to avenge myself. If Zola is acquitted, Paris will rise up, with me at their head. If Dreyfus sets foot in France, there will be 5,000 corpses of Jews in the streets of Paris.').[21] Murray, who saw in Esterhazy's terrible rage a measure of the depth of his terror, agreed with Zola's assessment that he was 'a bandit, a thorough-going bandit, but a brave bandit, and that he knew how to defend himself like a lion'.[22] When called to testify, Esterhazy declined to respond to any questions, standing in silence during the forty-minute interrogation, finally turning his back on the defense counsel as the compromising questions were relentlessly read into the record.

Esterhazy's disillusionment with Strong did not come until the following September in London, when the two had a bitter falling out. In the aftermath, Esterhazy, a master of invective, came to regard Strong with scorn as 'a loathsome character', an 'odious crook', a 'filthy cheat', 'a contemptible clown', 'an absolute swine', and 'one of the most despicable scoundrels' he was to encounter in the course of the entire affair. Recalling their first meeting, he wrote that Sherard had presented to him:

a little fellow with a red beard, whom he introduced as Mr. Rowland Strong, correspondent of English and American newspapers, and a ferocious enemy into the bargain of all Dreyfusards, past, present and future. The little man, whose cuffs were frayed and very dirty, smelled of alcohol ten feet away; but he greeted me at once with a warmth which I found extraordinary in an Englishman.

For the next 'seven or eight months' following their meeting, according to Esterhazy, he and 'the little red-haired fellow, Strong', were inseparable. Strong overwhelmed him with 'unbelievable demonstrations of friendship and devotion, fulminating against the Dreyfusards without letup, writing me daily, bombarding me with telegrams, importuning my friends by telephone when he had not seen me for a few hours to inquire what I had been doing, what I was going to do, why I did not come to see him', defending him in a dispute with a journalist from *Le Figaro*, and sending his secretary 'Hilley [Healy]' ('a bizarre individual'; 'a specimen of individual unspeakably vile and disgusting') to maintain constant communication with him. More importantly, 'this Hilley insinuated himself among the friends and supporters of Zola and Mathieu Dreyfus and Madame Dreyfus and reported to Strong everything that he was able to learn from these sources'. Esterhazy and Strong met regularly at the latter's favorite resort, a bar called the Horse Shoe. 'I confess that I have often found him in a bar which he frequented', Esterhazy recalled, 'where he tossed down 15 or 20 whiskies with a nonchalance that was equalled only by his capacity, after which he was always dead drunk every evening, or more or less so, every time I saw him at night.'[23]

Shortly after Strong's introduction to Esterhazy, Strong in turn introduced Esterhazy to Wilde, again 'in a bar in the Rue St. Honoré'. Healy, who claims to have been present, recalled that 'Wilde regaled them with a flow of his gayest witticisms' and established an immediate rapport with Esterhazy.[24] As a fictional villain in a fin-de-siècle melodrama, the fantastic self-styled Count Esterhazy, with a physical appearance to match his villainy, would seem overdrawn in both respects. Photographs at the time show him as gaunt and tubercular, with a long, black military mustache, a hook nose ('a bird-of-prey beak'), prominent cheek bones and piercing dark deep-set eyes, glowering in a fixed and menacing scowl. Early in his military career, he had served in the Papal Army, the French Foreign Legion, and the Zouaves, a background which, together with his striking appearance, a facility for foreign languages, and an urbane and cosmopolitan manner, gave him an exotic air. Julien Benda recorded the impression Esterhazy made on him when as a youth Benda was performing his military service, a few years prior to the affair: 'tall, thin, a little bent, the face sallow, bony and lined . . . a careworn air. He might have been an elegant and treacherous gypsy, or, better, a great wild beast, alert and master of itself. Charmed by his distinction, I could not take my eyes from him.'[25] Aptly described as a 'specialist in mental prestidigitation', Esterhazy possessed a quick intelligence, a sardonic sense of humor, an active, energetic, and enterprising temperament and a fertile and endlessly inventive imagination. An inveterate speculator and perennial loser on the Bourse, his marriage to the daughter of the Marquis de Nettancourt-Vaubecourt, designed to restore his fortune, did not long survive the dissipation of a dowry of 200,000 francs. As incorrigible in his pursuit of women as he was in his financial speculations, he combined the two interests by investing in a *maison de rendezvous*, a line of business he found congenial enough to resume later in exile in England. At the time he came to public attention in the Dreyfus case, he was about to turn fifty, on the inactive list owing to chronic poor health, and barely managing to hold his creditors at bay with funds embezzled from a young nephew (who felt himself hypnotized) and the latter's widowed mother.

Esterhazy's life in disintegration had been accompanied by so many shameful acts of desperation that he had reason enough, aside from his dealings with Schwartzkoppen, to wish to keep to the shadows. As the attention of the world press began to turn to the case, and interest inevitably focused on him, he veered wildly from the paralysis of despair, in which he contemplated suicide, to acts of extreme audacity, in which he was capable of threatening the president of the Republic that if he were denied protection he would turn for help to the emperor of Germany, whom he fancifully claimed to be the ancient suzerain of the Esterhazy family. The press was quick to publicize his liaison with his twenty-seven-year-old mistress, Marguerite Pays, a registered prostitute known as Four-Fingered Margaret whom he had picked up at the Moulin Rouge. His long-suffering and already estranged wife finally broke with him entirely and obtained a divorce.

To his employer Schwartzkoppen, his paid spy Esterhazy was 'the most marvellous, audacious & wonderful *canaille* that it was possible to imagine, either in fiction or history, & capable of any & every villainy, including murder'.[26] Even Blacker felt bound to admit to F. C. Conybeare that as a villain he found Esterhazy in his incredible audacity 'superb and magnificent'.[27] Ernest La Jeunesse, companion and chronicler of Wilde's final days, thought that it would require the pen of Voltaire to describe the dinners and symposia of Wilde and Esterhazy in the months following their initial meeting. Esterhazy's panic-inspired rage as he felt the case closing round him, his extravagant outbursts, and theatrical tirades both amused and fascinated Wilde. La Jeunesse recalled 'Le Commandant'—as Wilde, 'with a tender irony and hint of admiration' called him—saying to Wilde in one memorable exchange: 'We are the two greatest martyrs in all humanity, but (after a hesitant silence) I have suffered more.'[28] When Henry Davray, Wilde's French translator, remonstrated with him for his intimacy with such a 'crapule', Wilde excused the friendship on the ground that since his release from prison he had been obliged to frequent the society of thieves and assassins. 'If Esterhazy had been innocent', he explained, 'I should have had nothing to do with him.'[29]

3

Conybeare's response to Blacker's letter was disappointing in its failure to match the fire and enthusiasm that had so animated Blacker. 'I promptly wrote to E. T. Cook, editor of the *Daily News*', Conybeare replied, asking him, without naming Blacker, if he would publish the facsimiles. 'Of all the English papers the *Daily News* has been best informed & most sympathetic with Zola', he added.[30] Cook thought that publication of the documents 'would not seem to carry things much forward', and he accordingly advised Conybeare to tell his anonymous friend (Blacker) to spare himself the trouble of coming to England. Instead, he advised that the friend consult Cook's Paris correspondents, Mrs Crawford and David Christie Murray, who would be able to judge the value of the documents.[31] Discouraged by the seemingly cool response from Conybeare but unwilling to enlarge the circle of those privy to the secret plan, as recommended by Cook, Blacker was preoccupied by how best to proceed when he noted in the *Herald* on 3 March the publication of 'The Ballad of Reading Gaol'. Momentarily diverted, braving frightful weather ('snowing badly . . . very bad, rainy weather, cold, nasty'), he immediately went in search of a copy at the principal English booksellers in

Paris—Brentano's, Neal's, and Galignani's—but found that it had been sold out everywhere.

In Italy, Constance Wilde had written to her brother a few days after publication that she was 'frightfully upset by this wonderful poem of Oscar's.... It is frightfully tragic and makes one cry.'[32] Although resigned to permanent estrangement, she remained constant in her love and concern for her husband. 'Oscar is or at least was in Paris at the Hotel de Nice, Rue des Beaux Arts', she wrote to Blacker on 4 March:

> Would it be at all possible for you to go and see him there or is it asking too much of you? He has as you know behaved exceedingly badly both to myself and my children and all possibility of our living together has come to an end, but I am interested in him, as is my way with anyone that I have once known. Have you seen his new poem, and would you like a copy, as if so I will send you one? His publisher lately sent me a copy which I conclude came from him. Can you find this out for me and if you do see him tell him that I think the Ballad exquisite, and I hope that the great success it has had in London at all events will urge him on to write more. I hear that he does nothing now but drink and I heard that he had left Lord A. and had received £200 from Lady Q. on condition that he did not see him again, but of course this may be untrue. Is Lord A. in Paris? Do what seems right to you.... But I write to you on the chance of your seeing Oscar.[33]

The source of Constance's information about her husband's movements and whereabouts from time to time was undoubtedly Robbie Ross, whom she had come to admire for his 'exceeding unselfishness...for which I am indeed grateful. I have never seen anything in a man like him'. She admitted to Blacker that at first she could scarcely believe in Ross's unselfish devotion to her husband, 'but now I not only believe it, but admire and am astounded at it'.[34]

Having had no communication with Wilde since the previous September, Blacker was less ready than Constance to overlook his cruel and heartless behavior to her. Unaware that Wilde and Douglas had separated, he accordingly felt unable to comply with Constance's request that he see him, as he wrote to inform Wilde: '[8 March] Wrote letter to Oscar telling him what his wife had written to me and telling him how sorry I was that I could not see him as he had chosen his way in life.'

The same day, Blacker recorded a deeply upsetting encounter: 'Met Grandmaison in Rue St. Honoré and had long conversation with him

as far as the Chambre des Deputés about Dreyfus affair.' Since Conybeare's disappointingly lukewarm response to his recent letter, Blacker
had been casting about for an alternative on how best to proceed. The
chance encounter with his old friend Georges de Grandmaison, whom
he had known for seventeen years, suddenly appeared to offer the
alternative he was seeking. As a deputy, Grandmaison seemed the ideal
person, ideally situated, to implement the plan and Blacker impulsively
sought to enlist him in it. The abrupt and surprising overture was to
disturb their long friendship seriously when Grandmaison, viewing
Blacker's proposal as of the utmost importance, later asked to be
allowed to testify about their meeting before the Cour de Cassation
and again at Dreyfus's second court-martial at Rennes the following
year. According to Grandmaison, on parting after an exchange of
greetings, Blacker (an 'homme de lettres anglais' whom Grandmaison
regarded as a particularly warm partisan of revision of the court-martial
verdict) apparently on a sudden afterthought, turned back and said that
he had something of great importance to tell him. He thereupon
informed Grandmaison of the existence of the Esterhazy facsimiles,
among other things, and told him that he was seeking a French
political figure ('you for example') who would be willing to make
use of the documents in the interest of establishing Dreyfus's innocence. Grandmaison stiffly declared himself to be satisfied with
the verdict of the court-martial, and, as the conversation warmed,
stated his opinion that foreigners should not meddle in French affairs.
After a further brief exchange, the two parted with coolness on both
sides.[35] Blacker's diary entry for the stressful day concludes: 'Walked
home. . . . Had bottle of old claret.' A copy of the 'Ballad' had arrived
that morning and his wife Carrie read it aloud to him; afterwards, he in
turn read it aloud to his brother.

Constance responded promptly to Blacker's scruples regarding the
presence of Douglas:

I naturally would not have asked you to see Oscar, if I had thought there was
any chance of your meeting that person whom I know that very naturally you
loathe. I heard long ago that Oscar was not with him, and that he is on the
Riviera with his Mother, and that his allowance stops altogether if he ever
lives with O. again. The result of your writing to O. is that he has written to
me more or less demanding money as his right. Fortunately for him hearing
that he was in great straits, I had yesterday or rather the day before sent him
£40 through Robbie Ross. He says that I owe him £78 and hopes that I will

send it. I know that he is in great poverty, but I don't care to be written to as though it were my fault. He says that he loved too much and that is better than hate! This is true abstractly, but his was an unnatural love, a madness that I think is worse than hate. I have no hatred for him, but I confess that I am afraid of him.

Looking towards the coming summer that she would not live to see, Constance closed with the thought that 'it would be very nice to be at Tittisee this summer if you were there, and Cyril could come on there from Villeneuve.'[36]

Wilde added his own reassurance about Douglas in reply to Blacker's letter in a note in which he expressed his gratitude for Blacker's kindness to Constance and the children. 'My dear Carlos', he wrote:

I cannot express to you how thrilled and touched by emotion I was when I saw your handwriting last night. Please come and see me tomorrow (Thursday) at five o'clock if you possibly can: if not, pray make some other appointment: I want particularly to see you, and long to shake you by the hand again, and to thank you for all the sweet and wonderful kindness you and your wife have shown to Constance and the boys. I am living here quite alone: in one room, I need hardly say, but there is an armchair for you. I have not seen Alfred Douglas for three months. . . . I don't think it probable that we shall ever see each other again. . . . I have had for some weeks a copy [of the 'Ballad'] for you—of the first edition—by me, which I long to present to you.[37]

'[9 March] I received a letter from Oscar asking me to go to see him tomorrow at 5 and that he had separated from his vile friend.' Another, more serious, impediment to a meeting remained, however, in the form of Carrie's strenuous objection to her husband's having anything whatever to do with Wilde, long a matter of contention between them. The final outrage of Wilde's desertion of wife and children for Douglas had only recently brought Blacker round to sharing his wife's view. Faced now with the combined entreaties of both Constance and Oscar, however, and with the obstacle of Douglas's presence removed, he felt unable to resist Wilde's appeal for a meeting. With the unsettling encounter with Grandmaison the day before still much on his mind, he waited until the end of the day to broach the touchy subject of Wilde with Carrie: 'Bed at 12 with conversation with Carrie about going to see Oscar.'

The next day, 10 March, the king of Italy sent for Panizzardi in order to learn at first hand the truth of the Dreyfus affair in detail.

Blacker and Panizzardi decided to take advantage of the opportunity to correct a major flaw in their plan, one that entailed a considerable risk for Panizzardi and his military career. This was the lack of authorization by either the German or the Italian government to make use of the Esterhazy facsimiles in Panizzardi's possession. Thus preoccupied, Blacker deferred the proposed meeting with Wilde, informing him by telegram that he would see him the following Sunday:

We decided that [Panizzardi] would also avail himself of this opportunity to ask the King of Italy to write to the German Emperor requesting him as a personal favour to allow some of Esterhazy's documents to be handed to Panizzardi with a view to their being published in a neutral country, Switzerland, Belgium or England. With this intention he left for Rome, subsequently went to Berlin, & was back in Paris ten days later the 20th March. . . . In Berlin he was told that the Emperor had been much irritated at the way in which his official declarations had been received by the French Government & people. He was told that not all the publications in the world would be of the slightest avail under the condition of things in France & that under any circumstances the Emperor having made a statement, he did not like to bring proofs to prove that what he said was true when his word sufficed. There was therefore nothing to be done.

While considering what to do next, the rapid pace of events overtook the conspirators. 'Panizzardi authorized me to publish what he had told me, but this would have injured him—as he subsequently suffered, & I being in Paris with my mother & family, it was impossible to know what trouble this might have brought upon them, though the trouble & worry duly came afterwards.'[38]

While waiting for Panizzardi's return to Paris, Blacker, in anticipation of his meeting with Wilde, was drawn by curiosity to the dingy Hôtel de Nice to see where he was living: '[12 March] Out . . . in morning to Bon Marché. Afterwards walked and saw Oscar's hotel. Walked home.' The following day, their long-deferred reunion took place: '[13 March] At 4 called on Oscar and saw him for the first time since 19th February 95.' Wilde had then been at the summit of his glory, poised on the edge of the abyss. He had come that day to the Sackville Hotel in response to Blacker's call to try to relieve the gloom of Blacker's dreaded appearance in Bankruptcy Court the next day.

The bleak contrast between past and present in the reversal of their fortunes could not have been lost on either of them at the emotionally charged meeting. Blacker, like Constance, had been convinced from the outset that Wilde's only hope of salvaging the wreckage of his life was to resume writing. Fired by his own passionate commitment to Dreyfus's cause, and exhilarated by the recent promising turn of events with Panizzardi's summons to Rome, he became convinced in the course of the euphoric reunion that the same intellectual and moral stimulus would point the way to salvation for Wilde. Secure in the affection and trust of their long friendship, Blacker was moved to disclose the extent of his own involvement in the affair, including the secret information he had received from Panizzardi and the details of the plan they were developing to expose Esterhazy in the English press, everything in short except the identity of his informant, assumed by Wilde to be Schwartzkoppen. The reunion with his 'dear old friend' was for Wilde a rare solace. He had by now, however, come to accept the fact that his fate was indeed like Humpty Dumpty's, as Constance had foreseen a year before, 'quite as tragic and quite as impossible to put right'.[39] He knew himself to be broken beyond any real hope of recovery and that he would never write again. 'Life, that I have loved so much—too much—has torn me like a tiger', he had written to Blacker a few days before their meeting, 'so when you come and see me, you will see the ruin and wreck of what once was wonderful and brilliant... I don't think I shall ever write again: *la joie de vivre* is gone.'[40]

With the recent breach in their friendship healed, Wilde presented Blacker with a copy of the 'Ballad', which he inscribed, 'From the author: in affectionate remembrance of many kind messages. Paris. 98. Oscar Wilde.' The copy was not, however, of the first edition, as promised, but of the fourth edition, which had been printed a few days earlier. Wilde had already presented a less-warmly inscribed copy of the first edition to Strong ('with the compliments of the author. Oscar Wilde.'98').[41]

The interview was proceeding to a close in the warmth of their reestablished intimacy when Blacker became aware that Wilde was not in fact living 'quite alone', as he had stated in his letter, but that he had a young companion—most likely Maurice Gilbert, whom Wilde had recently 'met by chance' and who, as he had informed his publisher a week before, 'grows dearer to me daily'. Whether the encounter was by mischance or intentional on the part of Wilde, adamantly unapologetic about an aspect of his life for which he had paid so dearly, is uncertain. Blacker was deeply troubled by the revelation and reported the distressing news to his wife and to Constance. '[14 March] Spoke with Carrie about Oscar's not having been made better by his experience.... Wrote to Mrs. Holland about my interview with Oscar.' Constance, although still in love with her husband, was by now painfully free of past illusions about their marriage and received Blacker's report with resignation. 'Many thanks for your letter', she replied, 'tho' your account of Oscar is a very sad one. Still I am glad that he is in Paris, for I know that he does require intellectual stimulus always. He would have been bored to death with family life, though he does not seem at present to realize this! What could either the children or I have given him?'[42] Conybeare, who was planning to come to Paris, was less restrained in his response: 'In view of the facts you state in your letter about O.W.', he wrote:

I am really not sure your wife's judgment is not sound.... He is clearly without any sense of responsibility or self-respect.... I am sure to your kindly disposition it must be awfully painful. I should, were I in your place, write to him & say that you *were* fully prepared to preserve relations with him after he came out, if he seriously set himself to alleviate the pain & shame he had inflicted on his wife & children; but that, as he is doing just the opposite, your relations with him *must* cease.... I really do not think you will ever regret that you have been guided by [Carrie] in this matter.... In view of his jeune homme blonde, I should, if I were you, certainly take your wife's advice.... Probably the best thing he can do is to drink himself to death, or better yet— shoot himself right off.... It is all the same dreadfully sad.[43]

While Blacker was profoundly disturbed at the outcome of the meeting, Wilde, unaware, was cheered and his spirits were buoyed to be reconciled with 'the only old friend I have in Paris'. He promptly asked Blacker for a loan. '[15 March] Bad temper. Letter from Oscar asking me to let him have 200 francs which I took to him at the café in the Place du Théâtre Français as I was driving to the theatre with Carrie and felt in the most frightful rage all the time. Did not enjoy it at all. Left after 4th act.... Very bad temper.' Wilde was grateful for the loan and the two planned to meet again the following day, but Carrie, in light of what her husband had reported, objected all the more emphatically to his having any further contact with Wilde. '[16 March] Letter from Oscar thanking me for francs 150.... Bad temper again today.... Was to have gone to see Oscar but Carrie would not let me.' Disappointed, Wilde wrote to say that he was 'in dreadful straits', having been forced to pay his hotel bill with the money Blacker had lent him, and that he had heard from Robbie Ross that Constance '*will not* pay the arrears of my allowance'. Blacker replied with a further advance ('[18 March] Left 100 francs for Oscar at café') and sent Wilde's letter to Constance. 'I did send £40 to Mr. Ross', Constance responded immediately:

but he would not, and I expect rightly would not, send more than £10 at a time to him! I enclose you letters that I have had from Robbie which at any rate are truthful which I know that Oscar is not.... Oscar is so pathetic and such a born actor, and I am hardened when I am away from him. No words will describe my horror of that BEAST, for I will call him nothing else, A.D. Fancy Robbie receiving abusive letters from him, and you know perfectly well that they were sent with Oscar's knowledge and consent. I do not wish him dead, but considering how he used to go on about [his brother] Willie's extravagance and about his cruelty in forcing his mother to give him money, I think that he might leave his wife and his children alone.... You will say in the face of all this why did I ask you to go and see him in Paris? Well I thought you would have nothing to do with his money affairs, and I strongly advise you to leave them alone. I knew that you were not in your own house, and therefore could not ask him to dinner, and I was silly enough to think that you would give him merely the intellectual stimulus he needed.[44]

Meanwhile, Blacker's wish to see Wilde, in response to the latter's pleas for a meeting, served only to aggravate the long-standing discord on the subject between himself and Carrie: '[19 March] Out in morning with Carrie with friction because she would not allow me to see Oscar.' Constance wrote reassuringly to Carrie in support of what she assumed to be the reason for her opposition: 'You are perfectly right to want your husband to be independent of Oscar, who I am afraid would be a drag on anybody, from his apparently hopeless ineptitude to grasp money matters at all.... If he had plenty of money he would drink himself to death and do no work.... Everything seems to turn out wrong with him.'[45]

Wilde attributed the recent reinstatement of his allowance to Blacker's intercession on his behalf with Constance. 'A thousand thanks for your great kindness', he wrote. 'Really you have saved my life for me, for a little at any rate, and your friendship and interest give me hope.' He was prompted to appeal again for a meeting. 'I do hope to see you soon. Could we dine together at some little restaurant; ... just you and I together.'[46] On the strength of the reinstated allowance, Wilde moved to the Hôtel d'Alsace, where he took two rooms ('same street, much cleaner', he informed Blacker).[47] At the same time, he was involved in an accident in a fiacre in which he was injured and he begged Blacker once more to come to see him.[48] '[28 March] During lunch a carte telegram came from Oscar telling me that he had had an accident, cut his mouth badly, asking me to go to see him in the afternoon. Carrie would not allow me to go.... Sent telegram to Oscar telling him I can't go to him.'

Puzzled by the unexplained change of heart on Blacker's part since their emotional reunion more than two weeks earlier, Wilde, routinely shunned and cut by former friends, had become painfully aware that Blacker, like the rest of the world, was avoiding him. 'I am so sorry that you can't come to see me', he wrote in reply to Blacker's latest refusal. 'What happened to me was simply that through the horse coming down I was thrown almost through the front window of a fiacre, and cut my lower lip almost in two. It was quite dreadful, and, of course, a hideous shock to my nerves. It is so horrible to have no one to look after one, or to see one, when one is cooped up in a wretched hotel.' To the note of self-pity, Wilde teasingly added a bit of ominous information that was certain to cause Blacker alarm: 'I have not been out since Friday, except one night when I was dragged out to meet Esterhazy at dinner! The Commandant was astonishing. I will tell you all he said some day. Of course he talked of nothing but Dreyfus *et Cie*.' Wilde's bitter response to the rebuff of his pitiful appeal was immediate and final, spelling disaster for Blacker and the end of their once cherished friendship. Rowland Strong, in an article in *The New York Times* datelined the following day, 'Paris, March 29', under the heading 'A Probability of New Revelations in the Dreyfus Case to be Made in London', reported having been told on excellent authority:

that an English gentleman connected with the aristocracy named Blacker has obtained from Col. von Schwartzkoppen's own lips a statement to the effect that Major Esterhazy [had sold documents to the German military attaché]...The Englishman...has secured through the good offices of Major Panizzardi copies of a certain number of the documents, and these are to be published shortly in The Daily News or The Daily Chronicle. Of course, Major Esterhazy, whom I have questioned on this subject on behalf of *The New York Times*, declares that the documents, if they exist, are forgeries.[49]

Owing to the time-lag between Paris and New York, the article did not appear until 10 April. While devastating to Blacker personally and ultimately fatal to his and Panizzardi's plan, the explosive article proved a triumph for Strong, adding to his public reputation as a journalist 'to be reckoned with' in the Dreyfus affair, as noted in his obituary in the London *Times* twenty-six years later:

The Dreyfus case he followed from the beginning and some of his articles doubtless helped to bring the affair to a head. His spirited style and his fearless pugnacity made him one of the foreign correspondents in Paris who were to be reckoned with, and he plunged into the Dreyfus controversy with his customary courage.[50]

Constance, about to enter a clinic for an operation on her spine, in a final demonstration of concern for her husband wished to ensure that the allowance she had been giving him would continue to be paid for as long as he lived. 'I am going to give Oscar £10 a month', she wrote to Carrie, 'and I am putting a codicil to my will so that the allowance may continue after my death.' Then forty, Constance died less than two weeks later.[51]

8

'Paradoxes Are Always Dyngerous Things'

I

The high expectations raised in the initial reunion with Blacker ('always my staunch friend [who] stood by my side for many years')[1] having faded for Wilde, he made no further appeals. 'I thought I had got back my friend', he later observed ruefully to Robbie Ross of a loss that was as hurtful to him as it was unexpected. 'Considering our ancient friendship and how I stuck to him in his troubles', he noted with an uncharacteristic show of pique, 'he treated me with utter indifference, never invited me to have bit [sic] or sup with him at a café or elsewhere, and in the course of five months only came four times to see me'.[2] Of the torment of his deepening isolation, he confessed to Ross that, 'I cannot bear being alone.'[3] Recalling Wilde's 'curious prevision' that he would not survive the century, Rowland Strong observed years later that, '[Wilde] had no reason to feel that he was slipping away from the world, but was inwardly conscious that the world was slipping away from him.'[4] Another close observer, Vincent O'Sullivan, referring to the effect of the slights and rebuffs by former friends and other humiliations to which he was daily exposed, concluded that, 'Wilde endured too much cruelty in the Paris of his time; he received too many wounds, hardly ever resented them openly, but finally died of them.'[5] No wound was more grievous, or more deeply resented, than what he perceived to be his abandonment by Blacker, 'an old friend for whom I had made many sacrifices'. Of the painful end of the 'ancient friendship', he concluded with bitter resignation: 'One cannot demand friendship as a right. One cannot extort affection with a knife. To awaken gratitude in the ungrateful were as vain as to try to wake the dead by cries.'[6]

Elizabeth Robins, a young American actress friend of Wilde's, in a tribute to their friendship which had flourished at a time when Wilde was at the height of his fame ('I could do nothing for him; he could and did do everything in his power for me'), noted his capacity for retaliation when angered, describing him as 'brilliant beyond the power of report, overbearing yet urbane, unless crossed, and then most alarming'.[7] Wounded and brooding over Blacker's neglect, Wilde's response could not have been more alarming. Since his arrival in Paris the previous month, his attention had been largely devoted to the publication in England of his successful 'Ballad of Reading Gaol' as it passed through multiple editions. Prior to his meeting with Blacker, he appears to have had no more than a passing interest in the Dreyfus case from his close association with the journalists Healy and Strong, both of whom were absorbed in the drama. At his initial meeting with Blacker, Wilde would have recognized in the fervor of his total dedication to the cause of the unjustly condemned officer the qualities he so admired in him: his 'chivalry of nature . . . limitless generosity . . . quick intellectual sympathies'. The warmth and solace of their emotional reunion after not having seen one another for three years held a promise for Wilde that made Blacker's abrupt and inexplicable abandonment all the more unexpected and harder to bear. Whether his revelation of the confidential information he had received from Blacker to his more faithful, albeit more recent, friends, Healy and Strong, with as scant regard for his solemn bond of silence as Blacker had shown for the claims of 'his oldest and most faithful friend', was in fact a desperate act of retaliation or an alcoholic lapse—as Blacker himself professed to believe—is not entirely certain. Healy promptly went with the information to Zola, with results of critical importance to the Dreyfusard cause, while, in a grand paradox that may have had its own appeal for Wilde, Strong repeated everything to Esterhazy. 'Paradoxes', Wilde had noted in *The Decay of Lying*, 'are always dangerous things'— and the present instance proved to be no exception.[8]

2

The confidential information that Healy and Strong separately carried to Zola and Esterhazy was not long in reaching the public. On 4 April, six days before Strong's article appeared in *The New York Times*, the newspaper *Le Siècle* published the first of four documents that proved to be of decisive importance in exposing the guilt of Esterhazy in a series of dramatic revelations. The appearance of the first of the documents, 'La Vérité sur Esterhazy', or, as it came to be known by its more celebrated title, the 'Lettre d'un Diplomate', took Blacker totally by surprise. To his dismay, he found that the letter 'substantially contained' the secret information he had received from Panizzardi, which 'then became generally known for the first time', thus anticipating a crucial element of their plan. The document 'created a great sensation', in Blacker's words, enabling the Dreyfusard cause overnight to regain the initiative that had been lost with Zola's conviction several weeks earlier.[9]

Blacker had no doubt as to the source of the published information, as he told Salomon Reinach—one of only four others who were privy to the Blacker/Panizzardi plan. According to Reinach, in a report of his confidential conversations with Blacker ('he knows everything'), 'Blacker confided in four persons: 1—Conybeare of Oxford; 2—Paton, an Oxford Hellenist resident on Samos; 3—myself; and 4—Oscar Wilde.' In his report, submitted anonymously in a handwriting not his own and apparently without Blacker's knowledge, to the Cour de Cassation the following November, when the court was considering revision of Dreyfus's court-martial, Salomon Reinach disclosed that, 'Zola got some of his information from Oscar Wilde, who had got it from Blacker, the intimate friend of Panizzardi. Wilde betrayed the confidence of his compatriot, but this did not lessen the great value of the information obtained.'[10] Salomon Reinach's brother Joseph, sworn to secrecy as to Blacker's identity, states in a footnote in his history of the affair, without naming Blacker, that the 'Lettre d'un Diplomate' was written in his home by two prominent Dreyfusards, Yves Guyot and Francis de Pressensé, 'based on notes provided by Zola', without disclosing where Zola got the new information—information not available to him and his well-informed supporters at the time of his trial.[11] Blacker appears by name only once, in an unrelated footnote, in Joseph Reinach's exhaustive and meticulously documented seven-volume history.[12]

Chris Healy offered a key to the mystery of where Zola had obtained his information in an article in the English journal *To-day*, published a week after Zola's death in September 1902, in which he claimed credit for Wilde as 'one of the direct instruments in freeing Alfred Dreyfus'.[13] In his expanded account of the circumstances in his *Confessions* two years later, Healy extends his original claim to the right of writing 'at least one chapter' of the secret history of the Dreyfus affair to 'at least two or three chapters'. He relates that:

it was my fortune to see much of Émile Zola at a time when every newspaper in the world was giving his adventures the leading place in its columns . . . and, indeed, [I] was admitted to an interview on many occasions when other journalists were turned away. On one occasion I saw Zola's servant express his master's regret to David Christie Murray at being unable to see him that evening, and then lead me to the room where Zola was waiting to see me.[14]

According to Healy, Wilde confided to him the secret information that he had received from 'a friend [Blacker] who was familiar with Colonel von Schwartzkoppen [assumed by Wilde to be Blacker's informant]'. Healy 'immediately went to Zola and told him all. . . . Zola was anxious to meet Wilde, but the latter refused to see him, on the curious ground that Zola was a writer of immoral romances. . . . But the successful agitation [that followed] was all due to the information Oscar Wilde had given.' Whether Healy's further statement that 'the dramatic change in the tide of affairs . . . was planned by Zola and—Oscar Wilde' was intended to suggest that the two acted in concert is doubtful.[15] While Healy was puzzled by Wilde's refusal to meet Zola, Wilde had good reason not to wish to see the French writer, who, during Wilde's imprisonment, had declined to sign a petition circulated among men of letters in Paris for mitigation of his harsh prison sentence. 'I look upon Zola', Wilde told Healy, 'as a third-rate Flaubert. Zola is never artistic, and often disgusting.'[16] Seven years before, Robert Sherard, then working on a biography of Zola, had taken Wilde and Blacker to meet the French author, who had regarded the visit as 'a great honor'. Later, in London in 1893, Zola recorded the pleasure of passing an hour at the Alhambra and speaking with 'the very charming and remarkable poet Oscar Wilde, who had very thoughtfully sent a basket of flowers to my wife' at the Savoy Hotel.[17] Following Wilde's conviction, however, according to Sherard, Zola's 'indignation was so violent against Wilde that one might have fancied him the editor of a religious magazine, or the writer of moral text-books'.[18]

On the appearance of the 'Lettre d'un Diplomate', 'unfortunately', Blacker wrote:

I was considered the author of it, & it was attributed to me. Then commenced my troubles. I was attacked by the low and infamous press, & for days my family & I were insulted & dragged through the most filthy dirt. Anonymous and foul letters were addressed to me threatening me with assaults & death to myself & my family. I was followed & tracked without a moment's intermission for months & it was only on the frontier when I left France that I finally saw two men leaving the train who had been watching me from the next carriage.[19]

While the 'Lettre d'un Diplomate' rallied the Dreyfusard cause and marked a turning point in the affair, the appearance of Strong's article in *The New York Times* on April 10 struck a telling blow for the anti-Dreyfusards. The premature disclosure of the essential element of the plan so long in preparation by Blacker and Panizzardi, with Esterhazy's preemptive denial and charge of forgery, destroyed any remaining hope of success. 'The project unhappily fell through at the last moment', Conybeare wrote cryptically of their disappointment, 'because the conditions of secrecy, under which alone we could work, were menaced by the rashness of outsiders.'[20]

The cross-purposes to which Healy and Strong put the information obtained from Wilde brought their association to an abrupt end. Having incurred 'Esterhazy's enmity' and the 'hatred' of Strong, Healy left for England to pursue his journalistic career in London and was succeeded in the position of Strong's 'so-called secretary', as Esterhazy mockingly phrased it, by Maurice Gilbert.[21] Nameless but unmistakably identified in Healy's *Confessions* by reference to his relationship to Chateaubriand, Strong is described in uncomplimentary terms as 'a Parisian journalist who carried on the campaign against Dreyfus in the English press'; 'a fierce anti-Semite'; and a 'Jew-baiter'. Strong, for his part, described Healy as 'a born stool-pigeon' in whose presence he warned Esterhazy to be careful about what he said.[22]

Amid the turmoil, Wilde was in a deeply troubled state when Healy parted from him. 'The last time I saw Wilde', Healy recalled, 'he was kneeling in the Church of Nôtre Dame. The sun streamed through the windows, the organ was pealing a majestic chant, and his head was bowed, almost hidden. Perhaps some vision of what his life might have been came to him and scourged his soul anew. I only know that when

I left him he was still kneeling before the altar, his face hidden by his hands.'[23]

3

Although Blacker was gradually confirmed in his suspicion of Wilde, he did not immediately confront him with it, attributing the betrayal of trust to Wilde's 'having again become a drunkard [who] repeated everything [he] had told him to Strong, another drunkard'.[24] They were briefly reunited on news of the sudden and unexpected death of Constance in Genoa on April 7. 'I suppose you have heard the terrible news. Constance is dead', Wilde informed Blacker. 'I would like to see you tomorrow (Wednesday) at any hour you like.'[25] Blacker responded immediately. '[12 April] Carte telegram from Oscar saying that his wife Mrs. Holland was dead.... Went immediately to see Oscar but he was not in.' In the meantime, Blacker was under increasing stress as matters reached a critical stage following the appearance of the 'Lettre d'un Diplomate' and, a few days later, the first installment of Casella's deposition. Panizzardi, under attack in the anti-Dreyfusard press and the target of anonymous threats, was at the breaking point. '[12 April] Panizzardi came in great excitement while we were at dinner. Told me about other things appearing about him. Gave him some sandwiches, etc. He remained until past 12 and was very excited.' The next day, alarmed at the escalating crisis and the attacks on Panizzardi, and he himself beginning to be 'glanced at' by the press, Blacker went again to see Wilde. His suspicion of Wilde's role as informant of his fellow-drunkard Strong offered the prospect of a strained meeting, for which Blacker undoubtedly welcomed the diverting presence of Robbie Ross. '[13 April] Went to see Oscar, found Robbie Ross there.... Afterwards called on Panizzardi to see if everything was right with him.... Panizzardi to dinner. Talked till past 12'; '[14 April] Robbie Ross to lunch. Long conversation with him afterwards. Went to Oscar's for an hour. He had to go to his tailor.... Panizzardi to dinner.'

Panizzardi's presence in Paris having become untenable, he left the following day. In the hope that use might still be made of the incriminating facsimiles in Esterhazy's handwriting, and 'afraid they might in some way be got hold of', he wished to leave them in Blacker's care.

Blacker, however, was himself increasingly anxious about his own and his family's safety in the highly charged and threatening atmosphere and felt unable to accept the responsibility. Panizzardi accordingly took the documents with him. Whatever their subsequent fate, they were never to be seen again. In the absence of this compelling evidence, Blacker and Conybeare, who had arrived in Paris a few days before, were left to salvage what they could of the abortive plan. As an alternative course, they agreed that Conybeare, fully informed by Blacker, would write a detailed account of Esterhazy's dealings with Schwartzkoppen, but concealing Panizzardi's identity as the ultimate source of the information, and arrange for its publication in England. Conybeare, combative by nature, was fully committed to the plan by the time he left Paris on 23 April and eager to put it in execution.

As the breakup of the friendship between Blacker and Wilde became clear, Robbie Ross tended to sympathize with Blacker, whose genuine concern for Wilde's welfare he fully appreciated. '[16 April] Mrs. Holland's death appeared in *Temps*. . . . Robbie Ross to lunch. He told me that he had arranged with Oscar about not seeing him any more unless it was for his benefit. Long talk with him. . . . Said goodbye to him as he was leaving tomorrow.' Ross was concerned that Wilde's notoriety would bring him under police scrutiny and that his scandalous life might result in his being expelled from the country. Ross had earlier advised Wilde about the people to whom he should send copies of the limited 'Author's Edition', the third edition of the 'Ballad'— 'people who have been kind to me and about me', Wilde described them to Smithers, informing his publisher that Ross would bring him the list.[26] High on Ross's list of such people was Carlos Blacker to whom, on his return to London, Ross sent copy number 3 of the ninety-nine copies printed of the 'Author's Edition', inscribed, albeit with less warmth than on the earlier occasion at the Hôtel de Nice: 'To Carlos Blacker from his friend the author.'[27]

Communication between Wilde and Blacker petered out in sporadic appeals from Wilde for money: '[7 May] Sent Oscar frcs 50 which he had asked for'; '[9 May] Letter from Oscar thanking me for 50 francs and saying that he had had an operation. Letter from Vivian, torn letter asking me to give his love to his father. . . . Letter from Oscar asking for advance of £37.10 on his quarterly allowance'; '[10 May] Received letter from Ross asking me to go to see Oscar. I wrote to him [&] told him what was being said about Oscar here.' What was being said had caused all of Wilde's former French friends to shun him. Vincent O'Sullivan recalled that such former friends as Stuart Merrill, who had sponsored the petition for leniency by French men of letters during Wilde's imprisonment, and Marcel Schwob and others 'were constantly begging me to get Wilde's English friends to make him realize that he was ruining what sympathy was left for him among the Parisians by shewing himself drunk on the Boulevards in such a place as "The Kalasaya" Bar with sodomist outcasts, who were sometimes even dangerous in other ways'.[28] O'Sullivan felt that he himself was too young to dare to speak to Wilde about it. Ross, however, ventured a cautionary note on the subject, to which Wilde replied: 'my dear Robbie, do not listen to stories about my being expelled from Paris; they are childish. I live a very ordinary life.... I suppose Carlos is the author of the *canard*? It is unkind of him.'[29] Blacker in exasperation decided that he had had enough: '[13 May] Wrote to ... Ross about Oscar saying I could in future only buy what works he produced but could not go on advancing him money.' In earnest of the new direction his support was to take, Blacker promptly purchased two copies of the 'Ballad' for friends. He did not see Wilde again until a final confrontation two months later ended in their total estrangement.

4

Zola had in the meantime appealed his conviction and on 2 April the verdict against him was overturned by the Cour de Cassation, to the consternation of the anti-Dreyfusard camp. The judges in the Ester-hazy court-martial who had been defamed in *J'Accuse* immediately filed another suit against Zola, limiting their complaint to a single sentence in *J'Accuse* in which Zola had stated that the court-martial had acquitted Esterhazy 'on command'. Wishing to avoid a repetition of the tumult and riot surrounding the first trial, the court ordered the opening hearing in the case to be held on 23 May in the presumably less volatile political atmosphere of Versailles.

Esterhazy, mistrusted and abandoned by his military protectors to whom he had become an embarrassment, welcomed the opportunity to make a public display of outraged innocence on the opening day of the hearings, at which he appeared in the front rank of an unruly mob of anti-Zola demonstrators. 'Major Esterhazy drove down to Versailles on an English mail coach which had been specially chartered for the purpose by an English friend', Strong (the likely 'English friend') reported in the *New York Times* the following day:

It started from Campbell's restaurant in the Rue St. Honoré at 10 A. M., and drew up in front of the Palais de Justice at 11:30, amid a great blowing of the horn. The Major's ostentatious intention in coming to Versailles was to seek out ex-Col. Picquart [his principal accuser in the military] and fall on him with fists and feet; but the Colonel was nowhere to be found. All that happened then was that the Major and his friends lunched quietly at the Hotel de la Chasse and drove back in a distinctly gay mood, to judge from the shouting and the horn blowing, to their point of departure. There was an American, together with an English journalist, on board the coach, (the latter being Mr. Arthur Lynch of The London Daily Mail,) and the quantity of whiskey and soda consumed en route was quite remarkable.[30]

Wilde was otherwise occupied on the day, attending the trial of a husband and wife who had murdered a debt-collector, for which the husband was sentenced to death and his wife to life-imprisonment. He did, however, witness the deplorable aftermath of the Versailles outing which had started and ended in Campbell's Bar. Here, he and Douglas, who had reappeared in Paris the previous month—'very angelic and quiet'—later ran into Sherard, disheveled and distraught. 'Robert looked quite dreadful', Wilde reported to Ross, 'all covered with cigar-ash, stains of spilt whisky, and mud. He was unshaven, and his face in a dreadful state. He had no money, and borrowed a franc from Bosie.' Sherard had fallen victim to the passions unleashed at the Versailles hearing, when, prompted by his anti-Dreyfusard sentiments, 'he created a horrible scene in Campbell's Bar by bawling out "*A bas les juifs*," and insulting and assaulting someone whom he said was a Jew. The fight continued in the street, and Robert tried to create an Anti-Semite, Anti-Dreyfusard demonstration. He succeeded, and was ultimately felled to the ground by the Jew!'[31] Sherard's refusal on an earlier occasion to call on Wilde because of the presence of Maurice Gilbert was the same deeply resented offense of which Blacker had been guilty, and the two offenders were similarly rewarded for their 'monstrous moralising'.[32] Ten days after the humiliating spectacle presented by Sherard, Blacker, after voicing his disapproval of Wilde's association with Douglas ('no one should know such an infamous person'),was to find himself, to Wilde's satisfaction, 'tumbled into the mud in Paris as completely as he did in London'.[33]

The day after Zola's appearance at the Versailles hearing, the second installment of Casella's abortive deposition appeared in *Le Siècle* but, in Blacker's estimation, added nothing new: '[24 May] Casella's 2nd letter appeared in the *Siècle* in which he only recapitulated what was known before.' A week later, on 1 June, the long-planned article by Conybeare, titled 'The Truth About Dreyfus', was published in the *National Review* in London under the nom de plume 'Huguenot'. 'This article', in the words of George Barlow, a contemporary historian of the affair, 'was destined to exercise a remarkable influence upon events.'[34] Four days after its appearance, Joseph Reinach published extensive excerpts from it with an approving commentary in *Le Siècle*, for which the Minister of War ordered him as an officer in the reserve to appear before a military Court of Enquiry for insulting the General Staff.

The appearance of Reinach's article provoked an immediate attack on him by Esterhazy's most active champion among French journalists, André de Boisandré of the *Libre Parole*. In the gathering storm, as the identity of 'Huguenot' of the *National Review* came under scrutiny, Blacker decided to leave the threatening atmosphere of Paris with his family. He had from the outset demonstrated an overriding concern for secrecy and anonymity, for himself as well as for Panizzardi. While his confidant Salomon Reinach was puzzled by Blacker's refusal to take a public stand, Strong thought he knew the reason for it. 'It was Strong who told me of the role played by a certain Carlos Blacker in this affair', according to Esterhazy:

an extremely shady role that consisted of digging up bogus information in Germany and passing it on to his friend Conybeare—the Conybeare so acclaimed by Reinach and Yves Guyot. . . . Blacker did not dare to act openly himself as there had been some rather unpleasant scandals in his past, Strong told me, and he modestly contented himself with the role of informer, leaving to his friend Conybeare that of dispenser of justice.[35]

On the eve of his departure from Paris, Blacker went to see Wilde, twice the same day, for what proved to be their final encounters. They had not seen one another for two months. Wilde was then staying at a small riverside inn called *A l'Idée* on the banks of the Marne ('a little inn where poor poets go, like *L'Ermitage* in literature'),[36] where he had credit. It was a half-hour by rail from Paris, at Le Perreux, Nogent-sur-Marne, a favorite warm-weather retreat of Wilde and his intimate circle—Bosie Douglas, Rowland Strong, and Maurice Gilbert—and where they were occasionally joined by Esterhazy, for whom Wilde and Douglas were 'deux hommes de beaucoup d'esprit'. The precise reason for Blacker's visits is not clear from the accounts both he and Wilde left of them. Convinced as Blacker was of Wilde's complicity with his enemies, it seems likely that in the face of the menacing newspaper attacks and the possibility that the dreaded specter of his troubles with Newcastle might be raised, he came to plead with Wilde to stop fueling the press campaign with information. If this were in fact the reason for the visits, his mission proved unsuccessful. Blacker's most recent act of betrayal, in Wilde's eyes, had been his unfavorable report to Robbie Ross on 'what was being said' about Wilde in Paris that exposed him to possible expulsion from the country. Wilde could now report to Ross on what was being said about Blacker whose own activity had rendered him liable to the same ignominious treatment. '[Blacker] has got into a mess here through being [Joseph] Reinach's "*homme de paille*" in his Dreyfus-Syndicate campaign', Wilde wrote to Ross from Nogent three weeks after Blacker's visits, 'and I should not wonder if he were expelled':

His connections with Conybeare—the author of the article insulting the 'état-major,' for which Reinach has been dismissed from the army—is well-known; it was of course really written by C.B. He has returned to Boulogne, so as to be near the coast . . . .

He came down to see me about a fortnight ago, enquired affectionately into my financial position, actually wept floods of tears, begged me to let him pay the balance of my hotel bill—a request that I did not think it right to refuse—and left me with violent protestations of devotion.

A week later he wrote me a Nonconformist conscience letter in which he said that as he did not approve of my knowing Bosie he thought it would be morally wrong of him to help me in any way except by advice!

He also added that his wife disapproved of my knowing Bosie!! So Tartuffe goes out of my life.[37]

The cryptic diary notes that Blacker made of the meetings are unenlightening: '[7 June] went to see Oscar who told me about Sherard, etc., as I had not seen him for 2 months. . . . After lunch went to see Oscar again at 4 to 6, had a long talk about several things'; '[8 June] Up at 9 after having a good laugh with Carrie at Oscar.' The 'good laugh' under the dire circumstances recalls Blacker's mirthless, bitter reaction to impending calamity at the time of his breakup with Sir Lewis

Molesworth, when the latter's note terminating relations 'made me laugh as I have not laughed for many a day'. Blacker left Paris for Boulogne with his family the following day.

In a report in *The New York Times*, datelined the day of Blacker's meetings with Wilde, Strong named Blacker, again 'on good authority', as the author of the *National Review* article:

The article in the National Review dealing with the question of Esterhazy's alleged guilt and Dreyfus's innocence has caused a lively sensation here, and people are asking who is the author of it. I am told on good authority that it is from the active pen of Mr. Carlos Blacker, who has already done yeoman service in attracting public attention to the persistent assertions of the German and French [*sic*] Attachés that Dreyfus was not a traitor. It was Mr. Blacker who inspired the articles signed a 'Diplomat,' which were addressed from Bern to the Siècle. He is the son of a wealthy Cuban merchant, and married into the English aristocracy. Persons intimate with the social life of London will remember the club incident connected with card playing which took place two or three years ago between Mr. Blacker and the Duke of Newcastle, resulting in the former being made bankrupt on the petition of the Duke for £10,000 money lent.[38]

Owing again to the time-lag between Paris and New York, Strong's 7 June article did not appear until 19 June. In the meantime, two days after Blacker's departure from Paris, André de Boisandré published an article in the *Libre Parole* titled 'A New Agent of the Syndicate', in which he gave a detailed account, without identifying Blacker by name, of the new agent's troubled career in England.[39] Suggesting that the anonymous agent, an Englishman whom he promised soon to name, was actually the author of the 'Lettre d'un Diplomate' and the *National Review* article, Boisandré went on to provide information of such an intimate nature—such as Blacker's alleged role in the marriage of Lord Francis Hope and May Yohe—that it was clear to Blacker that it could only have originated with Wilde. Although Boisandré promised to identify soon the 'nouvel agent anglo-dreyfusard' by name, he did not do so until two weeks later, possibly pursuant to an understanding with Strong, his source, that the latter's 'scoop' be allowed first to appear in *The New York Times*. The pleasant round of life in Boulogne ('sun, sea air, sands') was shattered for Blacker when informed of Boisandré's article by Conybeare: ['22 June] After lunch letter from Conybeare with news of article in *La Libre Parole*. Upset me very much. . . . Bad temper.' Two days later, despite a reassuring 'letter from Coney[beare] saying article in *La Libre Parole* was not with my name', Blacker, consumed by the shame and humiliation the article threatened, revealed a tortured state of mind in a unique notation in the diary entry for the day. Written in Greek, following the daily narrative in Pitman shorthand, are quotations from the *Odyssey* (Book XX, line 82: Odysseus's faithful wife Penelope, pressed by suitors in his prolonged absence and unaware as yet of his return, prays that she might die rather than 'gladden at all the thoughts of a baser man'); and from Sophocles, *Ajax* (lines 550–1): before killing himself for his regretted conduct, Ajax wishes for his son: 'My son, may you be more fortunate than your father / But be like him in all else [and you will not be base].' Blacker watched with mounting apprehension as the press attacks increased in intensity with the approach of Reinach's appearance before the Court of Enquiry.

In order to clear Reinach of the charge of complicity in the authorship of the *National Review* article, of which he was being accused along with Blacker in the anti-Dreyfusard press, Conybeare—at the request of Reinach's brother Salomon—wrote an open letter claiming authorship and signing himself by name, adding for weight the tag, 'of the University of Oxford'. It was as a friend of France, Conybeare wrote, that he had:

thought it well to publish the information on the subject of the Dreyfus affair, which I have obtained from the surest and most reliable sources. . . . I affirm to you that the French War Office is in danger of seeing published in foreign papers facsimiles of documents which have been sold by Esterhazy to Colonel Schwartzkoppen, and which are all written in Esterhazy's hand.

. . . I affirm to you that this very thing as nearly as possible happened in the month of February last, and that the sword of Damocles is always suspended over the head of the War Office.

In his appearance before the Court of Enquiry on 24 June, Reinach read Conybeare's letter, described by the historian George Barlow, as 'the terrible letter from Oxford which sealed Esterhazy's doom before the bar of the world's educated opinion'.[40] Despite the fact that the letter when 'reproduced by the press of the entire world created an immense sensation', according to Reinach, he was found guilty and stripped of his commission in the territorial army.[41] When the letter was reproduced in the *Libre Parole* the following day, Boisandré named Blacker for the first time.

The press attacks were unnerving to Blacker and he blamed Cony-beare's indiscreet use of certain information in his open letter for directing the unwelcome anti-Dreyfusard spotlight on himself and Panizzardi. Blacker's friend W. R. Paton sympathized with him:

You will have seen, I think, that before I heard from you to that effect, I felt practically certain that Conybeare had as regards his obligations to & consid-eration for yourself acted with indiscretion. Of course when he sent me his article (his corrected proof) I was under the impression that he had fully secured your approval in making his revelations & cut out certain things (among them the 2,000 francs a month [paid by Schwartzkoppen to Ester-hazy]) by your request. I can't, as things are, excuse him for having acted as he did, except on the ground on which you will excuse him, that he was tremendously excited by this appalling affair & I am sure would, if there had been any necessity for it have made any personal sacrifice. But of course he had no right at all to sacrifice your personality.... I feel inclined to give Conybeare a scolding, but it would serve no purpose & only pain him much, as he bears great affection to ourselves.[42]

Another close friend of Blacker's, Albert Curtis Clark, Regius Profes-sor of Latin at Oxford, joined in offering commiseration: 'I have been very grieved to hear that a recent publication has caused you pain. I did not see it until it was in print. I was then rather startled, but I was told that you had seen it, & did not cut out anything in it. I really do not think that there is anything in it which points to you, or indeed to the friend [Panizzardi] whom I met.'[43] Conybeare in his defense reminded Blacker that his identity had been known to the anti-Dreyfusard press for at least two months before Conybeare's letter: 'You will remember that even before I left Paris you were being glanced at in Ester[hazy]'s paper the *Jour*, and O.W., you said, had after his dinner with Ester. admitted to Strong that *his* informant was one C.B., viz: yourself.'[44] With regard to the *National Review* article, Conybeare voiced a further suspicion of Wilde: 'I suspect Wilde had been set on at pure random to sound yourself about the art. in the N. R.' at the time of Blacker's visit to Nogent. He assured Blacker that he was 'the pioneer of a noble cause and you must not be scared away from it by a few lines of obscure abuse levelled at you by Drumont [editor of the *Libre Parole*]. That really does you honour.' 'In conclusion', Conybeare wrote:

I hope you will castigate one O.W. who long ago betrayed your confidences to an Uhlan [Esterhazy] and early in June suggested to the same Uhlan that you were an English publicist.... Do you think that the mere circumstance that O.W. met me casually in your rooms in London some six years ago warrants his assuring Drumont that I am 'intime' with you as well as with various other people of whom I never before heard? Break his head.[45]

The attacks on Blacker were deeply upsetting to his mother, whose uncertain state of health was a cause of grave concern. 'I am regretful beyond power of words to hear that your mother was distressed', Conybeare wrote, adding, with a broad hint that the unfortunate turn of events might have been avoided had Blacker earlier heeded his advice: 'You must allow that when you told me that your wife disapproved of your seeing O.W., I wrote at once to you to follow her advice and that you would never regret having done so.'[46] More than ever convinced of the soundness of his advice, he offered it again through Carrie: 'Pray Carlos never to see that man (if I may call one lower than the animals) again. When he first told me that you were against it, I felt that your instinct was right, and advised him to decline an interview.'[47]

From Boulogne, Blacker wrote Wilde an accusing letter. Wilde indignantly denied the 'disgraceful accusation' and appealed to Ross, whose consistent support of Blacker was a source of annoyance: 'C. Blacker has behaved like a hypocritical ass to me, and finally wrote me a letter accusing me of having written some attack on him that appeared in some Paris paper. I need hardly say I never read the paper, or saw the attack, and that I never write anonymous attacks on people anywhere. I was so angry, I wrote him a very strong letter',[48] in which Wilde protested his innocence and demanded an apology, adding, for Blacker's instruction, 'a few truths about himself, which he can ponder on in exile':

It is a curious thing, dear absurd little Robbie', he complained, 'that you *now* always think that I am in the wrong. . . . Why not sometimes think that I may be in the right? Why, at once, take the side of "*le triste individu*"? . . . You think it good for me that you should never be on my side. The Goliaths who threaten me are always assisted by my David.[49]

No apology was forthcoming from Blacker, whose diary, under the heading for the day's entry, 'Letter from Oscar saying Good Bye', records with finality: '[25 June] After lunch just before dinner letter from Oscar which put an end to our friendship forever.' Conybeare's advice was, 'Let Carlos keep O.W.'s blackmailing letter and let him keep silence. It is beneath his dignity to answer attacks from such a quarter.'[50]

Blacker may have followed Conybeare's advice and kept Wilde's 'blackmailing letter'. Although the letter cannot now be found, an empty envelope preserved among Blacker's papers may once have contained it. The envelope bears an inscription in ink in Blacker's unmistakable hand: 'Letter from O.W.', with the date '22.1.20' and some faintly written, illegible notes in pencil. The date is significant for Blacker's having 'nearly died of "Spanish Flu" in January 1920', according to his son Pip in a notation on a letter addressed to Blacker from Anatole France, dated 24 January 1920.[51] 'I was with him in Florence [where Blacker and his wife were on holiday] at the time', Pip wrote, 'and I recall one night when we were doubtful if he would survive till the next day.'[52] In the belief that he was dying, Blacker may have destroyed the letter the envelope once contained, recording the date as was his habit. It is not apparent why he would have had a 'Letter from O.W.' with him in Florence under the circumstances or why he should have inscribed the date on the retained envelope; nor can the empty envelope be related to any of Wilde's surviving letters to him.

In accounting for the press attacks to a small circle of friends, Blacker confided his suspicions of Wilde's perfidy. In France, one of Wilde's earliest and most outspoken defenders, his friend, the prominent literary critic Henry Bauër, sympathized with Blacker: 'O. W. whom I have defended so ardently inspires me now only with contempt. . . . He betrays the friends who have stood by him and supported him. I turn away from this foul odour; he no longer exists for me.'[53] Salomon Reinach, while more philosophic was no less disapproving: 'from a purely moral view, he is not worse than many people who betray their friends, lie, slander—and do not go to gaol'.[54] Others of Blacker's intimate circle in England vented their indignation more forcefully. 'Words would fail me if I tried to express what I think of O. W.', wrote Albert Curtis Clark. 'This seems to me the very worst of his misdeeds. That he had no moral sense one knew, but I cannot conceive anyone so entirely lost to all sense of honour.'[55] Conybeare concluded that 'it is evident now that he is the basest of brutes fit only to perish miserably, which I hope he soon will'.[56]

W. R. Paton, then in Turkey, incensed by Blacker's report was roused to take precipitate action. 'Although I entered into an engagement with myself & you not to mention O.W., I must tell you what I did', Paton informed Blacker:

I wrote a letter to the papers narrating the facts with all the eloquence & ire I had. Then on second thoughts instead of sending it to a paper I sent it to [James] Bryce with whom I am in intimate correspondence as regards the Eastern question & said that he might send it to the papers if he thought fit; but that I wished at least to place my feelings on record by submitting it to him. He replies that it shocked more than surprised him, that after consideration he did not have it published, but has communicated it to several people including the late Home Secretary [Herbert Henry Asquith, Home Secretary at the time of Wilde's trials].[57]

The 'malevolent comment in London, where Wilde was accused of taking part on that side of the Dreyfus affair which was not popular in England', as noted by Robert Sherard, may have been owing as much to the circulation of Paton's letter among 'several people' of influence in England by the future Viscount Bryce as to Wilde's 'passing acquaintance' with Esterhazy, which Sherard suggested as the source of the 'malevolent comment'.[58]

Bitterness persisted on the part of both Wilde and Blacker and the two were never reconciled: '[30 June 1898] Talked with Carrie after dinner saying I never again would have to do with Oscar.'

9

'No One Should Know Such an Infamous Person as Bosie'

Blacker's 'Letter from Oscar saying Good bye' was followed a few days later by a salvo from Boisandré, who published further damaging 'biographical information' about Blacker and his troubles with Newcastle in the *Libre Parole* of 29 June. This was taken up by Boisandré's colleague Charles Roger who repeated the information in the equally hostile *Intransigeant*, as noted by Blacker: '[5 July] Carrie and I wrote to Conybeare in answer to his letter to me saying attacks had commenced again.' In his letter Conybeare had written that, 'it is clear that O.W. . . . told them that you and I were friends. In the last three days he has persuaded them that . . . I really get my news from you.'[1] Conybeare was 'awfully grieved' that Blacker was so distressed by the continuing attacks, as much for Panizzardi's sake as for his own, and he sought to reassure him that Panizzardi's identity as Blacker's informant was not suspected by the anti-Dreyfusard press. 'Drumont, Strong & Co. are the only set that know Carlos to have the innermost history of the case in his possession', he wrote to Carrie. 'But they are convinced equally that Schwartzkoppen & not Panizzardi is his informant as well as mine. Of Pan[izzardi] they do not dream.'[2] Nonetheless, the publication of the first installment of Casella's deposition, precipitating Panizzardi's recall from Paris, had seriously threatened his prospects in the army, the source of his livelihood. Badly shaken, he wished to be free from any further involvement in the affair in which he had taken such a buffeting. Writing from Rome at the end of June, he informed Blacker that he had nothing more to say or do about the matter, his present quest being for 'tranquility, always tranquility, nothing but tranquility'.[3]

At Nogent, Wilde observed the ongoing press attacks with bitter satisfaction. '[Blacker] is, I am glad to say, over in Paris', he wrote to Ross:

The *Libre Parole*, and the *Intransigeant*—the former one of the first papers in France—have published his *dossier* as it is called: . . . His whole *dossier* is paraded and he has tumbled into the mud in Paris as completely as he did in London. It is a great Nemesis on him. He treats me, his oldest and most faithful friend, with contempt because I am friends with Bosie and says that 'no one should know such an infamous person' as Bosie. A fortnight later he has to bolt to Boulogne because from a little corner—a very little corner of his own life—a veil is raised. The gods are sometimes just, and always humorous.[4]

On 5 July Wilde received a visit from a total stranger, a self-introduced admirer of his work, whose account of the 'perfect summer day' the two spent together at Nogent affords a curious glimpse of Wilde's state of mind at the time. The torment Blacker was suffering as a result of having the veil raised on 'a very little corner' of his past life, a corner that Wilde had shared as trusted friend and ally, and of which he was now betrayer, could never have been far from Wilde's thoughts. His visitor arrived for breakfast and was met by Wilde at the gate of the courtyard of *A L'Idée*. 'Snatcher, a lively dog lent to him by Mr. Rowland Strong, was present', the guest noted, 'and eagerly snapped up a morsel which Wilde rendered more appetizing by christening it Dreyfus.' In the course of a rambling, day-long conversation, Wilde told his visitor of knowing 'that remarkable man' Esterhazy and of his unhappy life. He talked of fear and of the guillotine, which he said he had witnessed in operation ('the victim . . . green with fright') and of the morgue ('a dignified place'). He said he had been struck by the power of a drama of betrayal he had seen enacted in which a murderer is betrayed by his mistress. As the latter beholds the 'venomous look' of hatred in the eyes of her betrayed and helpless lover when he is led away to his certain doom, she shrieks, 'J'ai peur, j'ai peur!' as the curtain falls. Entering into the role of the betrayer with feeling, 'Wilde delivered these words with a force that went into the marrow of my bones', his startled visitor recalled.[5]

Two days before, 'the sensation of the week in connection with the Dreyfus affair' had taken place in Paris, as reported by Strong in the

New York Times. Esterhazy finally caught up with his accuser, Colonel Picquart—the chief witness against him at his court-martial and again at the Zola trial, and who had refused to meet him in a duel—and assaulted him in the street. 'Major Esterhazy had been looking out for Col. Picquart for some weeks past', Strong reported, 'and had been exercising himself diligently at swordstick and foil play at a salle d'armes with this object in view':

He invariably carried with him a fairly thick stick made out of wild cherry wood, and painted cherry red. He is, I am told, very skillful both with the manipulation of a stick and with the sword, as well as being an adept at French boxing, or la savate, as it is called, which includes the use of the feet. He met Col. Picquart in the Avenue Bugeaud on Sunday last, and there was an animated tussle between them. Neither, I understand, was seriously hurt. Col. Picquart's hand bled, and he had it dressed at a neighboring chemist's shop. Major Esterhazy's hat was knocked off. The result of it will be a police prosecution, and the Major will be fined.[6]

In Conybeare's more colorful description of the incident, Esterhazy, 'maddened with absinth, rushed out of a drinking-shop and attacked Picquart with a club from behind. He thought he had taken him off his guard; but that officer was too quick for him, and with a few well-aimed strokes of his cane sent Esterhazy head foremost into the gutter, into which his hat had preceded him.'[7]

Meanwhile, in the turbulent aftermath of the publication of 'the terrible letter from Oxford', Esterhazy was trying to avoid being engulfed by yet another potential catastrophe. It had gradually dawned on his young cousin Christian that Esterhazy had embezzled funds entrusted to him for investment by Christian and his widowed mother and he confronted Esterhazy with his suspicions. Preoccupied by the larger, more terrible, struggle in which he was engaged, Esterhazy in a state of nervous exhaustion impatiently admitted everything, dismissed the matter without apology, and, in a fretful take-it-or-leave-it gesture, offered to make good out of the eventual proceeds of a contract he had for the publication of his memoirs. Christian was outraged, said he would agree to nothing until he had consulted a lawyer and further offended Esterhazy by refusing to shake hands with him in parting. At this, Esterhazy cried out after him in exasperation: 'Very well, then! Merde! I'm going to kill myself tonight.' Information furnished by Christian to Esterhazy's Nemesis, the examining magistrate Paul

Bertulus, who had been stalking the Commandant for several weeks, was all that was needed to lead to the uncovering of sufficient evidence for the arrest on 12 July of Esterhazy and his mistress Marguerite Pays on a charge of conspiracy to make use of forged documents in a matter peripheral to the Dreyfus case.[8]

2

As the summer of 1898 wore on, 'the sole subject of conversation in Paris is the heat', Strong noted in the *New York Times*, 'and certainly one is inclined to believe that it has never been so oppressively hot in the city before'.[9] Douglas, although now 'inseparable' from Maurice Gilbert, fled the heat in July to join his mother at the seaside, writing to Wilde soon after his departure that he was 'furious with Bobbie [Ross] for coming to Paris in that idiotic way; I am convinced that he purposely waited till I had gone in order that he might make an ass of himself with Maurice'. He requested that Strong send his servant to Nogent to pick up his things, as it was a bore having them there in case he suddenly decided to return to Paris.[10] Maurice Gilbert in the meantime was 'looking very ill', as Wilde informed Ross. 'He works, or rather overworks, with Strong from 9 a.m. till 9.45 p.m. in a stuffy room.'[11] With Douglas gone to the seaside, Esterhazy in prison, and Strong and Gilbert confined by work to a stuffy room, the carefree days of Wilde's Nogent circle came to an end. Years later, Strong looked back through a haze of nostalgia to the idyllic hours passed at *A L'Idée*: 'Oh, the joys of the little river-side *pavillon*, or cottage, with its big garden filled with flowers and vegetables and fruit-trees, *en plein rapport*, with laden branches. It was but a cab-drive to get there! No need of railways. Boating, fishing, and bathing, were the day-long amusements. . . . But all this is now a thing of the past.'[12]

Wilde suffered acutely from the heat and lamented that if only he could 'get away to the sea all would be well'. The Hôtel d'Alsace was 'a very poor and unsanitary place', he had complained to Ross in May of a condition that he knew was bound to get worse with the warm weather. 'People won't stay there as there is no drainage.'[13] Inadequate drains, even in hotels of the first category, were a notorious cause of complaint in Paris of the Belle Époque. 'No hotel can be recommended as first-class', the contemporary Baedeker *Handbook for*

Travellers cautioned, 'that is not satisfactory in its sanitary arrangements, which should include an abundant flush of water and a supply of proper toilette paper.'[14] This was a fact that Wilde was able to confirm from experience. 'The vital thing is the sanitary question', he reiterated to Ross. 'It is a real horror in life to live in an unsanitary house, especially now that summer is coming on.'[15] In the record-breaking heat of August, his worst fears were more than realized and the resulting misery forms a continuing refrain in his letters. 'Paris is hot and empty', he wrote to his publisher Leonard Smithers on 9 August. 'Perspiring English families are all that can be seen.'[16] Three days later, it was worse: 'It is so hot in Paris that I simply cannot write a letter. At night it is charming, but by day a tiger's mouth.'[17] Writing to Frank Harris from the Hôtel d'Alsace, he noted that, 'Paris is terrible in its heat. I walk in streets of brass, and there is no one here.'[18]

At the height of the heat wave, Esterhazy and Marguerite Pays were released from prison for lack of sufficient evidence for a prosecution. 'Major Esterhazy and his companion, Madame Pays, have been released', Strong reported in the *New York Times*. 'They have returned to their little apartment in the Rue Douai, where their poodle gave them an extraordinary welcome, and have closed their doors ruthlessly to all interviewers.'[19] The exclusion did not apply to Strong, however, who turned up at the apartment to welcome the couple home armed with two bottles of champagne, 'completely drunk', according to Esterhazy, 'having consumed, as was his habit, a prodigious amount of whiskey'.[20] A few nights later, with no relief from the awful heat, Wilde joined the party. He informed Ross, 'I dined last night with Strong, to meet Esterhazy and *la fille Pays*, who is a most charming woman—very clever and handsome. I am to dine with her and the *Commandant* on Thursday.'[21] The immediate bid by the harassed and secluded couple for more of Wilde's company suggests that Marguerite was as charmed by Wilde as he was by her and as the Commandant had been by Wilde's 'gay witticisms' at their first meeting. Wilde undoubt-edly raised the spirits of the troubled pair, as he had done for Carlos and Carrie Blacker three years earlier at the Sackville Hotel in London. If he had in fact succeeded in altering the aspect of Esterhazy's desperate situation, however, the *couleur de rose* faded quickly. At eight o'clock the following morning, Esterhazy received orders to appear before a military Court of Enquiry to consider his fitness to continue to serve as an officer.

Madame Louise Gérard, concierge at 49, rue de Douai, where the little one-room, first-floor apartment was located, was on intimate terms with Marguerite Pays and she and Esterhazy often dined with Madame Gérard and her husband in the kitchen of the concierge's lodge. As public attention began to focus on the Commandant and his mistress, Madame Gérard, aware that she was a witness to history-in-the-making, took to carrying a notebook in which she recorded in meticulous detail all that she saw and heard concerning the two. This record, which she later made available to the Cour de Cassation, gave an air of precision to her testimony, as evident in her notes of some critical disclosures made by the unsuspecting couple while Madame Gérard waited on them at dinner following their release from prison ('At the moment the Commandant and Mme. Pays spoke of these things, they were at the table, eating a chicken. It was nine o'clock at night'). In response to the question 'Who is this Mr. Strong?', she replied, 'He is an English journalist who was often with the Commandant, in the company of two other Englishmen, Messrs Cherald [Sherard] and Oscar Wilde. Mr. Cherald was also an English journalist. As for Mr. Oscar Wilde, he is the one whose conviction received so much notoriety. Mme. Pays', she added gratuitously, 'described to me in some detail the nature of the offenses of which he was convicted.' The Sunday after Wilde joined them for dinner for the second time, a terrible scene took place in the little apartment, witnessed—and later testified to—by Madame Gérard. Marguerite surprised the Commandant in the act of consulting a railway timetable and, suspecting his intention, flew into a rage, calling him 'a heartless coward and a scoundrel', and threatening to go to the Minister of War and tell everything. Esterhazy fell to his knees and begged her not to do it. Although he eventually succeeded in calming her, he remained convinced that flight was his only alternative to suicide.[22]

During the first day of hearings before the Court of Enquiry, things went badly for Esterhazy and it became evident to him that he would be dismissed from the army. He told Strong that evening that he was desperate and was considering suicide. Strong offered as a more appealing option the prospect of a rich reward in England for his version of events, which, based upon what Esterhazy had told him, Strong was sure would command a high price from the London journals with which he was associated. Although Esterhazy already had a contract with Fayard Frères in Paris for publication of his inside story, Strong's proposal had the added attraction for Esterhazy of removing him from the scene of his cousin Christian's action against him for fraud while at the same time providing him with a means of support while working on a more remunerative book-length account that he intended to write about the affair. He saw the projected book as not only a means of making his fortune but a means as well of settling the score with his despised military 'chiefs' who had abandoned him. Falling in with Strong's proposal, Esterhazy agreed to join him in London where Strong was to precede him to conclude arrangements for publication. With the most sensational story of the day within his grasp, Strong left for London in high spirits—and with even higher expectations—to negotiate for the most favorable terms with the *Pall Mall Gazette* and *The Observer*, leaving Maurice Gilbert to shadow the Commandant in his absence and prod him to follow Strong as soon as possible. Esterhazy later complained of his constant harassment at all hours by Strong's 'so-called secretary' Gilbert, whose bicycle—apparently a gift from Wilde—provided him with easy mobility for his importunate visits. Following a second day of hearings, the Court of Enquiry acquitted Esterhazy on two counts but found him guilty on a third, citing, among other examples of conduct unbefitting an officer, his interest in a house of assignation and his dealings on commission with marriage brokers. On 30 August, the court submitted its findings to the Minister of War who recommended to the president of the Republic that Esterhazy be dismissed from the army for habitual misconduct.

The same day, Lieutenant-Colonel Henry, Esterhazy's only remaining protector in the army, was arrested after confessing to having fabricated the *faux Henry*. The following evening, he was found dead in his prison cell in the fortress of Mont-Valérian with his throat cut and his razor in his hand, an apparent suicide. Esterhazy was convinced that Henry had been assassinated and that he himself was in imminent danger of sharing a similar fate. In panic, he determined to flee at once. On 2 September, eluding the agents of the Sûreté assigned to watch him, he boarded a tramway to Saint-Denis from where he proceeded by train to Chantilly. There he purchased a ready-made suit from an English tailor and a valise before continuing on to Soissons and then, by 'train omnibus', to Maubeuge, where he spent the night. The following day, he went on by train to Brussels from where he wired Strong that he was on his way with an 'enormous bombshell', signing himself 'de Bécourt'. To complete his disguise as the count de Bécourt, he shaved off his conspicuous military moustache.

'I doubt not that you are as jubilant as myself over the turn which events have taken in France', Conybeare wrote to Blacker, convinced that the suicide of Henry and the flight of Esterhazy meant the end of the case and that the Cour de Cassation would now simply annul the verdict against Dreyfus. He was then preparing an article for the *National Review* on 'The Moral Aspects of the Dreyfus Case' and for background asked Blacker if he might quote from his letter of the previous February, 'through which I became acquainted with the true history of the case? May I mention your name as that of the writer? Probably even Panizzardi will not now object to my mentioning him. Why do you not now declare yourself as the author of the Lettre d'un Diplomate from Berne? I suppose it was yours.' Alarmed at the suggestion, with the attendant threat of once again provoking hostile attention in the anti-Dreyfusard press, Blacker requested that Conybeare return his letter so that he might refresh his recollection about exactly what he had written that had so inspired Conybeare. 'My idea was to show to the public what a salutary influence you had exercised in the matter, but only of course with your consent & after the matter is—if ever—liquidated. . . . Let me have the letter again someday for when it is over I mean to bind them up in a book.' Conybeare was to wait in vain for the return of Blacker's letter which, like consent to the mention of his name, was never forthcoming.[23]

3

In London, Esterhazy joined Strong at 6 St James's Street, where Strong was staying as the guest of a friend of his, an American journalist named Thomas Fielders, and where a bed was set up for Esterhazy in Strong's room. Things went wrong almost from the start and during the next two weeks that Esterhazy shared the cramped quarters with the two journalists his relationship with Strong, and his nerves, steadily deteriorated. Unable to understand English and follow what was going on, he felt isolated and ignored, totally dependent upon Strong as translator, when Strong was not 'saturated with whiskey'. Strong had negotiated the sale of the inside story to *The Observer* for £500 on the basis of the sensational news value of Esterhazy's 'enormous bombshell': his admission (made to Strong in Paris) that he was the author of the famous *bordereau*. Since Dreyfus had been condemned for having been the author of the *bordereau*, Esterhazy's confession constituted a clear basis for reversal of the court-martial verdict. Esterhazy was reluctant to make his most sensational disclosure at the outset, wishing to secure a more long-term benefit from the book-length memoirs which were to follow and which he looked upon as a potential gold mine. He wished to hold his trump card in reserve for the future, enlivening his newspaper account in the meantime with smaller 'bombshells'. As the days passed, Strong continued to press Esterhazy to tell all he knew and, according to Esterhazy, 'even what I didn't know'. In the grip of a mounting paranoia, Esterhazy feared extradition in his cousin Christian's action for fraud and at the same time imagined that his life was in danger at the hands of the imaginary Dreyfus Syndicate. He became convinced that Strong had betrayed him when he discovered on being introduced to Mrs Rachel Beer, the proprietor of *The Observer*, that she was Jewish.

Continued haggling over the proposed publication ended finally in a heated altercation and complete break between Strong and Esterhazy, in the kind of farcical scene that Esterhazy had a knack for creating. Thomas Fielders shared Esterhazy's interest in boxing and on their first night together he set up a punching bag ('un ballon de boxe') for Esterhazy to demonstrate his French technique. Fielders described Esterhazy as 'a great admirer of "la boxe." He could box in French style, with his feet, and had a most dangerous side kick, but with his hands he was of no consequence, and, as he always crouched and held his head well forward, he would have been a very easy mark for an Englishman or American.' Later, in the course of an animated quarrel with Strong, Esterhazy suddenly assumed his menacing crouch position and challenged Strong: 'You miserable wretch. Defend yourself!' Wary of the Commandant's prowess at *la savate* and his dangerous side kick, Strong threw himself onto a sofa, raised his legs in the air and prudently declined to rise. Esterhazy, in 'a violent rage . . . made a dash at Mr. Strong', Fielders reported, 'and I was compelled to get between them. Nothing happened, however, except that Esterhazy said that he would have no further dealings with Mr. Strong.'[24] Esterhazy, who in the meantime had opened negotiations for publication of his book with Grant Richards, to whom he had been introduced earlier by

Strong, left Fielders's lodgings and moved to a small hotel catering to foreigners in Coventry Street, the Hotel Privatali.

Strong was unwilling to lose the story in which he had so much invested and, without Esterhazy's consent, went ahead with publication in *The Observer* of the Commandant's sensational disclosures, including his 'enormous bombshell'. Esterhazy immediately issued a denial and with the help of a solicitor—Arthur Newton, who had acted for Alfred Taylor at the time of Wilde's trials—won a retraction and £500 in damages from *The Observer*, plus costs. Sherard, who was in London, reported Strong's 'abominable treachery' to Boisandré, who found the 'infamous' conduct of his erstwhile ally 'truly inexplicable' and 'disconcerting'. Sherard and Boisandré immediately came to Esterhazy's defense in public attacks on Strong—by Sherard in an article in *London Life* and Boisandré in the *Libre Parole*. Boisandré came at once to London, where he found Esterhazy, by the latter's account, starving. With Sherard's assistance, more congenial lodgings were found for him in a boarding house at 15a Margaret Street, where he attempted to settle down to compose his memoirs in fulfillment of his commitments to Fayard Frères and Grant Richards. The task, however, proved to be beyond him in his agitated state and Boisandré, together with his colleague from the *Libre Parole*, Gaston Méry, undertook to produce an acceptable text for Fayard based on Esterhazy's rough notes. The resulting 'Les Dessous de l'affaire Dreyfus' was originally intended to appear in ten installments but after the third Fayard suspended publication when Esterhazy sold the same story to the London *Daily Chronicle*. Meanwhile, working from Fayard's galleys, which were brought to London by the faithful Marguerite Pays, Esterhazy supplied Grant Richards with sufficient copy for an English version of his memoirs to appear in book form. After this had been partially set in type, the project predictably collapsed in rancorous disagreement between author and publisher and the book never appeared.

Six months after his arrival in England, to begin a fugitive life in hiding that was to last until his death twenty-five years later, Esterhazy wrote to his lawyer of his precarious existence: 'I live in a moral solitude that is something atrocious . . . alone, alone, a thousand times more alone than in a desert solitude.'[25] Isolated and maddeningly frustrated by his ignorance of English in his desperate struggle for existence, for long periods he contemplated suicide and on at least one occasion narrowly escaped death in a near-successful attempt. 'If I told you that I did not know English on my arrival here', he recalled to a correspondent years later with characteristically mordant humor, 'it is because I did not know A WORD of English, except Water Closet, Whisky and Soda, Steeple Chase, God Save the Queen: remarkable learning but inadequate.'[26] He persisted to the end in stubbornly maintaining an improbable version of events—in which he may ultimately have come to believe—that portrayed him as the real victim in the Dreyfus affair whose only fault was having performed his duty as a soldier in the tradition of his distinguished military family—his father and an uncle having been generals in the French army—and having acted throughout in a manner consistent with his self-image as a 'soldier in the old sense of the word, Catholic, reactionary in the fullest force of the term'.[27]

In his adopted country, Esterhazy remained to the end a stranger in a strange land, living and dying under an assumed name. It was not until three months after his death on 21 May 1923 in the quiet village of Harpenden, where he had been living for the previous fifteen years as the comte de Voilement, that his true identity became known. At the approach of death, he wrote to his daughter Everilda, the object of a rare constancy of affection on his part whom he had not seen since the start of his exile, when she was ten: 'Goodbye, my very dear child. Despite all the misfortunes that have befallen you because of me, do not have too bad a memory of me. I have never deserved the infamous abuse that has overwhelmed me. I have been the victim over and over again of the most frightful, the most ironic bad luck that has ever afflicted a man; I have been pursued by a relentless fate.'[28] Everilda, who with her younger sister Valentine was disowned by her mother's aristocratic family at the time of their father's disgrace, remained faithful to his memory through a life of privation marked by some well-publicized instances in which she rallied with fury in defense of his name. Finally, in old age, she succeeded where he had failed and took her own life by drowning in the Seine.

4

In Aix-les-Bains with his mother, after several weeks at the seaside, Douglas found it difficult to follow recent developments. 'How extraordinary of Strong to go to England just when all the excitement about Dreyfus is on', he wrote to Wilde in late September. 'I am still unshaken in my anti-Dreyfus beliefs, but I must admit that things look rather bad!' Passing through Paris en route to Aix-les-Bains, he had unsuccessfully tried to locate Wilde. Informed at the Hôtel d'Alsace that Wilde was at Nogent, Douglas was on the point of joining him there. 'But luckily I didn't', he informed Wilde, 'as I should have been very disgusted to find no one but Albert [the inn-keeper] & Snatcher [Strong's dog].'[29]

Strong's unauthorized publication of Esterhazy's confession marked the beginning of the end of the once close friendship between Strong and Sherard, who remained steadfastly loyal to Esterhazy. 'Great rows here over Strong selling Esterhazy's confession', Wilde reported to Ross. 'He is violently attacked by his old *confrères*, and Robert Sherard writes terrific diatribes.'[30] Under 'the chilling torpedo-touch of Strong', Maurice Gilbert had been reduced to 'a state of silent fright-ened idiocy'.[31] Even Snatcher became caught up in the mêlée and enjoyed a moment of celebrity when he was featured in a newspaper account. In an interview with a reporter from *L'Aurore* about the attacks on him in the *Libre Parole*, Strong suggested that if the reporter wished to interview Snatcher—'who being of a proud race would certainly be sorry to see his name mixed up with such idle gossip'—the reporter would have to go to Bry-sur-Marne where Snatcher was then living *en pension* because at times he expressed his political opinions too loudly and frightened the children of Strong's neighbors in his Paris apartment house.[32]

From Wilde's close association with Strong, Conybeare mistakenly assumed that the two were in league in the 'abominable treachery' to Esterhazy. On the appearance in the London *Observer* of the disputed article containing Esterhazy's purported confession, Conybeare wrote to Blacker: 'I suppose the communiqué in last Sunday's *Observer* was by Oscar, who is ready to give away his new friend.'[33] As the quarrel continued to attract public attention in the international press, Cony-beare was confirmed in his belief in the complicity of Wilde: 'I am very glad that Strong & O.W. have turned on their friend Esterhazy. You know the proverb about thieves falling out.'[34] Blacker, however, was unable to share Conybeare's satisfaction. In the course of the public quarrel, his name had reappeared in the newspapers and he feared a resumption of the dreaded attacks that had been the source of such anguish. 'We are both very sorry to hear that your nerves are so disturbed', Conybeare commiserated:

I can well understand that they are.... Forgive me for being so frank, but I think you err greatly in taking to heart the libels of Drumont & Co. If you see your way someday to visit condign vengeance on the scoundrels, do so by all means; but pray remember firstly that by touching pitch one risks being defiled; 2° that none of your friends have either seen or, if they have, felt anything but disgust for the authors of such attacks; 3° that revenge is most satisfactory & complete, if the outraged person waits 5 or 10 years before taking it: by that time the authors of iniquity have as a rule gone to the devil their own way, & if not are so far towards it as to need little extra impetus to be given them.... I suppose if I went to Esterhazy with a few pounds in my pocket, I could get the whole truth out of him.[35]

He wrote reassuringly a week later from Oxford: 'Set your mind at rest, for no paper here so far as I know—& I look at all—has mentioned your name. I only saw quoted in the *Siècle* a letter of Esterhazy to Strong asking Est ce encore Blaker (sic) qui a écrit un article dans le Revue Nationale?...I do not think it is of any use to go to this scoundrel till he has exhausted the cash he gets from Grant Richards for his book. When that is ended, it may be worth while for some trusty person to visit him with a five pound note.'[36]

On 3 September, following the death of Lieutenant-Colonel Henry, Mme Dreyfus filed a request for an appeal of her husband's case with the Minister of Justice. The Chambre Criminelle, one of three divisions of the Cour de Cassation (the High Court of Appeal) accepted the case and on 29 October began to hold closed-session hearings for the revision of Dreyfus's court-martial. Called to testify about Esterhazy's purported confession of authorship of the *bordereau*, Strong gave a guarded account of his dealings with him, including how he came to be introduced to Esterhazy by Sherard at the offices of the *Libre Parole*. He testified that he had put Esterhazy in touch with 'un homme de lettres anglais, M. Melmoth [Oscar Wilde], qui connaissait un M. Blaker, ami de Conybeare',[37] and that this was how Esterhazy came to be informed about the plan to publish incriminating documents in an English journal. Esterhazy, invited to return from exile abroad under a safe conduct to appear as a witness, testified at length over three days in late January 1899. When he came to recount his dealings with the now despised Strong, he volunteered, with unmistakable innuendo: 'I should mention that Mr. Strong has as intimate friends, in whose company he is constantly to be found, two high-spirited fellows, Lord Alfred Douglas and Sir Oscar Wilde. Although I have been accused of every vice and crime in the world, I am not as yet guilty of the one that would make such relationships entirely agreeable.'[38] Eventually, on 3 June, the Chambre Criminelle having decided in favor of the appeal, the case was remanded for a second court-martial.

The government took elaborate precautions to ensure the secrecy of the proceedings of the Chambre Criminelle. The men employed at the Imprimerie Nationale were not permitted to leave the premises during the printing of the eighty-three copies that were produced of the two-volume report, each copy separately and intricately coded for identification. Despite these measures, the more sensational testimony, including Strong's, was published illegally in *Le Figaro* in April 1899. The appearance of the secret testimony brought Strong's quarrel with Sherard to a head and a violent altercation followed in which the two came to blows, resulting in their permanent estrangement. Boisandré, in a letter to Esterhazy several years later when the affair was becoming yesterday's news, inquired if he knew anything about their former collaborators, the 'scoundrel' Strong and the 'brave drunkard' Sherard, adding that he was curious to know what had become of them.[39]

5

In February 1900, Blacker received a telegram from Norman Forbes-Robertson, friend of Newcastle and companion of happy bachelor days whom he had not seen for four years, announcing his arrival in Paris. After talking 'about different things' at an initial meeting, the two met again the next day, the conversation continuing for several hours over lunch at the Maison Dorée. The substance of their talk is clear from Blacker's diary entry the following day: '[13 February] Temper with Carrie about reconciliation with Newcastle which I will not have.' Diary entries in the ensuing months trace the course of the patient negotiations conducted by Forbes-Robertson leading eventually to the successful outcome recorded the following July: '[London, 2 July] Went to fetch Norman lunched with Newcastle and saw him for first time since 7 years. . . . [4 July] Met Newcastle for 2nd time lunched at Savoy.'

The initial meetings were followed by an exchange of correspondence, all meticulously noted by Blacker in his diary, culminating in a reunion in Paris in late September when '[26 September] Newcastle and Francis came from London. First time...for many years.' Any lingering awkwardness from the long estrangement was finally dispelled by the duke in a long letter in which he offered the profound apology vainly sought by Wilde on Blacker's behalf years earlier. 'My dear old friend', Linny wrote on his return to London from Paris after several days in Blacker's company:

Everything yesterday went well from start to finish and it is just as well that I did not wait because it is blowing considerably today. What a lovely day yesterday was! The country, bathed in the radiant sunshine, was exquisite, and I never saw Chantilly look so beautiful. It made me quite sad when the daylight faded; the end of a glorious day is always melancholy in the country. I had a good dinner and decent champagne at Boulogne and plenty of time to enjoy them. The lady in charge of the buffet is a mash of mine and she always looks after me very well.... Now, old chap, I want to try to express on paper some things which I could not put into words, I am such a bad hand at expressing my feelings. I want to tell you how deeply I deplore all that you have suffered in the past through me. I never realized what my conduct had done until the other day when you were telling Francis and myself all that you had gone through. Even your troubles over Dreyfus are more or less due to me because if all had been well you would probably not have left England.

I don't know what could have possessed me seven years ago when I allowed a friendship which had always been so dear to me to be so cruelly severed, but I can assure you that during all these years I have always looked back with poignant regret to the time before 1893.

When Norman spoke about a reconciliation I thought, and told him, that it never could be. I said that I wished the past could be undone but that it seemed to me that a friendship, once severed, could never be renewed, that at the best we could only be acquaintances. Although, as I have said, I did not realize the extent of the wrongs you had endured, I knew from Norman that much suffering had been caused you through me, and I felt that it would be impossible for you ever to forgive this, that the remembrance of it must always place a barrier between us.

That I have been mistaken, that you, out of your great generosity, have shown me my mistake, and have proved by a kindness, which I have never deserved but shall certainly never forget, that our renewed friendship is as strong as the severed one of the past, is a cause of the deepest rejoicing.[40]

Although Linny's long-sought apology effectively sealed his reconciliation with Blacker ('the greatest friendship of my life'), memory of the painful episode was an occasional cause of lingering regret. 'It is too bad that you should suffer so much in spirit when in England', he wrote several years later, 'and I cannot but feel that I am in some way to blame for this through the terrible misunderstanding which separated us for so many wretched years and which caused you so much pain.'[41] When in 1906 the Dreyfus affair again became the focus of public attention, with the final judicial proceedings in the rehabilitation of the unjustly condemned officer, Linny cautioned Blacker, 'for goodness sake don't make an ass of yourself again over the Dreyfus affair; leave it severely alone and avoid Paris if there is the slightest chance of being dragged into it'.[42]

A further means of escape for Linny from the uncongenial atmosphere of Clumber was his acquisition in 1904 of Forest Farm, close to Windsor and Eton, thereafter his preferred residence. A near neighbor was the American author Howard Sturgis, a fellow Old Etonian, whose home, Qu'Acre, bordering Windsor Great Park, was at the time the center of a discriminating coterie of friends that included Henry James and Edith Wharton. Sturgis's novel *Belchamber*, on which he had worked for ten years, appeared in the year of Linny's purchase of Forest Farm. Set in the early 1890s, with an all-Etonian cast, the similarities between the real-life story of Linny, 'the little duke' remembered for his 'saintliness', and the fictional life of the 'little marquis' of Belchamber, known as Sainty, are sufficiently striking to suggest this to be more than mere coincidence.[43] Percy Lubbock in his *Diary of Arthur Christopher Benson*, an Old Etonian, writing of the 1890s, notes that, 'there were in those days two familiar houses on which a great deal of Eton converged in holiday-time . . . often with Howard Sturgis, a joint-host'.[44] Although there is no evidence of retiring Linny's presence on such occasions, as duke of Newcastle he was at the time a high-profile figure in Eton circles. It seems likely that rumors of his scandalous charges against his 'most excellent of pals' Carlos Blacker would inevitably have fed the gossip of the holiday-time gatherings of 'a great deal of Eton'.

The novel traces the misfortunes of well-meaning Sainty, crippled by a fall from his pony when a child and his distant, ambitious young wife Cissy, who finds her frail, physically handicapped husband 'repulsive' in their unconsummated marriage. Sainty's worldly, much admired cousin Claude occupies an influential place in the lives of the 'little marquis' and his mindless younger brother Arthur (Etonians all) reminiscent of the role played by Carlos Blacker in the lives of the 'little duke' and his profligate younger brother Francis. In love with impoverished Claude, Cissy has a child by him (accepted with full knowledge as his own by Sainty). Following the death of the child, however, Cissy is thwarted in her plan to leave Sainty and join Claude, who abandons her without a word to marry a wealthy heiress. 'Blackguard! Blackguard!' moans Cissy in stifled rage at the unexpected betrayal, echoing what may well have been the anguished cry of Blacker's 'unfortunate mistress' in like circumstances described by Wilde. In self-imposed exile in France, penniless and deeply in debt, Blacker, according to Wilde following their breakup, deserted his mistress 'to get engaged to a rich American girl. Never wrote to her, never did anything.'[45] Earlier in the novel, Claude had passed on his beautiful chorus-girl mistress Topsy Muggins to Sainty's younger brother and heir Arthur who, like Lord Francis Hope and Madcap May Yohe, takes her for his wife. Despairing Sainty has a prophetically haunting vision of feckless Arthur 'cutting down the trees and selling the books and pictures [at Belchamber] to buy more horses and lose bigger bets'. The dark, unpromising future awaiting 'the great historic house' of Belchamber is a foreshadowing of the ultimate fate of the great ducal house of Clumber.

Arthur Christopher Benson, like his friend Blacker a prolific diarist, describes an occasion at the Athenaeum on 29 April 1904, when 'H.J. [Henry James] and I talked of Howard's Belchamber' shortly after its appearance. Quoting at length James's incisive critical comments on the trials of 'the poor rat' Sainty, Benson notes in conclusion: 'I think I have got this marvellous tirade nearly correct.'[46] Two weeks earlier, an entry in Blacker's diary of questionable decipherability (a challenge to the best efforts of the shorthand transcribers) may possibly refer to the novel: '[Paris, 15 April 1904] Bad news about Bel[more?] from [H R?].'

10

'He Was a Great Genius. His Familiar Talk Was Golden'

I

Douglas's description of Wilde in his final years ('before he began to break up'), as 'a sort of show for the bohemians of Paris; the sport and mock of the Boulevard', recalls Proust's baron de Charlus—for whom Wilde served as a model—steering the bulk of his huge body, at times unsteadily in Wilde's case, through the streets of Paris, drawing in his wake 'sodomist outcasts' and other social pariahs, creating the spectacle that caused Stuart Merrill, Marcel Schwob, and most of Wilde's former French friends to shun him.[1] Even the devotedly loyal Robbie Ross and Reggie Turner tended to keep their distance, preferring to maintain contact through correspondence despite Wilde's pleas for their company. After rising about noon, according to Douglas, Wilde would customarily walk from the Hôtel d'Alsace, through the Louvre, to the Café de la Paix or the Grand Café, where he would drink apéritifs before going to lunch. In the afternoons, Douglas knew he could always find him at either the Café Julien or the Calisaya Bar, where he would drink until dinner time; then, in the evening, he would go 'where his friends might lead him, and some of them led him to pretty dreadful places'.[2] Edgar Saltus, a friend from his days of triumph in London, recalled seeing him in Paris in his last years when 'he looked like a drunken coachman'.[3] The pathos of Wilde at this time is brilliantly evoked in Ricardo Opisso's 1898 sketch of the social outcast in the company of Toulouse-Lautrec and Yvette Guilbert at the Moulin de la Galette, Montmartre.

Wilde described the Calisaya, an American bar on the Boulevard des Italiens, as 'the literary resort of myself and my friends: and we all gather there at five o'clock—Moréas, and La Jeunesse, and all the young poets'.[4] Among this company, Ernest La Jeunesse, to whom Strong awarded the title 'King of the Boulevard', provided unfailing entertainment.[5] Wilde had been 'greatly fascinated' by his *L'Imitation de notre-maître Napoléon*, which was among the books he had requested to have waiting for him on his release from prison and one of the first he read. Fantastic and unpredictable, La Jeunesse could also be 'more intolerable than ever', as Wilde reported to Ross on one occasion.[6] Robert Sherard considered La Jeunesse's essay on Wilde, published in the *Revue Blanche* two weeks after Wilde's death, to be 'the most valuable account of his last years which exists ... a pure gem of literature.'

2

In a diary entry for 18 November 1900, Blacker, then in Freiburg, noted 'Recommenced writing children's diary.' He had begun keeping a daily journal for Pip on the day he was born (8 December 1895) and continued it intermittently until what proved to be the final entry, for 25 November 1900, which breaks off in mid-sentence ('This is dictated by Pip on Monday 26th November 4.50 after—'), never to be resumed. Robbie Ross was at the time in the south of France with his mother when he received word from Reggie Turner that Wilde was dying. Before starting for Paris, Ross apparently notified Blacker by telegram, which may account for the abrupt interruption of Pip's diary. The entry in Blacker's own diary the following day, 27 November, states without preliminary, 'Left for Paris with Carrie.' While silent as to the reason for the sudden departure, indications are that Carrie was not made aware of the real object of the journey. The couple had for some time been considering finding an apartment in Paris, and on their arrival they 'went to see apartment in afternoon'. No other purpose is noted during their first three days in Paris. On the third day, the day of Wilde's death, Blacker's diary entry reads in part: '[30 November] Oscar Wilde's dying: ... At Brentano's man told me that Oscar was ill.'

Since Wilde's unforgivable act of treachery to Blacker, Carrie had remained more bitterly opposed than ever to her husband's having anything to do with him, an attitude in which she had been confirmed and fortified not only by Blacker himself but by the unanimous concurrence of those of their friends familiar with the circumstances of the breakup. If Blacker had in fact already known from Ross of Wilde's hopeless condition, he apparently had not shared the information with Carrie, who seems to have learned of it first in the chance encounter at the English booksellers, Brentano's. Whether or not Blacker used the opening to broach the idea to Carrie of going to see the dying man, it is clear that the subject had lost none of its contentious quality. That evening, as Blacker's diary entry for the date continues: 'Carrie while dressing very excited because I would not argue with her. Scissors.' The single word 'scissors' in the context appears to be a reference to a memorable quarrel between the two that had occurred less than a month after their marriage: '[2 March 1895] Slapping incident . . . serious friction . . . Carrie throwing scissors with violence.' They may have been unaware that Wilde had died earlier that afternoon.

With Wilde's death, Carrie's antipathy towards him appears to have softened. The following day, Blacker noted '[1 December] went to see . . . Oscar's body. In afternoon took him some violets from the children . . . very depressed.' The sight of the deathbed stirred old memories and bitterness gave way to tears of pity and regret. 'When I saw him on his bed', Blacker wrote to Wilde's brother-in-law Otho Holland, 'and considered the old days, and the sufferings he had endured and had caused others to suffer, I broke down and cried as I am almost ashamed to have cried.'[7] Blacker in tears at Wilde's deathbed recalls the lines from William Cory's *Heraclitus* ('I wept, as I remembered, how often you and I / Had tired the sun with talking and sent him down the sky'),[8] paraphrased by Wilde in his nostalgic letter to Blacker following his release from prison ('we tired many a moon with talk, and drank many a sun to rest with wine and words').[9] In an earlier letter to Holland, Blacker had written:

Though I had fallen out with Oscar Wilde and had not seen him for two years, I went to see his remains and I took him some flowers in his children's name, that he might bear something that came from them into his grave. It was all very terribly sad, for I had known him for many years and it was too pitiful to see how he had fallen, and what he had suffered.[10]

Writing again a week later, he added, 'I had known him for 20 years and for many years up to 1893 saw him daily. I need hardly therefore say what pain his fate has been to me. After 1895 I saw him a counted number of times, and then he treated me with gross cruelty and injustice and we parted. I always hoped that he would mend and that we would meet again, and therefore this final severance under the circumstances has grieved me deeply.'[11] Touching upon the regrettable meeting at which he had disclosed Panizzardi's information to Wilde, he wrote:

It was at [Constance's] request that I again saw Oscar in March 1898, though for her sake I think it would have been better if no 'rapprochement' had ever existed. She had invited him to Nervi, but he chose to go elsewhere with his former friend and source of his calamities. After thus returning to his vomit (forgive the expression), it was obvious that he was hopeless, and beyond redemption. However, I went to see him, as I say because your sister asked me to do so, and eventually when your letter reached him announcing her death he at once telegraphed to me to go and see him which I did.[12]

At the Hôtel d'Alsace, the undertaker, Randolph Gesling, was concerned that decomposition would begin very rapidly and he advised Ross to have the remains placed in the coffin as soon as possible. 'At 8:30 in the evening [1 December] the men came to screw it down', Ross informed Adey. 'An unsuccessful photograph of Oscar was taken by Maurice Gilbert at my request, the flashlight did not work properly.'[13] Turner recalled years later that 'Oscar's hands were decently laid by his side and his whole body covered with a white sheet . . . and only his head was showing. I have a photograph taken by flashlight by Maurice Gilbert on his death-bed—not very distinct but one clearly sees the placid face.'[14] Like Turner, Carlos Blacker kept by him to the end of his life Gilbert's blurred photograph of the shrouded figure of Wilde ready for burial, bearing the violets Blacker had brought in the name of the children.[15]

Although 'a good many people saw Oscar on his deathbed,' according to Turner, who 'at no time was . . . absent from the hotel & was nearly always in the room', he could recall only a few by name thirty-seven years later: 'André Gide (I feel sure but could not swear), Ernest La Jeunesse, [Léonard] Sarluis, Carlos Blacker, & many others whose names I don't recall at the present moment'.[16] Turner was mistaken about Gide who by his own account was in Algeria when he learned of Wilde's death in the newspapers.

On the morning of the funeral, Blacker noted, '[3 December] Out with Carrie at 9 to St. Germain des Prés and asked about Oscar's funeral.' Ross placed a laurel wreath at the head of the coffin inscribed, 'A tribute to his literary achievements and distinction', and tied inside it the names of 'those who had shown kindness to him during or after his imprisonment'. Unable to resolve the dilemma of relinquishing either his anonymity or his place on the wreath as the oldest of Wilde's friends among those named, Blacker chose 'by special request' to be included simply as 'a friend who wished to be known as "C.B."'[17] While consenting to be thus identified for the purpose of the laurel wreath, Blacker continued to guard his anonymity. In a detailed account of Wilde's death days later to his intimate friend More Adey, Ross, constrained by Blacker's wish, reported that around Wilde's neck was 'the blessed rosary which you gave me, and on the breast a Franciscan medal given me by one of the nuns, a few flowers placed there by myself and an anonymous friend who had brought some on behalf of the children'.[18] Following the funeral Mass at Saint-Germain-des-Prés, which Blacker assured Otho Holland had been 'well attended', and burial in the cemetery of Bagneux, Ross joined Blacker for dinner, and the two '[3 December] had a long talk about Oscar'. Before returning to Freiburg the next day, Blacker '[4 December] went to see Ross and said goodbye. Turner there also.'

Blacker had long been in the habit of confiding totally without reserve in his most intimate friend, W. R. Paton, from whom he kept no secrets and who, like Blacker, had known Wilde for twenty years. Profoundly shaken by his visits to the deathbed and the sight of Wilde—ravaged by 'how he had fallen, and what he had suffered'—Blacker wrote of the lacerating ordeal to Paton. Alarmed by the extreme agony of mind revealed in Blacker's letter, Paton pronounced it 'one of the most terrible letters' he had ever read, while citing the evident 'real affection' that Wilde, 'for all his faults', inspired in his friends. As the letter was 'sacred' and 'not meant for publicity', Paton asked that it be destroyed, as it apparently was by James Bryce to whom he sent it.[19] Blacker's more muted response four years earlier to the death of his well-loved father, from whom he had been estranged by his troubles ('[6 April 1896] Papa died. Regrets—remorse—') was in marked contrast to the effect reported to Paton of his visits to Wilde's deathbed. While the exact content of the missing letter remains open to speculation, the circumstances—combined with Paton's compelling description and what followed—strongly suggest that Blacker ('always the truest of friends'), grief-stricken and overcome with remorse and guilt for his abandonment of a cherished friend who 'had made many sacrifices' for him in the past, had been moved to bare his soul in a torment of regret. His silence regarding his lamentable failure to respond to Wilde's repeated appeals to see him had added vitriol to the anger and disgust with which Wilde's apparently unprovoked act of treachery to a trusting friend came to be viewed in Blacker's circle.

On receipt of Blacker's letter, Paton, as if by way of amends for the injury done Wilde by his earlier letter to James Bryce at the time of the breakup between Wilde and Blacker, immediately sent it on to Bryce, with a message for Asquith and the other recipients of his previous letter. 'You will remember my having once written to you about Oscar Wilde', Paton wrote:

& that I mentioned to you his conduct to my friend, who was his friend & marriage trustee. I cannot resist my impulse to send you this letter, which I received today from my friend. It will be obvious to you that it is not meant for publicity & is sacred. It is one of the most terrible letters I have ever read. Please destroy the letter after reading it, but mention to Mr. Asquith & others to whom you communicated my former letter that he was a man who with all his faults created real affection in his friends. You would be doing me a kindness if you would send me any obituary notices of him worth sending that appear.

WRP

He was a great genius. His familiar talk was golden.[20]

The 'real affection' cited by Paton that Wilde inspired in his friends proved to be undying in Blacker, as shown in diary entries following Wilde's death: '[12 December 1901] Went to Oscar's grave for first time'; '[5 January 1902] To Oscar's grave 2nd time'; '[6 January 1902] . . . to Oscar's grave 3rd time'; '[2 March 1902] To Bagneux for 4 [blotted by ink]'; '[7 April 1902] Bicycled . . . to Oscar's tomb 5th time'; '[12 April 1903] Bicycled to Oscar's tomb 7th time'; '[3 April 1904] Easter Sunday . . . Bicycled to Bagneux 8th time'; '[17 April 1904] Out bicycling . . . and back by Bagneux'; '[29 September 1906] Bicycled to Oscar's grave. Beautiful day.' The last of the quoted entries was made on Blacker's return to Paris from Oxford where a week earlier there had been an emotional parting from Pip, then ten, and Robin nine, who remained in England at Cothill boarding school ('[12 September 1906] Robin first put on his school clothes and abandoned his sailor suits'; '[14 September 1906] Robin photographed in new clothes'; '[17 September 1906] Carrie, Pip and Robin and I bicycled up to Cothill.... Pip much more sad than Robin who said of his mother that he loved her so much'). Preparations for the parting and the separation that followed are marked by frequent periods of depression on Blacker's part ('[5 January 1907] Very depressed, spoke to Carrie and Albertine [unidentified] about suicide'). Although the diary received only sporadic attention before it was abandoned altogether on 25 January 1907, one of the final entries indicates that Wilde was not far from Blacker's thoughts: '[12 January 1907] Read "De Profundis" before dinner.'

A more unexpected demonstration of Blacker's undying 'real affection' for Wilde, however, was to take place at the time of his death years later, in 1928.

3

The marriage of Carlos and Carrie was a long and happy one. In a note appended to a letter from Carlos on the eve of her arrival in England from America for their wedding in 1895—among the letters Carrie could not bring herself to destroy at the time of her husband's death—she wrote: 'The last letter I ever received from my beloved Carlos, on my arrival at Queenstown for our marriage—From this time to the end we were never parted for a day & so no other letters were ever exchanged between us.'[21] The death of their eighteen-year-old son Robin, killed in action in World War I, was a time of intense sorrow for them. Present in Torquay at the time to offer comfort to the grieving parents were faithful friends George Bernard Shaw and Robbie Ross. 'The news arrived this morning', Shaw reported to Robin's brother Pip, then on active duty in France, 'and by good luck Robbie Ross had arrived the night before, just the right man at the right time.... Robbie has been worth his weight in gold.'[22] The previous year, Shaw had presented the first draft of his highly controversial *Common Sense About the War* to Blacker, with the following inscription: 'It was written on the roof of The Hydro at Torquay and discussed as it proceeded with Carlos Blacker at Vane Tower there, as I seized every opportunity of spending the afternoon in his very congenial company. To him accordingly, I present this "scrap of paper" G. Bernard Shaw. 29th October 1914.'[23] Among Robin's effects found after he was killed was a notebook in which he had recorded his thoughts and impressions after leaving England for France a month before his death 'to partake in that universal lapse into barbarism and inhumanity (not to say imbecility and madness) which we call the Fight for Freedom and Peace against tyranny and militarism'. With a presciently dark vision of what was to come, reflecting the views of Shaw and his father, he noted on 30 August: 'There is one subject on which I try not to let my mind dwell as it irritates and disturbs me: that I, a human being, eighteen years old, the product of untold ages of evolution in humanity, should be in this place with the sole intent of putting to death other human beings—equally civilized, with similar ideals and similar beliefs.'[24]

Three years later, following the sudden death of Ross—'the very genius of friendship personified', according to his nephew-in-law in a letter to Blacker at the time—Ross's housekeeper, Nellie Burton, informed Blacker that 'his ashes are to be taken to Paris, & buried with his friend [Oscar Wilde].'[25] Ross had directed in his will that his remains:

shall be cremated at Golders Green Crematorium with the ordinary burial offices of the Catholic and Roman Church. And I direct that my ashes shall be placed in a suitable urn and taken to Paris and buried in the tomb of the said Oscar Fingal O'Flahertie Wills Wilde. If however it should prove impossible to obtain the licence of the necessary authorities for this I direct that my ashes shall be scattered in Père Lachaise.[26]

After a lengthy delay, Ross's wishes were finally realized thirty-two years later. In 1950, on the fiftieth anniversary of Wilde's death, his tomb in Père Lachaise cemetery was opened and Ross's ashes were placed inside.

Several years after the death of both his parents, Pip Blacker, confirming his mother's observation on their long and happy marriage, attested to the extraordinary bond that existed between them throughout their life together: 'My father and mother did not separate for a single night from their marriage in early 1895 to the date of his death in 1928.'[27] In view of the remarkably close relationship, it is all the more surprising that following Blacker's death at his home in Dinard, his devoted wife Carrie, acting on his expressed wish, consigned his body to the care of a single attendant who brought it to Père Lachaise cemetery for cremation. Waiting at the cemetery for the arrival of the body were one of Blacker's oldest friends, Italian Count Horace Guicciardi, and his son of the same name—Blacker's godson—who described what took place in a lengthy letter to Pip the same day:

We were at quarter to nine at the Père Lachaise but it is at nine only that the car bringing your Father arrived.

A young man accompanied the body and attended to everything. As soon as arrived the coffin was taken to a vaulted passage where it was opened and we saw your Father looking very peaceful and very much like himself: his complexion was only rather grayish. Both my father and me were painfully impressed when they took him out and placed him in a small wooden coffin and then on an elevator which brought him upstairs to the furnace. We went round the building and arrived to the furnace where the coffin was lying on a little wagon. The furnace was opened and the wagon slided into the fire. The door was closed and a violent noise of wood burning was heard.

We retired in a hall where people are generally waiting and everybody left us for an hour. It was foggy outside and very cold. After an hour the young man and some attendants came back and we went to the furnace again. It was open and the little wagon came out. On the red hot iron plate covered by an [illegible] sheet were lying the bones of the body on a bed of ashes and incompletely consumed wood particles. They let it cool and with a rake and a brush the wood pieces were sorted from the rest: bones and ashes were placed in an urn and for five minutes we waited until it was all cool. Then the remains were placed in a marble box a string was placed round it and sealed. Under the string the plate with the name which was on the coffin was inserted.

The marble box was carried on a little stretcher to the columbarium and placed in box number 1458. The columbarium box was closed and cemented: it was finished at 10.25 A.M.—It was the young man of the company charged with the whole thing who signed all papers.

When we left the fog was disappearing and the sky was clear and blue. The all ceremony was very sad for we thought of poor Carlos: my father of his old friend and me of that charming godfather of mine whom I loved and admired so much, but we admired him once more for that happy thought of his to be buried in that way. How sad it is to leave a friend of yours in the damp ground feeling that it will slowly disintegrate . . . here it had completely disappeared and his remembrance only was left so much more living and comforting: your father was right.

I give you all these details but I think you want to have them. I am glad nor your mother nor you were there for there were long and painful waiting.[28]

The failure of Carrie and Pip to accompany the body to Père Lachaise and witness the final disposition of Blacker's remains is unexplained. It may possibly have been out of deference on the part of Carrie, a devout Catholic, to the Church's disapproval of cremation, a ban not lifted until 1963.

As related by Blacker's godson, the urn containing Blacker's ashes was sealed in box number 1458 of the columbarium at Père Lachaise. 'Splendid in ashes', his remains, however, were destined not to remain long in the shadow of Wilde's celebrated tomb by Jacob Epstein in the neighboring cemetery division, among the most visited sites in Père Lachaise. Four months later, on 28 June 1928, at the direction of 'la famille de M. Carlos Blacker',[29] the urn containing the ashes was removed from the columbarium and, without further explanation, transferred to the American Cemetery at Saint-Germain-en-Laye.[30] The conventional setting of the American Cemetery may in Carrie's eyes have seemed a more fitting final resting place for her beloved Carlos than the shadow of Wilde's tomb, scene of an ongoing controversy since its unveiling in August 1914 over the figure of what Epstein called his 'winged demon angel'.[31]

Epilogue

In February 1940, with the German occupation of Paris impending, Paul Desachy, author of two seminal works on the Dreyfus affair, *Répertoire de l'affaire Dreyfus: 1894–1899* and *Bibliographie de l'affaire Dreyfus* (1905), noted in a memorandum an archive of manuscripts relating to Major Esterhazy of particular interest to him, described in a catalogue of the dealer Maurice Dussarp.[1] In July 1908, pursuant to an agreement with Desachy, Esterhazy had ceded to him all rights to his papers subject to the condition that Desachy leave them to the Bibliothèque Nationale, which he eventually did.[2] For an unknown reason, Desachy does not appear to have gained access to the archive which was still in the possession of Maurice Dussarp in the summer of 1946. I was working at the time with the American Delegation to the Paris Peace Conference, quartered in the Hôtel Meurice, from where it was a short walk down the rue du Mont Thabor to Maurice Dussarp's door at number 36. Having returned to Princeton the previous March with the intention of graduating, after a three-year absence in the Army, my search for a subject for the required thesis led me to Maurice Dussarp. In several unforgettable conversations with him, his passion for the Dreyfus case, which had fired his youth in the early years of the affair and in which he had retained a lively, well-informed interest, proved contagious and I acquired from him at the time the archive that had been the subject of Paul Desachy's memo. To this in the course of subsequent years has been added the accumulation of Blacker Papers (BP) on which the present work is largely based. All BP files are presently held in the Hand's Cove Library, Shoreham, Vermont.

The most rewarding aspect of such a long-sustained interest, not surprisingly, has been the many valued friendships formed in pursuit of it. Among descendants of individuals active in the Dreyfus affair to whom I am indebted, both for long years of friendship and for perspectives on the case developed over a lifetime, are the three grandchildren of Carlos Blacker: Carmen, Thetis, and John Blacker, all now deceased. Similarly, the late France Beck, esteemed collaborator and dear friend, whose lively interest in the case throughout her life was literally a birthright inherited from her grandfathers, Mathieu Dreyfus and Joseph Reinach, and from the latter's brother, Salomon Reinach, three of the most prominent figures in the affair. I am grateful as well to Merlin Holland, grandson of Oscar Wilde and editor of his collected letters, for our long and valued friendship as well as for his permission to quote from the letters of both his grandparents in the present work. For permission to quote from the letters of William Roger Paton, I am indebted to his grandson, David Paton, as well as for his friendship and generous hospitality. Both Charles Dreyfus, grandson of Alfred Dreyfus, and Colonel du Paty de Clam, grandson of Colonel Mercier du Paty de Clam, grew up with the affair which shaped the course of both their lives. I am grateful for the memorable hours spent in the company of each of them.

I owe a special debt to Olga Atkinson and Pamela Dunmore, multi-talented experts in the Shorthand Analysis Department at Pitman's Central College in London, for their brilliant work in transcribing the many hundreds of pages of Carlos Blacker's diary that are written in an early form of Pitman shorthand in which he was self-taught. Until the transcription, the shorthand pages had remained locked in an unreadable script from the time they were written almost a century earlier.

In 1928, the year of Blacker's death, Dulau & Company Limited of London published a valuable catalogue of *A Collection of Original Manuscripts Letters & Books of Oscar Wilde*, including the three letters from OW to Robbie Ross that contained the 'unimportant omissions' later made by Rupert Hart-Davis in the 1962 edition of the *Letters*, 'to avoid giving pain to descendants'.[3] The letters are only partially reproduced in the Dulau catalogue and the name of Carlos Blacker has in each instance been deleted. It was not until seventy-two years later that the omissions were restored in the 2000 edition of the *Letters*, with the result that the three redacted letters were finally printed as Wilde wrote them. While the restored letters present Wilde's version of the bitter breakup with Blacker, it was not until the transcription of the shorthand diaries that the surrounding circumstances of the painful episode became known, shedding light on the 'never-fully-explained ending of [Blacker's] friendship with Wilde', as the mystery was noted in Sotheby's catalogue at the time of the sale of a collection of Blacker's papers in 1986. The end of the 'ancient friendship' is described in a preliminary article of mine titled 'Oscar Wilde and the Dreyfus Affair', published in the journal *Victorian Studies* in 1997.

The present work has benefited greatly over the years from the help and support of many individuals and institutions. I have relied heavily on the extensive Oscar Wilde collection at the William Andrews Clark Memorial Library, University of California at Los Angeles, and wish to express my thanks to the successive librarians there, Thomas Wright and Bruce Whiteman, and to Carol Reid Briggs for their help. I am grateful as well to Michael Halls, King's College Library, Cambridge; to Michael Bott, Keeper of Rare Books & MSS, Reading University Library; to William Joyce, the Princeton University Library; to Ralph Franklin, director of the Beinecke Library at Yale; to William Bond and Roger Stoddard at the Houghton Library, Harvard; to John Bidwell and Herbert Cahoon at the Pierpont Morgan Library; and to librarians and staff members of the Bibliothèque Nationale, the British Library, the Bodleian, and the British National Archives for valuable help. I owe a special debt of gratitude to Pauline Robison and Martine Prieto for their exceptional help. For insightful comments and criticism on early drafts of the manuscript, I am indebted to Robert L. Hoffman, Katherine Bucknell, and David Levin.

I am immensely grateful as well to the following, named in alphabetical order, from whose interest and help I have benefited: Louis Begley, Antoinette Blum, Maureen Borland, Thomas Clark, Edward Colman, Roy Davids, Michel Drouin, Richard Ellmann, R. F. Foster, Mavis Gallant, Rupert Hart-Davis, Jeanne Hugueney, H. Montgomery Hyde, Mary Hyde, Norman L. Kleeblatt, Simone de Lassus, Michael Loewe, Cecily Maguire, George Maguire, Robert Maguire, Marcus McCorison, Ann Louise Strong, Stanley Weintraub, Douglas Johnson, Jacques de Spoelberch, and Patrick Viard. For the unfailing help and encouragement throughout the long history of this work, I am forever grateful to Pauline Maguire.

For a work so long in progress, inevitably the names of others who have been of help have been omitted through a regrettable lapse of memory, for which I offer my profound apology.

Appendix: Carlos Blacker's 'Private and Confidential' Memorandum on the Dreyfus Affair

Carlos Blacker's diary indicates that he 'commenced writing about Dreyfus affair' in Freiburg on 27 May 1899, apparently at the urging of Salomon Reinach, and completed his account two days later. The previous August, Reinach had introduced a passionate Dreyfusard to Blacker—'a French scholar of great repute . . . M. Brunot, professor of mediaeval French at the Sorbonne', recommending him warmly as 'the most trustworthy of men and the most discreet of advisers'. Blacker evidently provided Brunot a copy of his memorandum and on 22 July 1899 noted receipt of 'letter from M. Brunot asking me for more on the account of Dreyfus affair', in response to which, a week later, Blacker 'sent letter to M. Brunot about my experiences in Dreyfus affair'. When, the following month, Brunot asked Blacker to allow him to testify as a witness at Dreyfus's second court-martial at Rennes about the contents of the memorandum, Blacker declined. The memorandum exists in two states, exhibiting slight variations, one written prior to the release from prison of Colonel Picquart on 9 June 1899 and the other following his release a short time later. What follows is the later version, with some omitted words from the earlier draft shown in square brackets. The reference to 'the Club here' in the opening paragraph is to Freiburg, where Schwartzkoppen had spent the three years preceding his assignment to the German Embassy in Paris in 1891.

(Private & Confidential)

On the 25th of October 1897 [a gentleman] an officer came into the Club here saying that he had just seen the Commanding General & had heard him make a very interesting statement.

The General had told him that he had that morning received a letter from Schwartzkoppen in Paris, saying that he <u>knew</u> Dreyfus to be innocent, and that a terrible mistake had been made, that he was weighed down by the load of this secret, & that he intended to proclaim that Dreyfus was innocent, as soon as he was relieved of his post as Military Attaché in Paris.

Schwartzkoppen had been quartered here for three years before going to Paris, & thus had quite naturally written to his former General as a friend.

A few days after this I saw in the papers that Schwartzkoppen had been withdrawn from Paris.

On the 7th February 1898 I went [with my family] on a long visit to Paris. This was the first day of the Zola trial & Paris was in a ferment.

I immediately went to see my old & [very] intimate friend Panizzardi knowing that I would learn the whole truth from him, for it was evident that three beings alone knew the whole & entire truth, namely God, & the two Military Attachés.

I found Panizzardi very excited & distressed. He seemed aged & worn, & he unbosomed himself to me without [a moment's] hesitation, seeming to find [relief] comfort in so doing. He told me at once that Esterhazy was the guilty man, & that Dreyfus was perfectly innocent.

I then asked him why the error was not immediately addressed, & why Esterhazy was so protected.

He then explained that Esterhazy by his marriage had been brought into contact with the exalted members of the army. He had availed himself of this to acquire secret & important information in an informal manner, as for instance after dinner or out shooting, or on other similar occasions when the intimate nature of the opportunity served.

In this way & assisted by his unrivalled astuteness he had been able to make this information of use to himself without his informants knowing to what use he was putting it, namely communicating it to Schwartzkoppen against remuneration.

Consequently Esterhazy if prosecuted, would probably implicate Generals & superior officers who had at the worst been indiscreet but whom Esterhazy would probably denounce as worse. In short, what had been told to him in a spirit of friendship, would be given the complexion of treachery. Therefore it was that Esterhazy was protected & covered by those whom it concerned.

Neither Schwartzkoppen or Panizzardi, had ever seen or had anything to do with Dreyfus either directly, or indirectly or in any way whatever.

Esterhazy's treachery commenced in 1893 when he presented himself one day at Schwartzkoppen's rooms & gave him to understand that they could be mutually useful to each other. Schwartzkoppen however was circumspect & on his guard because of the extraordinarily secret information which he offered to reveal.

He thought he might be dealing with a counter-spy. He however accepted & paid for the information first offered. It was verified subsequently as correct, & from that time forward until November 1896 Esterhazy brought Schwartzkoppen all & every secret information he could procure. Schwartzkoppen in turn paid him a regular monthly allowance, & when a document of great & particular value was offered he paid something in excess of this allowance.

In this way Schwartzkoppen secured some 140 [documents] pieces of value, & in some cases of such value that some 30 of them were considered as of supreme interest & importance. Hence he was on several occasions congratulated by his war office in Berlin for the singular services which his zeal & vigilance rendered to his country.

Two characteristics invariably attended Esterhazy's visits to Schwartzkoppen's rooms in the Rue de Lille. The first that he always accompanied the delivery of information by stating the 'provenance' saying 'this piece I got from General X, or this other from Colonel Y' & so on.

The second characteristic was that he never failed to try to convince Schwartzkoppen that he was betraying the secrets of his country, not for the sake of gold, but because he had a deeply rooted hatred for everything that had to do with the French army & particularly its chiefs.

'Imbécile et canaille' fools & scoundrels were the epithets which he invariably made use of [when speaking of the] to qualify Generals & superior officers [to malign & traduce them], & he always had some anecdote ready to show that they were either fools, or scoundrels, or both.

He would say that his regret, his life-long regret was that he was not in the service of the German Army. That, he would say was an army indeed worth serving in, but since it was impossible for him to gratify this wish & ambition he nevertheless comforted himself by [working for] serving it as he did! The [remuneration] money he said was ['pour rendre des services à ces imbéciles et canailles'] to render services to those idiots & scoundrels, in order to coax their confidences, as money he said could do anything in the French army.

But Schwartzkoppen never shook hands with him!

I asked Panizzardi whether it could be considered right to make use of such services. He answered saying that it was wrong to approach a man & bribe him to obtain secret information, but that if a French officer offered his services, it was not only right but even his duty to accept them. For instance if a French officer offered to sell a copy of the treaty of alliance between France & Russia to an officer of the Triple Alliance, it was obviously his duty in his country's interest, to avail himself of the opportunity to secure such information.

Be this as it may Esterhazy continued to regularly betray the secrets of his country to [Schwartzkoppen] Germany from 1893 to 1896.

In September 1894 he wrote the now famous 'bordereau', & together with the documents enumerated therein left them with the porter of the German Embassy.

This man an Alsacian was in the pay of the French [secret intelligence department] War Office.

He abstracted the bordereau, tore it up, & took it to the French intelligence department of the War Office. The other documents enumerated in the bordereau were duly delivered to Schwartzkoppen & are now in his possession in Berlin together with the other [the 140 odd] documents he obtained from Esterhazy.

The porter at the Embassy tore up the bordereau for the following reasons. A document taken from the German Embassy was a document taken from German territory, & as such might lead to diplomatic complications. This indeed as it happens very nearly did occur.

By however tearing it up, it was made to appear as if Schwartzkoppen having read the letter had torn it up & thrown it into the waste paper basket, whence it might have fallen into the hands of some one outside the Embassy & thus out of the precincts of German territory.

The bordereau [in fragments as you know] having found its way to the War Office, was as you know attributed to Dreyfus. How & why this terrible mistake was made you will have read in the papers.[1]

Panizzardi told me that he had never himself had any relations with Esterhazy, but Schwartzkoppen both as friend & member of the triple alliance always communicated the important secrets he obtained from Esterhazy, without however mentioning 'his man's' name. [Hence Schwartzkoppen's excited visits to Panizzardi when the fear arose that 'his man' was caught.]

When however in October 1894 it commenced to be known that a French officer had been arrested for treachery to his country, Schwartzkoppen in great trepidation went to see Panizzardi & told him that he feared 'his man' was caught.

Two days afterwards it transpired that the officer in question was a Jew & he again went to see Panizzardi in order to tell him that 'his man' was not caught & that there evidently had been some other traitor at work, but that he knew nothing about him.

And so poor Dreyfus was tried, condemned & transported for life, as the author of the bordereau, without Schwartzkoppen or the general public knowing on what particular grounds he had been found guilty.

And so after this Esterhazy continued to act for Schwartzkoppen, & indeed some of his most valuable communications were made long after Dreyfus was on the Ile du Diable.

And so it continued until suddenly & mysteriously a photograph of the 'bordereau' appeared in the 'Matin' in November 1896.[2]

Then & only then Schwartzkoppen realized that Dreyfus had been wrongly condemned, & then it was that Esterhazy was seen rushing about the streets in the rain like a demented spirit.

Schwartzkoppen however could do nothing. Esterhazy ceased to communicate with him & retired on leave for reasons of ill health, & for a time travelled abroad, & disappeared.

Before this however in March 1896 Schwartzkoppen had himself addressed the famous 'petit bleu' to Esterhazy, disguising his handwriting, as was his custom when writing to him.[3]

He had written this in his rooms, intending to post it himself on his way to the Embassy where he had an appointment with his chief. This he forgot to do, & only remembered it when he found himself at the door of the Embassy already a little behind time.

To lose no time he took the 'petit-bleu' out of his pocket, handed it to the porter of the Embassy & told him to have it posted without delay. The porter as in the case of the bordereau again tore it up into small fragments, & it also found its way to the Intelligence department of the War office of which Picquart was now head.

As you know Picquart [has now been in prison since the 13th July 1898] was subsequently eleven months in prison charged with having forged this very 'petit-bleu,' for it was this document which first revealed the truth & which has played such an important part in the whole affair. All this however must be familiar to you.

Panizzardi then also told me that on Sunday 24th October 1897 Schwartzkoppen early in the morning broke into his (Panizzardi's) rooms to tell him that this time 'his man' was found out.

There was no doubt about it this time, & so to his great regret he would be compelled to leave Paris, with as little delay as possible. This it was necessary to do in order to avoid diplomatic complications & in conformity with regular & accepted usage, under similar circumstances.

Then it was that for the first time Schwartzkoppen mentioned 'his man's' name saying that it was Esterhazy, & [then described him as the most marvellous, audacious, & wonderful 'canaille' that it was possible to imagine either in fiction or history, & capable of any & every villainy, including murder] that he was the most marvellous, audacious & brutal scoundrel that it was possible to imagine in fact or fiction, & capable of any & every villainy & holding murder lightly.

He then told Panizzardi that on the preceding day October 23 at about 3 in the afternoon Esterhazy had suddenly appeared in his rooms (Schwartzkoppen's). He was livid, haggard & trembling with terror. He threw himself on a sofa, asked for brandy, & said that he had been found out. He [yelled] rolled out imprecations on God, humanity & himself & behaved like a [demon] creature from hell at bay.

Schwartzkoppen who had not seen him since the publication of the bordereau in the 'Matin' in November of the preceding year was dumbfounded. He [asked him to explain himself & to be a bit more composed, & tell him why he had come back to Paris] asked what on Earth had brought him to Paris, why he came to him again, & to steady him gave him brandy.

As soon as Esterhazy had recovered some composure he told Schwartzkoppen that being in the country he had the day before received an anonymous letter warning him that he was going to be denounced as being the author of the bordereau, & urging him to come to Paris in order to be prepared to meet the charge. He said on that very morning some one had called on him making a mysterious appointment for 6 o'clock at the Parc Montsouris & giving him a little slip of paper on which the hour & place of meeting was written down, & showing it to Schwartzkoppen.

But, he added, 'how do I know that this is not an ambush ["un guet-apens"], & while I am speaking to some person in that remote place in the dark, other men do not come from behind & seize me?' 'You must help me out of this difficulty, he said to Schwartzkoppen, you must go to the Dreyfus family & tell them that the bordereau was written by Dreyfus, that he was your informant & secret agent, & that it is futile trying to make any one else responsible for the "bordereau."'

Schwartzkoppen [could but smile at this suggestion] at this only shook his head, whereupon Esterhazy suddenly pulling out a revolver covered Schwartzkoppen saying 'unless you give me your word that you will do as I tell you, I will blow your brains out & mine afterwards.'

Schwartzkoppen with complete composure said 'You tell me that you have an appointment, & you [think it may be a guet-apens] fear it may be an ambush. Since however you are so well armed, it will be more opportune for you to commence firing when you are quite convinced that you are lost. It may however, he added, be quite the contrary & you may find [yourself protected] some friend or protector. Go there, & come back here afterwards to tell me the result.'

This quite disarmed Esterhazy & he [then after asking for drink, became more composed] said he would follow this advice. Then as if nothing unusual had happened he commenced to speak with his [accustomed vivacity & brilliancy as if nothing had happened] usual vivacity & fervour on the old theme of the stupidity & villainy of French officers, saying that anything might be expected from them.

[He left Schwartzkoppen promising to return after the interview in the Parc Montsouris,—in order to tell him the particulars.] He left at 4,—at 8 he returned.

This time he was radiant & almost beside himself with joy. 'I am protected,' he said. ['I have them now. I hold toute cette crapule entre les mains.'] 'I hold them now. They are afraid of me, I have all the brutes in my hand. I can now sleep on both ears. They dare not touch me.' He could hardly contain himself with high spirits & added 'I always told you they were a pack of cowards & scoundrels, now you will see to what lengths they will go to protect me.'

He then told him about the meeting; about the false beards, & spectacles, etc. [which you have read in the papers. But what has not appeared in the papers is that] He knew Paty du Clam from the first, though he did not recognize Gribelin [standing near him, or Henry in the cab in the dark] & Henry who held themselves at a distance & Henry remaining in the cab in the dark.[4]

He said that Paty du Clam had told him that he had nothing to fear, for even if Scheurer-Kestner[5] or Picquart or Mathieu Dreyfus denounced him, the Etat-Major would protect him through thick and through thin, [so that he only had to be quiet] & that he had to avoid doing anything rash, & must do just as he was told for he would then be perfectly safe. He was assured that protection came from the highest quarters & that all would be well.

To this Schwartzkoppen said 'Well I congratulate you for you must consider yourself very lucky. As it is though, I do not think there is any necessity for you to come here again. Adieu Monsieur. Portez vous bien!'

This then was what Schwartzkoppen told Panizzardi on that early morning of October 24th 1897 & then it was that for the first time Panizzardi knew that Schwartzkoppen had been employing a well known & notorious [spy] traitor, from whom any military attaché could obtain secret military information, if he chose to have it, & pay for it.

As a [spy] traitor he was as well known as intermediaries of another kind, or as a doctor for special diseases. Esterhazy & treachery were synonymous terms with the military attachés, but of course no one of them denounced him any more than they would have acknowledged having visited certain medical specialists.

In due course therefore, in November, Schwartzkoppen's request was granted & he was relieved of his functions in Paris after being decorated with the Legion of Honour by Félix Faure who at that time knew the whole & entire truth perfectly well.

On the night that he left Paris, he & Panizzardi dined together at a Restaurant. Between them lay a large sized Gladstone bag, which he afterwards kept on his knee in the cab, & which he treated as his pillow during the journey.

The bag contained the 140 odd pieces of treachery in Esterhazy's handwriting.

The above is an outline of facts learned [from Panizzardi] at first hand, on incontrovertible authority, the importance of which is manifest.

Panizzardi & I were constantly together & the subject of conversation was principally this terrible miscarriage of justice & discussions as to how this unhappy victim could be assisted.

This was exceedingly difficult since Panizzardi told me that the [Cabinet, Félix Faure] President & all the Ministers & most important political personages had been officially informed of the whole & the entire truth. Both the German & Italian Ambassadors had fully informed the Government under instructions from their respective Governments & Sovereigns [but they did not choose to act]. The truth therefore was & is known.

Public official declarations were also made & published, but they also were disregarded.

[It therefore seemed difficult to know how to act in order to be of some service when early in March 1898 the King of Italy sent for Panizzardi.] On the 10th of March 1898 the King of Italy sent for Panizzardi in order to learn the truth, with details, of the Dreyfus affair at first hand.

Panizzardi's position in Paris at this time was growing very difficult & he was meeting with scant courtesy from the Generals & officers he met. He was therefore going to avail himself of that opportunity to ask the King to relieve him of his post in Paris, where he had then been serving for 7 years.

This being the case we decided that he would [do what he could with the King of Italy to get the King to write to the German Emperor] also avail himself of this opportunity to ask the King of Italy to write to the German Emperor requesting him as a personal favour to allow some of Esterhazy's documents to be handed to Panizzardi with a view to their being published in a neutral country, [say England] Switzerland, Belgium or England.

With this intention he left for Rome, subsequently went to Berlin, & was back in Paris ten days later [the 15th] the 20th March.

He told me that the King of Italy had been much [interested &] pained to learn the facts, but he could not spare Panizzardi in Paris & told him to remain.

In Berlin he was told that the Emperor had been much irritated at the way in which his official declarations had been received by the French Government & people. He was told that not all the publications in the world would be of the slightest avail under the condition of things in France, & that under any circumstances the Emperor having made a statement, he did not like to bring proofs to prove that what he said was true when his word sufficed.

There was therefore nothing to be done. [Panizzardi authorized me to publish what he had told me, but this would have injured him,—as he subsequently suffered.] Personally I could not publish what Panizzardi had told me for this would have entailed Panizzardi's immediately having to leave Paris.

As for me, living in Paris with my family & my mother, there was no saying what the trouble to them might have been. The trouble & the worry duly came afterwards through no fault of my own & even this was bad enough, as I will in due course relate hereafter, to show what a condition of things prevailed in France at that time.

Panizzardi constantly dined with us, & he was always shadowed & watched. We could see the men in the street watching the house & waiting for him to leave, when they would jump on their bicycles & follow him as soon as he took a cab.

On April 4th appeared a letter signed 'un diplomate' in the <u>Siècle</u>. This substantially contained what I have written above, regarding the relations formerly existing between Schwartzkoppen & Esterhazy, & these then became generally known for the first time.

The article created a great sensation, but unfortunately for reasons which will appear in another part I was considered the author of it, & it was attributed to me [& the 'Presse Immonde' commenced a campaign against me & I was shadowed, tracked & followed, day & night & everywhere].

Then commenced my troubles. I was attacked by the low & infamous press, & for days my family and I were insulted & dragged through the most filthy dirt. Anonymous & foul letters were addressed to me threatening me with assaults & death to myself & my family. I was followed & tracked without a moment's intermission for months & it was only on the frontier when I left France that I finally saw two men leaving the train who had been watching me from the next carriage.

Four days after the publication of the 'Lettre d'un Diplomate' appeared an article signed by Casella in which he described interviews with Schwartzkoppen & Panizzardi, & what they had said to him regarding the innocence of Dreyfus.

Then Panizzardi's fate was sealed as far as remaining in Paris was concerned. [The 'Presse Immonde' covered him with filth, he was pestered with anonymous letters threatening death, & finally French officers publicly declared that if they met Panizzardi in a public place they would attack him.] The low press attacked him, anonymous letters poured in threatening to attack him & spit in his face in public & even his Ambassador was molested. From the 8th to the 15th of April he showed a bold front. He dined with us every night during this last week of his stay in Paris [and even wished to entrust me with all his secret papers & documents, there was therefore nothing connected with the Dreyfus affair which he kept from me, the above being only the outline & skeleton of what he told me]. He wished to entrust me with all his documents & papers, as he was afraid they might in some way be got hold of, but I could not accept the responsibility.

[Finally after a week's anxiety, he left Paris.] At length on the 15th April his position having become quite untenable he left Paris for Berne on the plea of a mission there. Eventually without being officially recalled from Paris he was given a regiment of Bersaglieri in Rome, where he now is [where from his letters he appears to be perfectly happy & above all perfectly convinced that the truth will be made manifest in France & that Dreyfus & Picquart will have justice meted out to them, as they deserve. One as an innocent victim, the other as the type of a noble man, with a 'soul of crystal'].

Since then we have been in constant correspondence, the principal subject being this unhappy affair & in every instance his predictions & anticipations & warnings have come true. This is due to his seven years' experience of the French people & an intimate acquaintance with their characteristics, merits & demerits.

[The above are facts, with which alone I intended to deal. General observations as to how & why such a perverse condition of things could have existed in France is matter for the historian.

I have also avoided mentioning names other than those of the principal actors. But if there is an immanent justice which has its time & its hour, it should go hard with some who are little better than that 'superb scoundrel' Esterhazy.]

Endnotes

INTRODUCTION

1. OW to CB, 12 July 1897, *Letters*, 911.
2. 'De Profundis', 688–9.
3. Ibid., 685–6.
4. Douglas to A. J. A. Symons, 31 July 1935, Clark [810] [Wilde D733L S988]. There is no record of Blacker's having matriculated at Oxford.
5. Max Beerbohm to Reggie Turner, 7 August 1894, in Rupert Hart-Davis (ed.), *Max Beerbohm: Letters to Reggie Turner* (London: Rupert Hart-Davis, 1964), 95.
6. CB Diary.
7. *The Yellow Book, An Illustrated Quarterly*, 4 (January 1895), 275.
8. Vincent O'Sullivan, *Aspects of Wilde* (London: Constable & Co. Ltd, 1936), 182.
9. Robert Harborough Sherard, *Oscar Wilde: The Story of an Unhappy Friendship* (London: Privately Printed, The Hermes Press, 1902), 30.
10. Salomon Reinach to C. P. Blacker, 17 February 1928, BP.
11. Loring Walton, 'Anatole France and the First World War: The Correspondence with Carlos Blacker', *PMLA*, 77 (September 1962), 471–81.
12. C. P. Blacker to Loring Walton, 29 September 1957, BP.
13. Otho Holland to CB, 13 January 1901, BP.
14. Richard Ellmann, *Oscar Wilde* (London: Hamish Hamilton, 1987), 529.
15. '[Wilde's] best friend, his marriage trustee [Blacker], was and is my best friend & I used whenever I went to London have the inestimable privilege of hearing Oscar Wilde talk to us very intimately every day.' William Roger Paton to Oscar Browning, 13 June 1897, King's College.
16. C. P. Blacker to John Paton, 22 August 1954, in the possession of David Paton.
17. CB Diary, 23 February 1896, BP. The dates of quoted entries from CB's diary are contained in brackets.
18. John Blacker (ed.), *Have You Forgotten Yet? The First World War Memoirs of C. P. Blacker* (Barnsley, S. Yorkshire: Leo Cooper, Pen & Sword Books, 2000), 2–3. C. P. 'Pip' Blacker and his brother Robin served as officers in the Coldstream Guards in World War I. Robin was killed in the battle of

Loos when barely eighteen in September 1915, four months after Oscar Wilde's son Cyril was killed by a sniper at Neuve Chapelle. Robin's Eton obituary contains an observation by 'a late Oxford Tutor' that undoubtedly reflects the undoubtedly reflects the admirable tutelage Pip and Robin received early in life from their father: 'I think he must have been steeped in good literature from his childhood, for he possessed, to a degree quite unusual in a boy of 17, the flair for what was worth reading and remembering.' *The Eton College Chronicle* (4 November 1915).

19. Hesketh Pearson and Malcolm Muggeridge, *About Kingsmill* (London: Methuen & Co. Ltd, 1951), 139.

20. Note by C. P. Blacker, 14 August 1973, in his seventy-eighth year, BP. Unless otherwise indicated, reference hereinafter to letters from CB to Carrie is to copies of letters now missing.

21. Carrie to CB, 1 January 1895, BP.

22. OW to Robert Ross [July 1898], *Letters*, 1087.

23. Carrie to CB, 28 April 1894, BP.

24. Déposition de Grandmaison, Déposition Strong Rowland [Rowland Strong], 2ᵉ Déposition Périnet, Femme Gérard, *La Révision du procès Dreyfus*, 3 vols. (Paris : P.-V. Stock, 1899), I: 735, 741, 787.

25. *L'Affaire Dreyfus: Dictionnaire sous la direction de Michel Drouin* (Paris: Flammarion, 2006), end cover.

26. CB Memo. See Appendix.

27. C. P. Blacker to John Paton, 22 August 1954, in the possession of David Paton.

28. CB to Otho Holland, 21 December 1900 (retained copy), BP.

29. Rupert Hart-Davis (ed.), *The Letters of Oscar Wilde* (New York: Harcourt, Brace & World, Inc. 1962), xii.

30. Sotheby's sale cat., *Melmoth* (London, 10 and 11 July 1986), introduction to 'The Property of the Blacker Family'.

31. Frederick C. Conybeare to Carrie, 6 July 1898, BP.

CHAPTER 1: 'THE GREATEST FRIENDSHIP OF MY LIFE'

1. Lord Alfred Douglas, *Without Apology* (London: Martin Secker, 1938), 167–8, 173.

2. John Fletcher, *Ornament of Sherwood Forest: From Ducal Estate to Public Park* (Bakewell, Derbyshire: Country Books, 2005), 12.

3. Newcastle to CB, 7 July 1907, BP.

4. 'In Memoriam, the Late Duke of Newcastle', *The Eton College Chronicle* (7 June 1928).

5. Newcastle to CB, 4 July 1907, BP.

6. Newcastle to CB, 18 January 1924, BP.

7. Newcastle to CB, 16 March 1924, BP.

8. Newcastle to CB, 27 March and 15 June 1920, BP.

9. Newcastle to CB, 7 August 1922, BP.

10. Newcastle to CB, 26 July 1909, BP.

11. 'In Memoriam, the Late Duke of Newcastle', *The Eton College Chronicle* (7 June 1928).

12. *The New York Times* and *The Times* (London) (31 May 1928).

13. 'How I wish you were here with me', Newcastle wrote from Brighton in 1910, 'to renew our recollections of the Rupert and Toby days! Fancy, how the years have flown since then.' Six years later, he returned to the theme: 'We had a lovely Easter Week which I spent partly at Brighton, thinking often of Rupert and Toby 29 years ago.' And again, five years later: 'I always gaze regretfully at the spot where we made the acquaintance of Rupert and "Toby" nearly 34 years ago; and long vainly for those happier days to return.' 30 March 1910, 5 May 1916, 27 January 1921, BP.

14. Newcastle to CB, 'Eve of the Circumcision' 1923, BP.

15. *The Times* (31 May 1928).

16. Fletcher, *Sherwood Forest*, 12.

17. David Watkin, *Thomas Hope 1791–1831 and the Neo-Classical Idea* (London: Murray, 1968), 192.

18. Brian Masters, *The Dukes: The Origins, Ennoblement and History of 26 Families* (London: Frederick Muller, 1988), 366.

19. Newcastle to CB, 10 February 1890, BP.

20. Newcastle to CB, 15 February 1890, BP.

21. Newcastle to CB, 24 February 1890, BP.

22. Francis Hope to CB, 4 April 1890, BP.

23. Norman Forbes-Robertson to CB, 18 April 1890, BP.

24. Francis Hope to CB, 12 April 1890, BP.

25. CB to Newcastle, 28 March 1889, Nottingham, Ne C 14,241/1.

26. Fletcher, *Sherwood Forest*, 42–3.

27. Newcastle to Robert Sherard, 2 May 1928, Reading, MS 1047.

28. Robert Harborough Sherard, *Bernard Shaw, Frank Harris & Oscar Wilde* (New York: The Greystone Press, 1937), 124.

29. Laurence Housman, *Echo de Paris: A Study from Life* (London: Jonathan Cape, 1923), 37–8. In a letter dated 17 May 1937 to an unidentified 'Mr Murray', Housman says of his book, which purports to be a record of a conversation with Wilde in 1899, that 'only about one-tenth of it is a record of the things Wilde actually said; the rest is more or less invention, but inspired, of course, by his extraordinary gift as a conversationalist'. BP.

30. *The Times* (31 May 1928).

31. Kathleen Newcastle, 'Clumber', in A. H. Malan (ed.), *Other Famous Homes of Great Britain and Their Stories* (New York: G. P. Putnam's Sons, 1902), 170.

32. Newcastle to CB, 24 February 1890, BP.

33. Newcastle to CB, 2 March 1890, BP.

34. Newcastle to CB, 'Good Friday' 1890, BP.
35. 'De Profundis', 702.
36. OW to Robert Ross [November 1896]; to Arthur Hansell, 12 April 1897, *Letters*, 670 and 799.
37. John Juxon, *Lewis and Lewis* (New York: Ticknor & Fields, 1984), 275.

CHAPTER 2: 'SADNESS, DISAPPOINTMENT, UPSET, & WEARINESS'

1. Francis Hope to CB, 4 April 1890, BP.
2. Newcastle to CB, 4 December 1923, BP.
3. CB to Carrie, 27 November 1888, BP.
4. OW to CB, 12 July 1897, *Letters*, 911.
5. CB to Newcastle, 5 December 1888, Nottingham, Ne C 14,239.
6. OW to Ross [July 1898], *Letters*, 1087.
7. André de Boisandré, 'Un nouvel agent du syndicat,' *La Libre Parole*, 11 June 1898.
8. CB to Newcastle, 10 December 1889, Nottingham, Ne C 14,246.
9. Newcastle to CB, 15 February 1890, BP.
10. Thomas Hohler to Newcastle, 28 February 1890, Nottingham, Ne C 14,209.
11. Newcastle to CB, 'Good Friday'1890, BP.
12. CB to Newcastle, 2 May 1890, Nottingham, Ne C 14,259.
13. Newcastle to CB, 15 May 1890, BP.
14. CB to Newcastle, 28 July 1890, Nottingham, Ne C 14,260.
15. CB to Newcastle, 8 September 1890, Nottingham, Ne C 14,262.
16. CB to Sir Lewis Molesworth (his future brother-in-law), 2 September 1892, BP.
17. *The Times* (4 June 1894).
18. CB to Carrie, 28 December 1892, BP.
19. CB to Carrie 29 July 1892, BP.
20. CB to Sir Lewis Molesworth, 27 December 1892, BP.
21. CB to OW, 16 January 1893, Clark [127] [Wilde B6285L W6721].
22. Sotheby's sale cat. *Melmoth* (10 and 11 July 1986), lot 144.
23. CB to Newcastle, Saturday (c.June), 1892, Nottingham, Ne C 14,269.
24. *The Times* (1 November 1895).
25. *The Times* (20 December 1895).
26. CB to Newcastle, undated (c.September 1893), Nottingham, Ne C 14,271.
27. CB to Carrie, 28 December 1892, BP.
28. CB to Newcastle, 28 March 1889, Nottingham, Ne C 14,241.
29. John Fletcher, *Ornament of Sherwood Forest: From Ducal Estate to Public Park* (Bakewell, Derbyshire: Country Books, 2005), 50–1.
30. CB to Carrie, 25 June 1892, BP.
31. Fletcher, *Ornament of Sherwood Forest*, 51.

32. CB to Carrie, 28 December 1892, BP.
33. CB to Carrie, 10 November 1894, BP.
34. CB to Newcastle, 3 December 1889, Nottingham, Ne C 14,245.
35. *The Times* (18 January 1895).
36. *The Times* (1 November 1895).
37. The Garrick Club records show that Blacker ceased to be a member on 3 January 1894. Although the reason noted is 'Bankrupt', he was not actually adjudicated bankrupt until more than a year later, on 12 February 1895. He was re-elected to membership in 1916—at which time the record may have been corrected—proposed by the duke himself, who had long since retracted his charge and duly apologized, and seconded by Norman Forbes-Robertson. Ten years before, the mollified duke had written to Blacker: 'Norman tells me that you have consented to stand again for the Garrick: he and I are delighted and we must have a royal drunk together there when you are elected.' 23 May 1906, BP.
38. CB to 'My Dear Luigi [Sir Lewis Molesworth]', 5 April 1893, BP.
39. CB to Carrie, 3 May 1892, BP.
40. CB to Carrie, 6 May 1892, BP.
41. Carrie to CB, 28 November 1894, BP.
42. CB to Carrie, 2 December 1893, BP.
43. Carrie to CB, 4 December 1893, BP.
44. CB to Carrie, 4 December 1893, BP.
45. Carrie to CB, 22 December 1893, BP.
46. CB to Carrie, 'Christmas Day' 1893, BP.
47. CB to Carrie, 14 December 1893, BP.
48. Carrie to CB, 16 December 1893, BP.
49. 'De Profundis', 693.
50. OW to More Adey, 7 April 1897, *Letters*, 795.
51. 'De Profundis', 693.
52. CB to Carrie, 1 December 1893, BP.
53. Carrie to CB, [3] December 1893, BP.
54. CB to Carrie, 3 December 1893, BP.
55. CB to Carrie, 4–5 December 1893, BP.
56. Carrie to CB, 2–3 December 1893, BP.
57. CB to Carrie, 6 December 1893, BP.
58. Carrie to CB, 8 December 1893, BP.
59. CB to Carrie, 21 December 1893, BP.
60. Charles S. Ricketts, *Self-portrait* (London: P. Davies, 1939), 124.
61. Lewis to H. Weller Richards, 13 January 1894, appended to Richards to OW, 15 January 1894, Clark [1762] [Wilde R5155L W6721].
62. Richards to OW, 15 January 1894, Clark [1762] [Wilde R5155L W6721].
63. Richards to OW, 16 February 1894, Clark [1763] [Wilde R5155L W6721].
64. Richards to OW, 18 May, 1894, Clark [1764] [Wilde R5155L W6721].

65. W. R. Paton to OW, 22 June 1894, Clark [1681] [Wilde P2955L W6721].

66. W. R. Paton to OW, 3 July 1894, Clark [1682] [Wilde P2955L W6721].

67. CB to Carrie, undated [? November 1894], BP.

68. Carrie to CB, 27 April 1894, BP.

69. CB to Carrie, 7 August 1894, BP.

70. CB to Carrie, 8 August 1894, BP.

71. CB to Carrie, 3 September 1894, BP.

72. OW to Robert Ross [July 1898], *Letters*, 1087–8.

73. CB to Carrie, 12 November 1894, BP.

74. Carrie to CB, 5 August 1894, BP.

75. CB to Jane Molesworth, 13 August 1894, BP.

76. Quoted 'verbatim' in letter from CB to Carrie, 22 September 1894, BP.

77. Carrie to CB, 17 September 1894, BP.

78. Carrie to CB, 24 September 1894, BP.

79. CB to Carrie, 30 September 1894, BP.

80. Carrie to CB, 1 January 1895, BP.

81. CB to Carrie, 30 September 1894, BP.

82. Daniel M. Frost to Carrie, 26 September 1894, BP.

83. Graham Frost to CB, 18 October 1894, BP.

84. CB to Carrie, 1 October 1894, BP.

85. CB to Carrie, 25 November 1894, BP.

86. CB to Carrie, 1 November 1894, BP.

87. Daniel M. Frost to CB, 11 November 1894, BP.

88. CB to Carrie, 30 November 1894, BP.

CHAPTER 3: 'THE GIRL WITH THE FOGHORN VOICE'

1. *The New York Times* (28 August 1938).

2. Henry Leyford Gates, *The Mystery of the Hope Diamond: From the Personal Narrative of Lady Francis Hope (May Yohe)* (New York: International Copyright Bureau, 1921), 91–3. May was actually twenty-five at the time, having been born on 6 April 1869.

3. *The New York Times* (28 August 1938).

4. André de Boisandré, 'Un nouvel agent du syndicat', *La Libre Parole* (11 June 1898).

5. CB to Carrie, 10 December 1894, BP.

6. Gates, *Mystery of the Hope Diamond*, 100.

7. Ibid., 211.

8. Ibid., 221.

9. Ibid., 244–5.

10. Ibid., 209.

11. 'Spouse Shot as Diamond Curse Trails May Yohe', *Los Angeles Evening Herald* (20 November 1924).

12. *The New York Times* (28 August 1938).

13. CB to Carrie, 14 December 1894, BP.

14. CB to Carrie, 24 January 1895, BP.

15. OW to Robert Ross [July 1898], *Letters*, 1088.

16. Diary entries for February 17 and following to March 14, with a few incidental exceptions, are in Carrie's hand.

17. André Gide, *If It Die...*, trans. Dorothy Bussy (London: Secker and Warburg, 1950), 276.

18. OW to More Adey, 7 April 1897, *Letters*, 795.

19. Lord Alfred Douglas, *Without Apology* (London: Martin Secker, 1938), 75.

20. '[24 April 1895] To theatre to see Othello. Supper at Gordon-Cumming'; '[30 April 1895] Met Gordon-Cumming.' It is not clear whether the entries refer to Sir William.

21. [22 May 1895], CB Diary, BP.

22. [5 August 1895], CB Diary, BP.

23. [19 October 1895], CB Diary, BP.

24. [13 November 1895], CB Diary, BP.

25. *Galignani Messenger*, 15 November 1895.

26. [4 November 1895], CB Diary, BP.

27. CB to Carrie, 26 August 1894, BP.

28. When the baby was ten days old, Blacker recorded in his diary: '[17 December 1895] Carrie first made Pip say his prayers: Please God, bless Pip & make him a good boy & a comfort to his parents.' In the course of a productive life that included four years of service as an infantry officer in the Coldstream Guards in World War I, and three years in World War II as medical officer in the same regiment, Pip gained eminence as a highly gifted psychiatrist and fully answered his mother's prayer, remaining for both parents throughout their lives an unfailing source of comfort. In the early months of World War II he was posted at Dieppe, an experience he later described in a letter to Paton's son John in which he noted that he had been unaware at the time of the associations the place had with Oscar Wilde. 'It is noteworthy that several of the letters (indeed most of them) written by Wilde to my father from Berneval were written, as is the letter to your father, on the note-paper of Dieppe cafés. Most come from the Café Suisse, as does that to your father. One comes from the Café des Tribuneaux, at the other end of Dieppes's Grande Rue. It is peculiar that I was posted at Dieppe, with No 1 General Hospital, from September 1939 to January 1940. I knew both these cafés, and many are the cups of tisane which I have drunk at the Café des Tribuneaux after dinner in the last few months of 1939. I had no idea then that Wilde had frequented these same cafés.' C. P. Blacker to John Paton, 22 August 1954, letter in the possession of David Paton.

29. Francis Hope to CB, 17 December 1895, BP. Francis's uncle at Windsor was Lord Edward Pelham-Clinton, Groom-in-Waiting to Queen Victoria and at the time Master of the Household.

CHAPTER 4: 'HE HAS BEEN MAD THE LAST 3 YEARS'

1. Lord Alfred Douglas, *The Autobiography of Lord Alfred Douglas* (London: Martin Secker, 1929), 121.
2. OW to More Adey, 7 April 1897, *Letters*, 796.
3. OW to Douglas [20 May 1895], *Letters*, 652.
4. 'De Profundis', 688.
5. Bankruptcy no. 724 of 1895, High Court of Bankruptcy, PRO-Chancery Lane, London, B9/428–9.
6. Otho Holland Lloyd to his wife Mary, describing the reaction of Sidney Hargrove, the Lloyd family solicitor, to Wilde's letter, 10 September 1895, *Letters* (1962 ed.), 872.
7. Douglas to Ada Leverson, 13 September 1895, Violet Wyndham, *The Sphinx and Her Circle: A Memoir of Ada Leverson* (London: André Deutsch, 1963), 54.
8. Constance Wilde to Sherard, 21 September 1895, reproduced in facsimile in Robert Harborough Sherard, *The Real Oscar Wilde* (London: T. W. Laurie Ltd, 1916), 173.
9. Robert Harborough Sherard, *Oscar Wilde: The Story of an Unhappy Friendship* (London: Privately Printed, Hermes Press, 1902), 210.
10. PRO-Kew, PCOM 8/432.
11. 'De Profundis', 717.
12. Douglas to Sherard [October 1895], MS 1047/1/1, Reading.
13. OW to Adey, 8 March 1897, *Letters*, 679–80.
14. Report of Dr R. F. Quinton, Medical Officer, 18 September 1895, PRO-Kew, PCOM 8/432.
15. 'De Profundis', 722.
16. Ross to Oscar Browning, 21 October 1895, King's College.
17. Douglas to Sherard, 22 September 1895, MS 1047/1/1, Reading.
18. Ross to Browning, 21 October 1895, King's College.
19. Clifton to CB, 8 October 1895, BP.
20. Clifton to Adey, 22 September 1895, BP.
21. PRO-Kew, PCOM 8/433.
22. Ibid.
23. Hargrove to CB, 7 November 1895, BP.
24. Ross to Browning, November 13 [1895], King's College.
25. Hargrove to CB, 11 November 1895, BP.
26. Ross to Browning, November 13 [1895], King's College.
27. Hargrove to CB, 13 November 1895, BP.

CHAPTER 5: 'LETTERS FROM TWO IDIOTS TO A LUNATIC'

1. Hargrove to CB, 13 November [1895], BP.
2. Clifton to Adey, 13 December [1895], BP.
3. OW to Adey, 16 December [1896], *Letters*, 675.
4. OW to A. D. Hansell, 12 April 1897, *Letters*, 799.
5. OW to George Alexander [February 1895], *Letters*, 633.
6. OW to Ada Leverson [*c*.13 March 1895], *Letters*, 635.
7. Maurice Sisley, 'La *Salomé* de M. Oscar Wilde', *Le Galois* (29 June 1892); E. H. Mikhail (ed.), *Oscar Wilde: Interviews and Recollections*, 2 vols. (London: Macmillan Press Ltd, 1979), I, 190.
8. Schuster to Adey, 1 February 1896, Clark [1944] [Wilde S395L A233].
9. Schuster to Adey, 15 May [1896], Clark [1956] [Wilde S395L A233].
10. Schuster to Adey, 2 December [1895], Clark [1933] [Wilde S395l A233].
11. Presentation copy of Frank Harris, *Oscar Wilde: His Life and Confessions* (New York: Printed and Published by the Author, 1916), front endpaper, dated September 1916, BP.
12. Schuster to Adey, 13 August 1896, Clark [1984] [S395L A233].
13. Schuster to Adey, 20 March 1896, Clark [1946] [Wilde S395L A233].
14. OW to Adey, 7 April 1897, *Letters*, 796.
15. OW to Adey, 12 May 1897, *Letters*, 814.
16. OW to Adey, 18 February 1897, *Letters*, 677.
17. OW to Adey, 7 April 1897, *Letters*, 796.
18. OW to Adey, 12 May 1897, *Letters*, 814.
19. Leverson to OW, 17 May 1897, *Letters*, 827.
20. 'De Profundis', 738.
21. OW to Ross, 1 April 1897, *Letters*, 782.
22. Siegfried Sassoon, *Siegfried's Journey: 1916–1920* (New York: Faber and Faber Ltd, 1946), 54. Wilde characteristically took a more indulgent view of Adey's eccentricity, writing to him from Rome shortly before his own death: 'I should like to go with you to the Vatican, where I hope you will some day walk gravely in mediaeval dress, with the gold chain of office, and guide pilgrims to the feet of the Pope.' OW to Adey [postmark 26 April 1900], *Letters*, 1184.
23. 'De Profundis', 762.
24. PRO-Kew, PCOM 8/433.
25. Constance to Otho Holland, *Letters*, 652 n.4.
26. OW to Ross, 13 May [1897], *Letters*, 818.
27. OW to Ross, 10 March 1896, *Letters*, 652.
28. Adey to Constance Wilde, draft of a letter [June 1895?], Clark [52] [Wilde A 233Z N911].
29. Ross to Adey, Margery Ross (ed.), *Robert Ross: Friend of Friends* (London: Jonathan Cape, 1952), 39.

30. Robert Harborough Sherard, *Oscar Wilde: The Story of an Unhappy Friendship* (London: Privately Printed, Hermes Press, 1902), 222.

31. Schuster to Adey, 1 June 1896, Clark [1957] [Wilde S395L A233].

32. Schuster to Adey, 4 June 1896, Clark [1958] [Wilde S395L A233].

33. Schuster to Adey, 2 December [1895], Clark [1933] [Wilde S395L A233].

34. Schuster to Adey, 29 February [1896], Clark [1945] [Wilde S395L A233].

35. Schuster to Adey, 20 March 1896, Clark [1946] [Wilde S395L A233].

36. Adey to Schuster [draft endorsed: 'Copy to Miss Schuster, April 14, 96'], Clark [28] [Wilde A233L S395].

37. OW to Adey [postmark 21 November 1897], *Letters*, 989.

38. Sotheby, Wilkinson & Hodge, London, sale cat., 11 November 1897. The curious history of John Blacker's collection of Hagué bindings is told in detail in Mirjam M. Foot, Carmen Blacker (great-granddaughter of John Blacker), and Nicholas Poole-Wilson, 'Collector, Dealer and Forger: A Fragment of Nineteenth-Century Binding History', in Mirjam M. Foot (ed.), *Eloquent Witnesses: Bookbindings and their History* (London: The Bibliographical Society of London, The British Library and Oak Knoll Press, 2004), 264–81.

39. CB Diary, 29 April 1896, BP. Panizzardi was accredited as military attaché to the Italian legations in Brussels and Berne as well as the embassy in Paris. Hagué was last known to have been living in Brussels. Howard M. Nixon, 'Binding Forgeries', *VI International Congress of Bibliophiles* (Vienna: International Congress of Bibliophiles, Conferences, 1971), 80.

40. Adey to Schuster [draft endorsed: 'Copy to Miss Schuster, April 14, 96'], Clark [28] [Wilde A233L S395].

41. Undated memorandum in Adey's hand, information to be communicated to Wilde, Clark [52] [Wilde A233Z N911].

42. Adey to Clifton [draft], undated [May 1896], BP.

43. Adey, 'Account of money paid into Bank' [1896?], Clark [27] [Wilde A233L S395].

44. Adey to Schuster [unsigned draft] [1896?], Clark [27] [A233L S395].The donors to the fund were Dalhousie Young, a composer and pianist (£50); J. Ellis McTaggart, the Cambridge philosopher (£50); Digby LaMotte, an assistant master at St Paul's School (£25); 'Warry', a friend of the latter's (£25); Rev. R. C. Tillingham (£10); plus £10 left over from the earlier bankruptcy fund raised by Ross in Cambridge. BP.

45. Ross to Adey [30 May 1896], Ross (ed.), *Robert Ross*, 39–41.

46. OW to Ross [30 May 1896], *Letters*, 654–5.

47. Schuster to Adey, 13 June [1896], Clark [1962] [Wilde S395 A233].

48. PRO-Kew, PCOM 8/433.

49. OW to the Home Secretary, 2 July 1896, *Letters*, 656–9.

50. Autograph fragment (in French), Adey to OW, unsigned and undated [1896] a, Clark [44] [Wilde A233L W6721].

51. Autograph fragment (in English—2 pages), Adey to OW, unsigned and undated [1896] b, Clark [45] [Wilde A233L W6721].
52. OW to Sherard [26 August 1896], *Letters*, 662.
53. Adey to OW, 23 September 1896, *Letters*, 664.
54. OW to Adey [25 September 1896], *Letters*, 666.
55. Sherard, *Story of an Unhappy Friendship*, 224–5.
56. PRO-Chancery Lane, London, B9/428–9.
57. Schuster to Adey, 11 August [1896], Clark [1982] [Wilde S395L A233].
58. Schuster to Adey, 12 August 1896, Clark [1983] [Wilde S395L A233].
59. Schuster to Adey, 13 August 1896, Clark [1984] [Wilde S395L A233].
60. Schuster to Adey, 17 August [1896], Clark [1985] [Wilde S395L A233].
61. The claims represented in the adoption of the resolution included those of the trustees of the marriage settlement (£1,557.16.02), the marquess of Queensberry (£677.03.08) and David Nutt, publisher of *The Happy Prince* (£7.00.04), amounting to £2,242.00.02 out of a total indebtedness of £3,591.09.09. PRO-Chancery Lane, London, B9/428–9.
62. Schuster to Adey, 28 August [1896], Clark [1988] [Wilde S395L A233].
63. Adey to Martin Holman [draft], 6 January 1897, Clark [12] [Wilde A233L H747].
64. Adey to OW [draft of part of letter now lost] 23 September 1896, *Letters*, 663 n. 3.
65. OW to Ross, 6 April [1897], *Letters*, 786.
66. OW to Adey, 16 December [1896], *Letters*, 671–2.
67. OW to Ross, 13 May [1897], *Letters*, 819.
68. OW to Adey, 16 December [1896], *Letters*, 672.
69. OW to Adey, 18 February 1897, *Letters*, 677.
70. OW to Adey, 8 March 1897, *Letters*, 680.
71. Adey to Schuster [draft], 16 March 1897, Clark [29] [Wilde A233L S395].
72. OW to Adey, 7 April 1897, *Letters*, 794.
73. OW to Adey, 7 April 1897, *Letters*, 797. Edgar Saltus describes an incident from a happier time, 'in the rooms of Francis Hope': 'Someone else entered and Hope asked what was new in the City. "Money is very tight, came the reply. Ah, yes, Wilde cut in. And of a tightness that has been felt even in Tite Street [where Wilde lived]."' Edgar Saltus, *Oscar Wilde: An Idler's Impression* (Chicago: Brothers of the Book, 1917), 18–19.
74. OW to Adey, 16 December [1896], *Letters*, 672.
75. Deed of Separation, Sotheby's sale cat. (London, 22 and 23 July 1985), lot 159.
76. OW to Adey [postmark 21 November 1897], *Letters*, 990.
77. OW to Adey, 1 May [1897], *Letters*, 807.
78. OW to Adey, 12 May 1897, *Letters*, 815.
79. Ibid., 811, 814.
80. Adey, autograph notes referring to OW's life interest in the marriage settlement [1896], Clark [52] [Wilde A233Z N911].

81. OW to Ross, 13 May [1897], *Letters*, 823.
82. OW to Adey [15 May 1897], *Letters*, 825.
83. OW to Ross [17 May 1897], *Letters*, 835–6.
84. Unfinished introductory reminiscence to Ross's proposed collection of post-prison letters from Wilde, *Letters*, 842.

CHAPTER 6: 'THE MOST BITTER EXPERIENCE OF A BITTER LIFE'

1. OW to Ross, 19 May 1897, *Letters*, 844.
2. Unfinished introductory reminiscence to Ross's proposed collection of post-prison letters from Wilde, *Letters*, 844.
3. Constance to Otho Holland, 26 March 1897, Holland.
4. CB to Otho Holland, 21 December 1900 (retained copy), BP.
5. Otho Holland to CB, 13 January 1901, BP.
6. OW to Ross [29–30 May 1897], *Letters*, 865.
7. Constance Holland to CB, 12 June 1897, BP.
8. OW to Ross, 1 April 1897, *Letters*, 782.
9. OW to CB, 12 July 1897, *Letters*, 911–12.
10. W. R. Paton to CB [? July], 1897 BP.
11. Paton to Carrie, 13 June [1897], BP.
12. Paton to CB, 8 November 1896, BP.
13. Paton to Oscar Browning, 13 June 1897, King's College.
14. Paton to CB, 10 July 1897, BP.
15. Paton to OW [? July 1897], BP.
16. OW to Paton [? early August 1897], *Letters*, 922.
17. Although her second son was christened 'Vyvyan', Constance consistently used the spelling 'Vivian'.
18. Constance Holland to CB, 11 July 1897, BP.
19. Constance Holland to CB, 18 July 1897, BP.
20. OW to CB, 29 July 1897, *Letters*, 920.
21. OW to CB [postmark 4 August 1897], *Letters*, 921.
22. Constance Holland to CB, 3 August 1897, BP.
23. Constance Holland to her son Cyril, 21 September 1897, BP.
24. Constance Holland to CB, 25 September 1897, BP.
25. OW to Reggie Turner [postmark 17 May 1897], *Letters*, 832.
26. Constance to Otho Holland, 26 March [1897], *Letters*, 783 n. 2.
27. OW to Ross [postmark 16 August 1898], *Letters*, 1095.
28. OW to Ross [28 May 1897], *Letters*, 858.
29. OW to Ross [29–30 May 1897], *Letters*, 865.
30. OW to Douglas, 7 [July 1897], *Letters*, 910.
31. OW to Douglas, 4 June [1897], *Letters*, 880.
32. OW to Douglas, 16 June [1897], *Letters*, 899.
33. OW to Ross, 19 June [1897], *Letters*, 903.

34. Martin Holman to Adey, 10 May 1897, British Library, Add. MS 81754 A-F.
35. OW to Ross, (Postcard) 18 June [1897], *Letters*, 902.
36. OW to Douglas, 17 June [1897], *Letters*, 902.
37. OW to Will Rothenstein, 24 August 1897, *Letters*, 931.
38. OW to Douglas [? 31 August 1897], *Letters*, 932–3.
39. OW to Ross [1 June 1897], *Letters*, 869.
40. OW to Ross, 4 September 1897, *Letters*, 934.
41. OW to CB [postmark 6 September 1897], *Letters*, 935.
42. OW to CB [postmark 13 September 1897], *Letter*, 936.
43. Constance Holland to CB, 25 September 1897, BP.
44. Constance Holland to CB, 26 September 1897 (first letter), BP.
45. Constance Holland to CB, 26 September 1897 (second letter), BP. Wilde later described his wife's letter to him in harsher terms to More Adey: 'My wife wrote me a very violent letter on September 29 last saying: "I *forbid* you to see Lord Alfred Douglas. I forbid you to return to your filthy, insane life. I forbid you to live at Naples. I will not allow you to come to Genoa." I quote her words.' [postmark 27 November 1897], *Letters*, 994.
46. OW to CB, 22 September [1897], *Letters*, 947.
47. Constance Holland to CB, 30 September 1897, BP.
48. Constance Holland to CB, 1 October 1897, BP.
49. Richard Ellmann, *Oscar Wilde* (London: Hamish Hamilton, 1987), 513.
50. OW to CB, 12 July 1897, *Letters*, 912.
51. Ross to Schuster, 23 December 1900, *Letters*, 1229.
52. CB to Otho Holland, 21 December 1900 (retained copy), BP.
53. OW to CB, 22 September [1897], *Letters*, 947.
54. Paton to CB, 29 October 1897, BP.
55. Paton to Carrie, 3 November 1897, BP.
56. OW to Turner [postmark 23 September 1897], *Letters*, 948.
57. OW to Turner [? *c.*1 October 1897], *Letters*, 951.
58. OW to Turner, Friday [15 October 1897], *Letters*, 961.
59. OW to Vincent O'Sullivan, 19 October 1897, *Letters*, 964.
60. OW to Ross [July 1898], *Letters*, 1087.
61. OW to Ross, 27 June [1898], *Letters*, 1086.
62. OW to Ross [? 3 October 1897], *Letters*, 954.
63. OW to Turner [postmark 30 October 1897], *Letters*, 976.
64. OW to Leonard Smithers [postmark 22 October 1897, Letter no. 2], *Letters*, 970.
65. OW to Adey [postmark 27 November 1897], *Letters*, 994.
66. OW to Ada Leverson, 16 November 1897, *Letters*, 981.
67. OW to Ross [? 2 March 1898], *Letters*, 1029.
68. OW to Smithers, 9 January 1898, *Letters*, 1011.
69. OW to Smithers [9 February 1898], *Letters*, 1013.

CHAPTER 7: 'THE DREYFUS–CASE PARIS CANNOT BE FIGURED
BY THE PARIS OF TODAY'

1. CB 'Private and Confidential' Memorandum on the Dreyfus Affair, see Appendix.
2. Panizzardi to Schwartzkoppen, 29 January 1898, Bernhard Schwertfeger (ed.), *The Truth about Dreyfus from the Schwartzkoppen Papers* (London & New York: Putnam, 1931), 118.
3. Panizzardi to Schwartzkoppen, 29 January 1898, Schwertfeger (ed.), *The Truth about Dreyfus*, 122–3.
4. Archives Nationales, BB^{19} 84.
5. Panizzardi to Schwartzkoppen, 9 December 1897, Schwertfeger, *The Truth about Dreyfus*, 108–9.
6. Ministère de la Guerre, Etat Major de l'Armée, Archives Historiques, Dossier Secret nos. 236 à 317.
7. Panizzardi to Schwartzkoppen, 9 December 1897, Schwertfeger, *The Truth about Dreyfus*, 109–10.
8. CB to F. C. Conybeare (retained copy), 22 February 1898, BP.
9. Panizzardi to Schwartzkoppen, 22 February 1898, Schwertfeger, *The Truth About Dreyfus*, 124–6.
10. CB Memo, see Appendix.
11. Vincent O'Sullivan, *Aspects of Wilde* (London: Constable & Co. Ltd, 1936), 197–8.
12. Ross to Schuster, *Letters*, 1229.
13. Robert Harborough Sherard, *Oscar Wilde: The Story of an Unhappy Friendship* (London: Privately Printed, The Hermes Press, 1902), 263.
14. OW to Ross [? 20 February 1898], *Letters*, 1022.
15. 'Death of Mr. Rowland Strong, Suspected Foul Play', *The Times*, dateline Paris, 7 January 1924 (8 January 1924).
16. Grant Richards, *Memories of a Misspent Youth* (London: William Heinemann Ltd, 1932), 179–80.
17. Rowland Strong, *Where and How to Dine in Paris: With Notes on Paris Hotels, Waiters and their Tips, Paris Theatres, Minor Theatres, Music Halls, Racing Round Paris, etc* (London: Grant Richards, 1900).
18. Rowland Strong, 'Major Esterhazy a Wreck', *The New York Times*, dateline Paris, 8 February 1898 (20 February 1898).
19. F. Walsin-Esterhazy, *Les Dessous de l'affaire Dreyfus par Esterhazy* (Paris: Fayard Frères, Éditeurs, 1898), 80.
20. E. T. Cook to David Christie Murray, 3 February 1898, BP.
21. Esterhazy, *Les Dessous de l'affaire Dreyfus*, 80; *Daily News*, 17 February 1898.
22. David Christie Murray, 'Some Notes on the Zola Case', *The Contemporary Review* (New York, April 1898), 486.

23. Esterhazy MS, BP. Corrected typescript, 101 pages (October to November 1898), of incomplete English translation of Esterhazy's version of the Dreyfus Affair, published in France by Fayard Frères (Paris, 1898) under the title, *Les Dessous de l'affaire Dreyfus*, which appeared serially in three installments, beginning in November 1898. The English translation is incomplete, negotiations having broken down between Esterhazy and Grant Richards, the English publisher, before the latter received the complete manuscript. The first thirty-eight pages of the English publication (which was never published) were set in type from this typescript (which bears printer's instructions) and corrected proof. Esterhazy had left England in October 1898 and was completing his manuscript in Rotterdam.

24. Chris Healy, *Confessions of a Journalist* (London: Chatto & Windus, 1904), 157.

25. Julien Benda, *La Jeunesse d'un clerc* (Paris: Gallimard, 1936), 181.

26. CB Memo, see Appendix.

27. CB to Conybeare, 22 February 1898, BP.

28. Ernest La Jeunesse, 'Oscar Wilde', *La Revue Blanche* (15 December 1900), 593.

29. Arnold Bennett, *The Journal of Arnold Bennett*, 3 vols. (New York: The Viking Press, 1932), I, 215.

30. Conybeare to CB, 25 February 1898, BP.

31. Cook to Conybeare, 24 February 1898, BP.

32. Constance to Otho Holland, 19 February 1898, Holland.

33. Constance Holland to CB, 4 [March] 1898, BP.

34. Constance Holland to CB, 8 March 1898, BP.

35. 'Déposition de Grandmaison', *La Révision du procès Dreyfus*, 3 vols. (Paris: P. V. Stock, 1899), I, 735. When Grandmaison's testimony at Rennes was made public, Salomon Reinach wrote to Blacker: 'I have just read the stupid deposition of your friend G. and do not congratulate you for your insight in having chosen such a notorious donkey as your confidant. He is one of the most ridiculous fellows of this ridiculous period of history.' 25 August 1899, BP.

36. Constance Holland to CB, 10 March 1898, BP.

37. OW to CB [postmark 9 March 1898], *Letters*, 1035.

38. Early draft version of CB Memo, see Appendix.

39. Constance to Otho Holland, 26 March [1897], *Letters*, 783 n. 2.

40. OW to CB [postmark 9 March 1898], *Letters*, 1035.

41. The rear end-paper of the copy inscribed to Blacker on this occasion bears the following unexplained pencil notation in Blacker's distinctive Pitman shorthand: '26-2-09. Very depressed. Someone's picture came.' The notation may be related to an event reported at length in the press in February 1909: a supposed sighting of Wilde in Turin, Italy. Among Blacker's papers at the time of his death was a clipping of a double-

column account of this from an unidentified Italian newspaper under the banner headline: 'Is Oscar Wilde Still Alive?' The sighting, one of many, followed the well-publicized dinner at the Ritz Hotel in London two months before in honor of Robbie Ross, to celebrate the publication of the first collected edition of Wilde's works and mark the eighth anniversary of the author's death. Among the more than 200 guests present, Blacker was noticeably absent.

42. Constance Holland to CB, 18 March 1898, BP.
43. Conybeare to CB, 21 March 1898, BP.
44. Constance Holland to CB, 20 March 1898, BP.
45. Constance Holland to Carrie, 26 March 1898, BP.
46. OW to CB [postmark 25 March 1898], *Letters*, 1050.
47. OW to CB ('petit bleu') [? 28 March 1898], *Letters*, 1050.
48. OW to CB [? 28 March 1898], *Letters*, 1051.
49. 'A Probability of New Revelations in the Dreyfus Case to be Made in London', *The New York Times*, dateline Paris, 29 March 1898 (10 April 1898).
50. *The Times* (8 January 1924).
51. Constance Holland to Carrie, 26 March 1898, BP.

CHAPTER 8: 'PARADOXES ARE ALWAYS DANGEROUS THINGS'

1. OW to CB, 12 July 1897, *Letters*, 911.
2. OW to Ross [1898], *Letters*, 1086–8.
3. OW to Ross [14 May 1898], *Letters*, 1068.
4. Rowland Strong, *The Diary of an English Resident in France during Twenty-two Weeks of War Time* (London: Eveleigh Nash, 1915), 46–7.
5. Vincent O'Sullivan, *Aspects of Wilde* (London: Constable & Co. Ltd, 1936), 199.
6. OW to Ross [1898], *Letters*, 1087.
7. Elizabeth Robins, 'Oscar Wilde: An Appreciation', a memoir, ed. and commentary by Kerry Powell, *Nineteenth-Century Theatre* (Winter 1993), 101, 102.
8. Oscar Wilde, *Intentions: The Decay of Lying; Pen, Pencil and Poison; The Critic as Artist; The Truth of Masks* (London: Osgood, Macilvaine, 1891), 31.
9. CB Memo, see Appendix. Two of the four documents, the first and the fourth in order of appearance in the Dreyfusard newspaper *Le Siècle*, were based upon information provided by Blacker. The second and third documents consisted of Henri Casella's deposition, published in two installments, of his interviews with Panizzardi and Schwartzkoppen. The deposition had been taken on behalf of Zola but was not admitted at his trial. The four documents were published as a collection later in the year under the title *La Trahison: Esterhazy et Schwartzkoppen* by Jean Testis [F. Isaac] (Paris: P.-V. Stock, 1898).

10. 'Extrait de conversations d'un archéologue avec un helléniste anglais ami de Panizzardi tiré de lettres confidentielles', Archives Nationales, BB[19] 19/95. The document is printed in full in J. Robert Maguire and France Beck, 'Chronique Dreyfusienne: un document inédit de l'Affaire Dreyfus: les confidences de Carlos Blacker à Salomon Reinach', Les Cahiers Naturalistes, 67 (1993), 333.

11. Joseph Reinach, Histoire de l'affaire Dreyfus, 7 vols. (Paris: Librarie Charpentier et Fasquelle, 1901–1911), III, 559 n. 5.

12. Reinach, Histoire de L'Affaire Dreyfus, III, 295 n. 3.

13. Chris Healy, Confessions of a Journalist (London: Chatto & Windus, 1904), 130, see also 157.

14. Ibid., 121, 124.

15. Ibid., 125–6.

16. Ibid., 136.

17. Colin Burns, 'Le Voyage de Zola à Londres en 1893', Les Cahiers Naturalistes, 60 (1986), 60, 65.

18. Robert Harborough Sherard, The Real Oscar Wilde (London: T. Werner Laurie Ltd, 1915), 199.

19. CB Memo, see Appendix.

20. Fred C. Conybeare, The Dreyfus Case (London: George Allen, 1898), 267.

21. F. Walsin-Esterhazy, Les Dessous de l'affaire Dreyfus (printer's galleys; omitted from the published text), BP.

22. Healy, Confessions, 173, 157, 164, 171.

23. Ibid., 137.

24. Maguire and Beck, 'Extrait de conversations', 333.

25. OW to CB ('petit bleu') [postmark 12 April 1898], Letters, 1055.

26. OW to Smithers [postmark 28 February 1898], Letters, 1026.

27. Sotheby's sale cat. Melmoth (10 and 11 July 1986), lot 145.

28. Vincent O'Sullivan, Some Letters of Vincent O'Sullivan to A.J.A. Symons (Edinburgh: Tragara Press, 1975), 7.

29. OW to Ross, 24 May [1898], Letters, 1072.

30. Rowland Strong, 'Esterhazy's English Coach', The New York Times, dateline Paris, 24 May 1898 (5 June 1898).

31. OW to Ross [c.28 May 1898], Letters, 1076.

32. Ibid.

33. OW to Ross [July 1898], Letters, 1087.

34. George Barlow, A History of the Dreyfus Case (London: Simpkin, Marshall, Hamilton, Kent & Co. Ltd, 1899), 277.

35. Esterhazy, Les Dessous de l'affaire Dreyfus (printer's galleys; omitted from the published text), BP.

36. OW to Henry D. Davray [Date of receipt 20 June 1898], Letters, 1084.

37. OW to Ross, 27 June [1898], Letters, 1085–6.

38. Rowland Strong, The New York Times, dateline Paris 7 June 1898 (19 June 1898).

39. André de Boisandré, 'Un nouvel agent du syndicat', *La Libre Parole* (11 June 1898).

40. Barlow, *A History of the Dreyfus Case*, 285, 286–7.

41. 'I had the satisfaction of seeing my letter reproduced *in extenso* in nearly two hundred daily French papers'. Conybeare, *The Dreyfus Case*, 271.

42. W. R. Paton to CB, 11 September 1898, BP.

43. Albert Curtis Clark to CB [*c*.28 June 1898], BP.

44. Conybeare to CB [*c*.28 June 1898], BP.

45. Conybeare to CB [30 June 1898], BP.

46. Conybeare to CB, 3 July 1898, BP.

47. Conybeare to Carrie, 6 July 1898, BP.

48. OW to Ross, Monday, 27 June [1898], *Letters*, 1085.

49. OW to Ross [July 1898], *Letters*, 1087.

50. Conybeare to Carrie, 6 July 1898, BP.

51. C. P. Blacker, annotation on letter from Anatole France to CB, 24 January 1920, BP.

52. C. P. Blacker to Loring Walton, 25 September 1964, BP.

53. Henry Bauër to CB, 2 August 1898, BP. After twenty years as a journalist with *L'Echo de Paris*, Bauër resigned from the paper in July 1898 over its anti-Dreyfusard stance.

54. Salomon Reinach to CB [July 1898], BP. Reinach's brother Joseph, although fully informed of the facts, treats the episode obliquely in his otherwise meticulously documented history of the affair, protectively concealing the identity of Blacker, while referring scornfully to 'this wretched Oscar Wilde, a subtle and profound thinker, who had been condemned in London for sodomy...the most refined and the most perverted of men'. Joseph Reinach, *Histoire de L'affaire Dreyfus*, III, 295–6.

55. Albert Curtis Clark to CB [*c*.28 June 1898], BP.

56. Conybeare to CB, 3 July 1898, BP.

57. W. R. Paton to Blacker, 11 September 1898, BP.

58. Robert Harborough Sherard, *Twenty Years in Paris* (London: Hutchinson & Co., 1905), 440.

CHAPTER 9: 'NO ONE SHOULD KNOW SUCH AN INFAMOUS PERSON AS BOSIE'

1. Conybeare to CB, 3 July 1898, BP.

2. Conybeare to Carrie, 6 July 1898, BP.

3. Panizzardi to CB, 30 June 1898, BP.

4. OW to Ross [July 1898], *Letters*, 1087.

5. Wilfred Hugh Chesson, 'A Reminiscence of 1898', *The Bookman*, 34(4) (December 1911), 389–94.

6. Rowland Strong, 'Major Esterhazy's Performance', *The New York Times*, dateline Paris, 5 July 1898 (17 July 1898).

7. Conybeare, *The Dreyfus Case* (London: George Allen, 1898), 266.
8. Christian Esterhazy, *La Plainte en escroquerie contre le Commandant Esterhazy: mémoire de Christian Esterhazy* (Paris: P.-V. Stock, 1899), 84.
9. *The New York Times* (28 August 1898).
10. Douglas to OW, 22 July 1897 [?], Clark [although dated 1897, this is clearly an error as the events described occurred in 1898], Clark [873] [Wilde D733L W6721].
11. OW to Ross [July 1898], *Letters*, 1090.
12. Rowland Strong, *Sensations of Paris* (London: John Long Ltd, 1912), 187.
13. OW to Ross, 24 May [1898], *Letters*, 1071.
14. Karl Baedeker, *Paris and Environs . . . Handbook for Travellers* (Leipzig: Karl Baedeker Publisher, 1898), 3.
15. OW to Ross, 25 May 1898, *Letters*, 1074.
16. OW to Smithers [postmark 9 August 1898], *Letters*, 1092.
17. OW to Smithers [12 August 1898], *Letters*, 1093.
18. OW to Frank Harris [postmark 13 August 1898], *Letters*, 1094.
19. *The New York Times* (28 August 1898).
20. 'Déposition Esterhazy', *La Révision du procès Dreyfus*, 3 vols. (Paris : P.-V. Stock, 1899), I, 599.
21. OW to Ross [postmark 16 August 1898], *Letters*, 1094.
22. '2ᵉ Déposition Périnet, Femme Gérard', *La Révision du procès Dreyfus*, I, 785, 787–8.
23. Conybeare to CB, 5 September 1898, BP.
24. Thomas Fielders, 'Esterhazy and the Bordereau', *The New York Times* (11 June 1899).
25. Esterhazy to Me Cabanes, 6 March 1899, BN, NAF 24902.
26. Esterhazy to Raymond de la Ville de Rigné, 28 July 1921, BN, NAF 16801 f. 47.
27. Esterhazy to Me Robinet de Clery, 18 June 1904, BN, NAF 16456 f. 62.
28. Esterhazy to his daughter Everilda, 10 May 1923, BN, NAF 16801.
29. Douglas to OW, 20 September 1898, Clark [874] [Wilde D733L W6721].
30. OW to Ross, 3 October 1898, *Letters*, 1098.
31. OW to Ross [25 November 1898], *Letters*, 1102.
32. 'Chez M. Strong: Réponse à La Libre Parole', *L'Aurore* (3 February 1899).
33. Conybeare to CB, 25 September 1898, BP.
34. Conybeare to CB, 3 October 1898, BP.
35. Conybeare to CB, 25 September and 3 October 1898, BP.
36. Conybeare to CB, 25 September and 10 October 1898, BP.
37. 'Déposition Strong Rowland [Rowland Strong]', *La Révision du procès Dreyfus*, I, 741.
38. 'Déposition Esterhazy', *La Révision du procès Dreyfus*, I, 598–9.
39. Boisandré to Esterhazy, 27 September 1903, BN, NAF 16453.
40. Newcastle to CB, 8 October 1900, BP.
41. Newcastle to CB, 7 July 1907, BP.

42. Newcastle to CB, 23 May 1906, BP.

43. Howard Sturgis, *Belchamber* (New York: New York Review of Books, 2008).

44. Percy Lubbock (ed.), *The Diary of Arthur Christopher Benson* (London: Hutchinson & Co. Ltd, 1927), 38.

45. OW to Ross [July 1898], *Letters*, 1088.

46. Lubbock (ed.), *The Diary of Arthur Christopher Benson*, 82.

CHAPTER 10: 'HE WAS A GREAT GENIUS. HIS FAMILIAR TALK WAS GOLDEN'

1. Lord Alfred Douglas, *Oscar Wilde and Myself* (New York: Duffield & Company, 1914), 134–6.

2. Ibid., 135–6.

3. Edgar Saltus, *Oscar Wilde: An Idler's Impression* (Chicago: Brothers of the Book, 1917), 23.

4. OW to Turner [postmark 6 December 1898], *Letters*, 1108.

5. Rowland Strong, *Sensations of Paris* (London: John Long Ltd, 1912), 25.

6. OW to Ross [25 November 1898], *Letters*, 1102.

7. CB to Otho Holland, 21 December 1900, BP.

8. Faith Compton Mackenzie, *William Cory: A Biography* (London: Constable, 1950), 174.

9. OW to CB, 12 July 1897, *Letters*, 911.

10. CB to Otho Holland, 13 December 1900, BP.

11. CB to Otho Holland, 21 December 1900, BP.

12. Ibid.

13. Ross to Adey, 14 December 1900, *Letters*, 1221–2.

14. Turner to Sherard, 9 December 1937, Reading.

15. 'Letter from Ross with photograph of dead Oscar', CB Diary, 14 December 1900; a second diary entry, for 30 October 1901, reads: 'Photographs of Oscar dead came from Robbie Ross', BP.

16. Turner to Sherard, 9 December 1937, Reading.

17. Ross to Adey, 14 December 1900, *Letters*, 1222.

18. Ibid., 1221.

19. W. R. Paton to James Bryce, 12 December 1900, MSS James Bryce, 115, Bodleian Library, Oxford.

20. Ibid.

21. Carrie, n.d., appended to letter to her from CB, 24 January 1895, BP.

22. G. B. Shaw to C. P. Blacker, 19 October 1915, Sotheby's sale cat. *Melmoth* (10 and 11 July 1986), lot 229.

23. Sotheby's sale cat. *Melmoth* (10 and 11 July 1986), lot 226.

24. 'Robin's Notebook and Last Letters', BP.

25. S. Squire to CB, 16 October 1915; Nellie Burton to CB, 15 October 1918, BP.

26. Maureen Borland, *Wilde's Devoted Friend* (Oxford: Lennard Publishing, 1990), 287–8.
27. C. P. Blacker to Loring Walton, 23 November 1958, BP.
28. Horace Guicciardi [Jr] to 'Pip' Blacker, 19 February 1928, BP.
29. Martine Lecuyer, Conservatrice, Cimetière du Père Lachaise, to Martine Prieto, 8 February 2012, BP.
30. Françoise Nottias, Adjointe de la Conservatrice, Père Lachaise, to Martine Prieto, 10 April 2012, BP.
31. Michael Pennington, *An Angel for a Martyr: Jacob Epstein's Tomb For Oscar Wilde* (The Whiteknights Press, University of Reading, 1987), xi.

EPILOGUE

1. Bibliothèque National, NAF 16, 459, f. 132. Described by Dussarp as a 'very important dossier', the archive contains 19 ALS of Esterhazy, a fugitive in Holland and England, to his mistress Mme de Guilhem, in the months immediately following his flight from France; a MS police report on Esterhazy's activities in Holland and the secret visits he received there from high-ranking officers in the French Army; ALS, Esterhazy, a violent and indignant response to the allegations made in the police report; 7 ALS, Colonel du Paty de Clam; ALS, Lieutenant-Colonel Marie-Georges Picquart.
2. Bibliothèque National, NAF 16, 444–16, 466.
3. *A Collection of Original Manuscripts Letters & Books of Oscar Wilde* (London: Dulau & Company Limited, 1928).

APPENDIX

1. Blacker's account of how the *bordereau* reached the War Office—i.e. through the Alsatian agent (Martin Brücker)—conflicts with the 'official' version, according to which it came by 'the ordinary route': Mme Bastian, a charwoman employed at the German embassy routinely delivered the contents of Schwartzkoppen's waste-paper basket to Major Henry at the War Office. Schwartzkoppen maintained to the end that never having received the bordereau it could not have ended up in his waste-paper basket. Dreyfus himself came to accept the version recounted by Blacker. Jean-Denis Bredin, *The Affair* (New York: George Braziller Inc., 1986), 60.
2. Pierre Teyssonières, one of three experts appointed to examine the handwriting of the *bordereau*, failed to return the photograph of the document as called for on completion of his assignment and, instead, sold it to the newspaper *Le Matin*. Guy Chapman, *The Dreyfus Case* (New York: Reynal & Company, 1955), 136.

3. Disagreement remains as to the disguised handwriting of Schwartzkoppen's *petit bleu* (carte-telegram) to Esterhazy which has been attributed to his mistress to whom he is thought to have dictated the message. Colonel Picquart was accused of having forged the document for which he was arrested and held in prison for eleven months.

4. At the rendezvous in the Parc Montsouris, Esterhazy, in panic as the case closed round him, was assured by Colonel du Paty de Clam that he would be protected. Like du Paty, Félix Gribelin, an archivist at the War Office, was in civilian clothes and disguised at the meeting: du Paty with a false beard and Gribelin wearing blue spectacles. Major Henry of the intelligence service remained out of sight in the cab that had brought them. Chapman, *The Dreyfus Case*, 149–50.

5. Senator Auguste Scheurer-Kestner, an Alsatian, and an influential Dreyfusard.

Bibliography

THE DREYFUS AFFAIR

L'Affaire Picquart devant La Cour de Cassation (Paris: P.-V. Stock, 1899).

Barlow, George, *A History of the Dreyfus Case* (London: Simpkin, Marshall, Hamilton, Kent & Co. Ltd, 1899).

Begley, Louis, *Why the Dreyfus Affair Matters* (New Haven & London: Yale University Press, 2009).

Benda, Julien, *La Jeunesse d'un clerc* (Paris: Gallimard, 1936).

Boisandré, André de. 'Un nouvel agent du syndicat.' *La Libre Parole.* 11 June 1898.

Bredin, Jean-Denis, *L'Affaire* (Paris: Julliard, 1983).

Chapman, Guy, *The Dreyfus Case: A Reassessment* (New York: Reynal & Company, 1955).

—— *The Dreyfus Trials* (New York: Stein and Day, 1972).

Conybeare, Fred C., *The Dreyfus Case* (London: George Allen, 1898).

Desachy, Paul, *Bibliographie de L'affaire Dreyfus* (Paris: Edouard Cornely et Cie, 1905).

—— *Répertoire de L'affaire Dreyfus 1894–1899* (Paris, 1905).

Dreyfus, Mathieu, *L'Affaire: telle que je l'ai vecue* (Paris: Bernard Grasset, 1978).

Drouin, Michel (ed.), *L'Affaire Dreyfus: dictionnaire sous la direction de Michel Drouin* (Paris: Flammarion, 2006).

Dubreuil, René, *L'Affaire Dreyfus devant La Cour de Cassation*, Edition populaire illustrée par H.-G. Ibels, Couturier et Léon Ruffe. Paris: P.-V.Stock, 1899.

Esterhazy, Christian, *Memoire, la plainte en escroquerie contre Commandant Esterhazy* (Paris: P.-V. Stock, 1899).

Harris, Ruth, *The Man on Devil's Island: Alfred Dreyfus and the Affair that Divided France* (London: Penguin, 2011).

Johnson, Douglas, *France and the Dreyfus Affair* (London: Blandford Press, 1966).

La Révision du procès Dreyfus, 3 vols. (Paris: P.-V. Stock, 1899).

Lazare, Bernard, *Une Erreur Judiciaire* (Paris, P.-V. Stock, 1897).

Leblois, Louis, *L'Affaire Dreyfus: l'iniquité, la réparation, les principaux faits et documents* (Paris: Librarie Aristide Quillet, 1929).

Lispschutz, Léon, *Une Bibliographie Dreyfusienne: bibliographie thematique et analytique de l'affaire Dreyfus* (Paris: Éditions Fasquelle, 1970).

Ministère de la Justice, Cour de Cassation, *Enquête de la Chambre Criminelle, l'affaire Dreyfus* (Paris: Imprimerie Nationale, 1899).

Murray, David Christie, 'Some Notes on the Zola Case', *The Contemporary Review* (April 1898).

Paléologue, Maurice, *An Intimate Journal of The Dreyfus Case* (New York: Criterion Books, 1957).

Reinach, Joseph, *Histoire de l'affaire Dreyfus*. 7 vols. (Paris: Librairie Charpentier et Fasquelle, 1902–11).

Schwertfeger, Bernhard (ed.), *The Truth About Dreyfus from the Schwartzkoppen Papers* (London & New York: Putnam, 1931).

Simon-Nahaum, Perrine and Vincent Duclert, *L'Affaire Dreyfus* (Paris: Larousse, 2009).

Steevens, G. W., *The Tragedy of Dreyfus* (London and New York: Harper and Brothers, 1899).

Thomas, Marcel, *L'Affaire sans Dreyfus* (Paris: A. Fayard, 1961).

—— *Esterhazy ou l'envers de l'affaire Dreyfus* (Paris: Vernal/Philippe le Baud, 1989).

Walsin-Esterhazy, Ferdinand, *Les Dessous de L'affaire Dreyfus par Esterhazy* (Paris: Fayard Frères, Éditeurs, 1898).

OSCAR WILDE AND CARLOS BLACKER

L'Aurore, 'Chez M. Strong: Réponse à La Libre Parole' (3 February 1899).

Baedeker, Karl, *Paris and Environs . . . Handbook for Travellers* (Leipzig: Karl Baedeker Publisher, 1898).

Bennett, Arnold, *The Journal of Arnold Bennett*. 3 vols. (New York: The Viking Press, 1932).

Blacker, John (ed.), *Have You Forgotten Yet? The First World War Memoirs of C. P. Blacker* (Barnsley, S. Yorkshire: Leo Cooper, Pen & Sword Books, 2000).

Borland, Maureen, *Wilde's Devoted Friend* (Oxford: Lennard Publishing, 1990).

Burns, Colin, 'Le Voyage de Zola à Londres en 1893', *Les Cahiers Naturalistes*, 60 (1986), 41–73.

Chesson, Wilfred Hugh, 'A Reminiscence of 1898', *The Bookman*, 34(4) (December 1911), 389–94.

Douglas, Lord Alfred, *Oscar Wilde And Myself* (New York: Duffield & Company, 1914).

—— *The Autobiography of Lord Alfred Douglas* (London: Martin Secker, 1929).

—— *Without Apology* (London: Martin Secker, 1938).

—— *Oscar Wilde: A Summing Up* (London: Duckworth, 1940).

Ellmann, Richard, *Oscar Wilde* (London: Hamish Hamilton, 1987).

The Eton College Chronicle, 'In Memoriam, the Late Duke of Newcastle' (7 June 1928).

Fielders, Thomas, 'Esterhazy and the Bordereau', *The New York Times* (11 June 1899).

Fletcher, John, *Ornament of Sherwood Forest: From Ducal Estate to Public Park* (Bakewell, Derbyshire: Country Books, 2005).

Foot, Mirjam M., Carmen Blacker, and Nicholas Poole-Wilson, 'Collector, Dealer and Forger: A Fragment of Nineteenth-Century Binding History', in Mirjam M. Foot (ed.), *Eloquent Witnesses: Bookbindings and their History* (London: The Bibliographical Society of London, The British Library and Oak Knoll Press, 2004), 264–81.

Gates, H. L., *The Mystery of the Hope Diamond: From the Personal Narrative of Lady Francis Hope (May Yohe)* (New York: International Copyright Bureau, 1921).

Gide, Andre, *If It Die . . .* (London: Secker & Warburg, 1950).

Harris, Frank, *Oscar Wilde: His Life and Confessions* (New York: Printed and Published by the Author, 1916).

Hart-Davis, Rupert (ed.), *The Letters of Oscar Wilde* (New York: Harcourt, Brace & World, Inc., 1962).

—— *Max Beerbohm: Letters to Reggie Turner* (London: Rupert Hart-Davis, 1964).

—— *More Letters of Oscar Wilde* (New York: The Vanguard Press, 1985).

Healy, Chris, *Confessions of a Journalist* (London: Chatto & Windus, 1904).

Holland, Merlin and Rupert Hart-Davis (eds.), *The Complete Letters of Oscar Wilde* (London: Fourth Estate, 2000).

Housman, Laurence, *Echo de Paris: A Study from Life* (London: Jonathan Cape, 1923).

Juxon, John, *Lewis and Lewis* (New York: Ticknor & Fields, 1984).

La Jeunesse, Ernest, 'Oscar Wilde', *La Revue Blanche* (15 December 1898).

Los Angeles Evening Herald, 'Spouse Shot as Diamond Curse Trails May Yohe' (20 November 1924).

Lubbock, Percy (ed.), *The Diary of Arthur Christopher Benson* (London: Hutchinson & Co. Ltd, 1927).

Mackenzie, Faith Compton, *William Cory: a Biography* (London: Constable, 1950).

Maguire, J. Robert and France Beck, 'Chronique Dreyfusienne: un document inédit de l'affaire Dreyfus: les confidences de Carlos Blacker à Salomon Reinach', *Les Cahiers Naturalistes*, 67 (1993), 326–34. (Includes transcription of *Extrait de conversations d'un archéologue avec un helléniste anglais ami de Panizzardi tiré de lettres confidentielles*, Archives Nationales, BB[19] 19/95.)

Mason, Stuart, *Bibliography of Oscar Wilde*. 2 vols. (London: T. Werner Laurie Ltd, 1914).

Masters, Brian, *The Dukes: The Origins, Ennoblement and History of 26 Families* (London: Frederick Muller, 1988).

Mikhail, E. H. (ed.), *Oscar Wilde: An Annotated Bibliography of Criticism* (London: The Macmillan Press Ltd, 1978).

—— *Oscar Wilde: Interviews and Recollections*, 2 vols. (London: The Macmillan Press Ltd, 1979).

Mikolyzk, Thomas A., *Oscar Wilde: An Annotated Bibliography* (Westport, CT and London: Greenwood Press, 1993).

Newcastle, Kathleen, '*Clumber': Other Famous Homes of Great Britain and Their Stories*, ed. A. H. Malan (New York: G. P. Putnam's Sons, 1902).

Nixon, Howard M., 'Binding Forgeries', *VI International Congress of Bibliophiles* (Vienna: International Congress of Bibliophiles, Conferences, 1971).

O'Sullivan, Vincent, *Aspects of Wilde* (London: Constable & Co. Ltd, 1936).

—— *Some Letters of Vincent O'Sullivan to A. J. A. Symons* (Edinburgh: Tragara Press, 1975).

Patch, Susanne Steinem, *Blue Mystery: The Story of the Hope Diamond* (Washington, DC: Smithsonian Institution Press, 1976).

Pearson, Hesketh and Malcolm Muggeridge, *About Kingsmill* (London: Methuen & Co. Ltd, 1951).

Renier, G. J., PhD, *Oscar Wilde* (London: Peter Davies, 1933).

Richards, Grant, *Memories of a Misspent Youth* (London: William Heinemann Ltd, 1932).

Ricketts, Charles S., *Self-portrait* (London: P. Davies, 1939).

Robins, Elizabeth, 'Oscar Wilde: An Appreciation', a memoir, ed. and commentary Kerry Powell, *Nineteenth Century Theatre* (Winter 1993), 101–13.

Ross, Margery (ed.), *Robert Ross: Friend of Friends* (London: Jonathan Cape, 1952).

Saltus, Edgar, *Oscar Wilde: An Idler's Impression* (Chicago: Brothers of the Book, 1917).

Sassoon, Siegfried, *Siegfried's Journey: 1916–1920* (New York: Faber and Faber Ltd, 1946).

Sherard, Robert Harborough, *Oscar Wilde: The Story of An Unhappy Friendship* (London: Privately Printed, The Hermes Press, 1902).

—— *Twenty Years in Paris* (London: Hutchinson & Co., 1905).

—— *The Life of Oscar Wilde* (London: T. Werner Laurie, 1906).

—— *My Friends the French* (London: T. Werner Laurie, 1909).

—— *The Real Oscar Wilde* (London: T. Werner Laurie Ltd, 1915).

—— *Bernard Shaw, Frank Harris & Oscar Wilde* (New York: The Greystone Press, 1937).

Sisley, Maurice, 'La *Salomé* de M. Oscar Wilde', *Le Galois* (29 June 1892).

Sotheby's, Sale catalogue, 22 and 23 July 1985 (London: Sotheby's, 1985).

—— Sale catalogue, *Melmoth*, 10 and 11 July 1986 (London: Sotheby's, 1986).

Speedie, Julie, *Wonderful Sphinx: The Biography of Ada Leverson* (London: Virago Press, 1993).

Strong, Rowland, 'Esterhazy Looks a Wreck', *The New York Times*, dateline Paris, 8 February 1898 (20 February 1898).

—— 'Esterhazy's English Coach', *The New York Times*, dateline Paris, 24 May 1898 (5 June 1898).

—— 'Major Esterhazy's Performance', *The New York Times*, dateline Paris, 5 July 1898 (17 July 1898).

—— *Where and How to Dine in Paris: With Notes on Paris Hotels, Waiters and their Tips, Paris Theatres, Minor Theatres, Music Halls, Racing round Paris, etc.* (London: Grant Richards, 1900).

—— *Sensations of Paris* (London: John Long, Limited, 1912).

—— *The Diary of an English Resident in France During Twenty-two Weeks of War Time* (London: Eveleigh Nash, 1915).

Sturgis, Howard, *Belchamber* (New York: New York Review of Books, 2008).

Testis, Jean [F. Isaac], *La Trahison: Esterhazy et Schwartzkoppen* (Paris: P.-V. Stock, 1898).

The Times (London), 'Death of Mr. Rowland Strong' (8 January 1924).

Walton, Loring B., 'Anatole France and the First World War: The Correspondence with Carlos Blacker', *PMLA*, 77 (September 1962), 471–81.

Watkin, David, *Thomas Hope 1791–1831 and the Neo-Classical Idea* (London: John Murray, 1968).

Wilde, Oscar, *A Collection of Original Manuscripts Letters & Books of Oscar Wilde* (London: Dulau & Company Limited, 1928).

—— *Intentions: The Decay of Lying; Pen, Pencil and Poison; The Critic as Artist; The Truth of Masks* (London: Osgood, Macilvaine, 1891).

Wyndham, Violet, *The Sphinx and Her Circle: A Memoir of Ada Leverson* (London: André Deutsch, 1963).

The Yellow Book, An Illustrated Quarterly, 4 (January 1895), 275–83.

Index